The Character Compass

A guide to transforming leadership for the 21st century, this is a book about a powerful and practical framework that leaders can use to help their organizations thrive, prosper, and improve the world around them: leader character.

Developed through extensive research, teaching, and outreach over the past decade, leader character is the foundation that leaders rely upon to help them make their most critical judgments. This book carries forward the authors' important work to the implementation stage on both the individual and organizational levels. Based on the authors' interactions with organizations in the public, private, and not-for-profit sectors around the world, they offer practical roadmaps for implementing leader character in such areas as leadership development, strategy, manifesting purpose, culture-building, executive recruitment and HR practices, EDI, risk management, and other key corporate activities. The result of these implementations is nothing less than sustained organizational excellence. Leader character is the compass that helps leaders steer their organizations through real, positive, and lasting change.

This actionable book will earn its place on the bookshelves of professionals and students in talent management, leadership development, HR, and organizational development, as well as leaders from the public, private, and not-for-profit . sectors.

Mary Crossan is a professor of strategic leadership at the Ivey Business School and was awarded Western University's highest honor—Distinguished University Professor—for sustained excellence in teaching, research, and service during her distinguished career at Western. In 2021, she was recognized on a global list representing the top 2 percent of the most cited scientists in her discipline. She was recognized for her life-time career achievement by the Academy of Management, receiving the 2023 Award for Distinguished Educator. She is a co-founder of Leader Character Associates Consulting and of the Virtuosity application.

Gerard Seijts is a professor of organizational behavior and was the inaugural executive director of the Ian O. Ihnatowycz Institute for Leadership. He received his PhD from the University of Toronto. Seijts has led and taught in numerous leadership programs, including customized offerings.

Bill Furlong is an executive in residence at the Ivey Business School, focusing on leader character within the Ian O. Ihnatowycz Institute for Leadership. He is a co-founder of Leader Character Associates Consulting and the founder of the *Question of Character* podcast, which he co-hosts with Mary Crossan. Bill is a director of the CAA Group of Companies and sits on the boards of their insurance subsidiaries. Bill is an adjudicator with the Capital Markets Tribunal and from 2015 to 2019 was a commissioner with the Ontario Securities Commission. Bill held senior global leadership roles at TD Securities, retiring in 2012 as vice chair.

The Character Compass

Transforming Leadership for the 21st Century

Mary Crossan, Gerard Seijts
and Bill Furlong

Routledge
Taylor & Francis Group

NEW YORK AND LONDON

Designed cover image: Getty

First published 2024
by Routledge
605 Third Avenue, New York, NY 10158

and by Routledge
4 Park Square, Milton Park, Abingdon, Oxon, OX14 4RN

Routledge is an imprint of the Taylor & Francis Group, an informa business

© 2024 Mary Crossan, Gerard Seijts, and Bill Furlong

ISBN: 978-1-032-37651-6 (hbk)
ISBN: 978-1-032-37648-6 (pbk)
ISBN: 978-1-003-34121-5 (ebk)

DOI: 10.4324/9781003341215

Typeset in Times New Roman
by Apex CoVantage, LLC

Contents

Dedication

To all those who have supported us to pursue our passions and helped the institute thrive. Through your support, you have not only enabled us to deepen our contributions to the student curriculum but also extended our outreach to those within the public, private, and not-for-profit-sectors. The lives of our students, colleagues, and clients are enriched by the opportunities you helped to create. Your support is instrumental in developing better citizens, better leaders, better organizations, and ultimately, a better world.

Mary Crossan, Gerard Seijts, and Bill Furlong

Character leadership resonated so deeply with me because I witnessed it on a daily basis in my parents, Betty and Terry O'Brien, the character contagion that extended to my many siblings, and the incredible community of family and friends that have supported me. My husband, daughter and son, and their partners have been an ongoing inspiration in my own character-development journey. To all these amazing people, I dedicate this book.

Mary Crossan

My parents, Piet and Nel, returned their borrowed
stardust to the universe a few years ago for reuse.
Their life lessons stayed and will never be forgotten.
I remain a flawed human being who needs to cultivate
his character on a daily basis. I thank Jana, Aiden, and
Arianna for helping me on that challenging journey:
to consider our obligations to each other, to the next
generations, and to Earth.

Gerard Seijts

To my parents, Constance and Myles Furlong, who
lived lives of character. To my Aunt Helen Carew, who,
at that one critical juncture in my life, would not let
me quit on myself. To my life partner, Erin—somehow,
things don't seem real until I share them with her.

Bill Furlong

Acknowledgements

We would like to acknowledge the many leaders from the public, private, and not-for-profit sectors who contributed to our intellectual stimulation over the past 15 years. A special thank-you goes out to Ian O. Ihnatowycz, President and CEO, First Generation Capital Inc.; Bill Troost, President and CEO, Peel Plastic Products; Walter Zuppinger, Chairman and CEO, Domco Foodservices Group of Canada Limited; and other donors for their ongoing interest in and financial support of our work that led to *The Character Compass*. We are grateful to the membership of the Leadership Council of the Ian O. Ihnatowycz Institute for Leadership and our Ivey colleagues for the insights they shared with us. We also like to highlight five leaders that were instrumental in writing the book: Steve Virgin, Sonia Cote, Jennifer Bitz, Corey Crossan, and Lawrence Hughes. All five put "skin in the game," so to speak, to get the book done. We appreciate the guidance and support provided by Meredith Norwich and Bethany Nelson from the Routledge Taylor & Francis Group throughout the writing of the book. We are indebted to Jeffrey Cruikshank for his superb editorial support in getting the book written. Thank you, Jeffrey! We are grateful to the Social Sciences and Humanities Research Council for the funding that has supported much of our research on which the book is based.

Introduction

Mercifully, the typhoon has passed.

But now, a new problem challenges the crew of the *Pequod*. The storm's intense electrical discharges have "turned the compass" of the ship—a fact that Captain Ahab realizes only this morning when the steersman asserts that the ship is headed east southeast. But as all can see, the sun is *behind* them. The compass has been destroyed. The *Pequod* is sailing west, not east.[1]

Fearing that this small disaster may push his already restive crew over the edge into mutiny, Ahab makes a show of constructing a homemade compass out of a lance, a needle, and thread. The skeptical crew watches his every move. The resulting crude tool—basically, a magnetized needle suspended on a thread—only *appears* to function as a compass.[2] But that's good enough for Ahab's purposes. "Look ye, for yourselves," he proclaims dramatically, "if Ahab not be the lord of the level loadstone! The sun is East, and that compass swears it!"

The crew is awed and intimidated by the display. At the same time, they are more aware than ever of Ahab's flaws as a leader. He holds the ship's fate, and their lives, in his hands. This is not a reassuring thought. "In his fiery eyes of scorn and triumph," narrator Ishmael concludes, "you saw then Ahab in all his fatal pride."

This is a book about *character*, especially in the context of organizations. More than ever before, our collective fate hinges on the character of those who direct and influence our organizations—"leader character," we call it. And this applies not only to senior leaders but to *every person* who is in a position to help bring about the transformational change for which we advocate in this book.

Why this conviction? There are lots of answers. Our technologies are racing out ahead of us, faster and more prolifically than ever before: AI, quantum computing, cryptocurrencies, genetic manipulations, and so on. But like the *Pequod's* compass, technologies can fail and deceive us and set us on bad courses. Sophisticated financial tools present their own challenges. Although they may have a clear utility in limited contexts, when they are wielded in ever-broader and more dangerous realms, they can help steer the world financial system toward the reefs.[3]

DOI: 10.4324/9781003341215-1

Meanwhile, there are new and more powerful storms brewing—among them climate change, commodity shortages, supply-chain failures, and many more—and we expect our major corporations and other organizations to help us ride them out and imagine a better way forward.[4] At the same time, social movements demand effective responses from our organizations: ESG, #MeToo, Black Lives Matter, and others. And a black swan event like the COVID-19 pandemic can arise to present fundamental challenges to society, and most visibly to the habits and structures of the workplace.

So how will our society rise to these challenges—both outside and inside our companies, not-for-profits, and other organizations?

One thing is certain: these organizations will need effective leadership on all levels. To be effective, those leaders will have to draw on what we will summarize as the three Cs: *competencies, commitment,* and *character.* All are prerequisites to wise judgments and actions—but they are not equally so under all circumstances, and they are interrelated in subtle and powerful ways.

Weighting the three Cs

Much of business education, and certainly much of our day-to-day lives in organizations, revolves around the notion of *competencies.* What are the people within the organization good at—and by extension, what is the organization good at? What can they get better at? In many cases, especially in modern-day start-ups, the answer hinges on some sort of breakthrough technology or esoteric financial instrument. In fact, much of the history of business organizations in the 20th century and in the early decades of this century has been about doubling down on ever-more-complex technologies and the increasingly arcane management systems that support them.

But like Ahab's compass, ever-more complex instruments present their own kinds of challenges. First, of course, they require hard-to-find specialists to deploy and maintain them. Second, they are subject to abuse by bad actors or even well-intentioned nonexperts. (In coming chapters, we'll look at examples of major companies that hit the metaphorical rocks when key players within them misused core technologies.) And finally, complex things tend to break down, often with catastrophic consequences—to the extent that even deep competencies can't make up for them. It's hard to salvage things that fall off a high cliff.

Commitment involves aspiration, engagement, and sacrifice. In *The Character Compass,* we will focus only lightly on commitment. This is in part because ambitious people in business tend to have an abundance, even an overabundance, of commitment. Think of all those stories of entrepreneurs who refused to take "no" for an answer, engaging in serial failures before finally succeeding.[5] Or think of those mainline CEOs—like Maple Leaf Foods' Michael McCain—who, when faced with an existential food-poisoning crisis involving several of that iconic Canadian company's meat products—stepped up, took complete ownership over what was happening, and worked energetically over time to help save the country's largest food-processing company.[6]

"Great leaders build great organizational culture," one observer wrote of McCain, "and the behaviour that supports that culture drives performance."[7] That requires time and commitment.

Conversely, those who really *don't* care all that much are sniffed out and rejected by ambitious organizations. And those who actually step down—who walk away from power—tend to be punished by their former constituents. Think back to 2009, when Alaska governor (and former vice-presidential candidate) Sarah Palin abruptly resigned her office. Certainly, some observers responded sympathetically to Palin's decision, but others faulted the governor for her lack of commitment to the job. "Good point guards don't quit and walk off the floor if the going gets tough," as a former senior strategist for Palin's running mate Senator John McCain commented to the *New York Times*. "People don't like a quitter."[8]

This brings us to *character*: a defined set of interconnected behaviors that satisfy a set of criteria as being virtuous, meaning that these are behaviors that deliver sustained excellence and well-being.[9] What we call "leader character" is the foundation that leaders rely upon to help them make their most critical judgments. Augmenting character with the word "leader" is more about the *disposition to lead* rather than occupying a formal position of leadership. It is about how any person can bring their best self to their endeavors.

Seen from this perspective, competencies are the *what*, and character is the *who*. They are intimately entangled.[10] But for now, let's simply assert that the stronger the character, the better the judgment and decisions, which means better outcomes for all. Yes, as noted previously, competence and commitment are also key, but they are both leveraged—for better or for worse!—by character.

Of course, putting this kind of explicit emphasis on character inevitably calls forth an array of myths, misconceptions, and objections, as with the following examples:

- *Character is "locked in" at birth—or in childhood, or at some other early developmental stage—and can't be changed.* This is not true. Rigorous science supports the hypothesis that character is merely a *habit*, which can be strengthened with intentional exercise. Conversely, when left unexercised, character can be weakened and molded in dysfunctional ways by external pressures and contexts. The truth is, it's never too late to strengthen character; indeed, it's a lifelong journey.
- *Character can't be taught, and so it shouldn't be a concern of academia or leadership development.* In fact, engaging in character education and development used to be a vibrant role of academic institutions. Over a century ago, most university administrators and faculty members would have said that building an integrated self was their most important task. We, your authors,

can't turn back the clock—but we can do our best to plug what we consider a gaping hole in the academic agenda.

- *Character can't be defined and assessed.* Again, not true! This is exactly what we've learned to do and taught others to do—including leaders from the public, private, and not-for-profit sectors—over the last decade. For example, we facilitate character-based interviews that create unique and valuable insights into a candidate—insights that can't necessarily be achieved through conventional executive interviewing, reference checking, and psychological testing processes.
- *Character is a nice-to-have and not really a core concern of hard-nosed business leaders.* No, we argue that leader character is foundational for sustained excellence. Consider the alternative. When character is *not* present, the result is very often personal and professional failure, leading in turn to massive organizational damage. The scandals at Boeing, Theranos, Volkswagen, and Wells Fargo—to cite only a few recent examples, some of which we'll return to in later chapters—were not failures of competencies but of character.

The three Cs have to be cultivated in thoughtful combination. Separately, they are ineffective—or worse, dangerous. "We look for three things when we hire people," Warren Buffett once told a group of students at the University of Georgia, speaking of hiring practices at Berkshire Hathaway. "We look for intelligence, we look for initiative or energy, and we look for integrity. And if they don't have the latter, the first two will kill you, because if you're going to get someone without integrity, you want them lazy and dumb."[11]

Buffett uses terms that are different from our own, but clearly and colorfully, he makes the case for leader character.

Who are we?

We are a team of scholars, writers, and practitioners who bring complementary perspectives and experiences to bear on the subject of leader character.

Mary Crossan is a professor of strategic leadership at the Ivey Business School and was awarded Western University's highest honor—Distinguished University Professor—for sustained excellence in teaching, research, and service during her distinguished career at Western. She teaches in Ivey's undergraduate, MBA, PhD, and executive education programs.

Her research on organizational learning and strategic renewal, leader character, and improvisation has been widely published: In 2021, she was recognized on a global list representing the top 2 percent of the most cited scientists in her discipline. Working with her colleagues, she has developed courses, cases, and a diagnostic assessment to develop leader character and is a co-creator of the Virtuosity™ character development app. The *Developing Leadership Character* book—discussed in depth in Chapter 2—summarizes the team's research on the subject.

Gerard Seijts is a professor of organizational behavior at the Ivey Business School. Seijts has led and taught in numerous national and international leadership programs, including customized offerings. His research activities—spanning journal articles, book chapters, blogs, and conference papers—comprise a wide range of topics, including leadership, leader character, organizational change, training and development, and performance management. He is a frequent speaker at national and international conferences, including professional associations in the public, private, and not-for-profit sectors, and is an award-winning researcher and teacher in both degree and executive education programs. He has authored and co-authored several books, including (with Crossan) *Developing Leadership Character*. He is the former executive director of the Ian O. Ihnatowycz Institute for Leadership.

Bill Furlong held senior global leadership roles at TD Securities—including global head of Asset Securitization, global head of Middle Office (UK), and global head of Trading Business Management—from 1994 to 2012. Furlong retired from TD Securities in 2012 as vice chair and has been an executive in residence at the Ivey Business School since 2013, focusing on leader character within the Ian O. Ihnatowycz Institute for Leadership. He has co-authored thought-leading essays on leader character that have been published by *MIT Sloan Management Review*, *Business Law International*, and the *Global Risk Institute*. Furlong has also presented leader character to numerous organizations, regulators, associations, and conferences reaching audiences around the world. In 2020, Furlong founded and with Mary Crossan co-hosts *Question of Character*, a podcast dedicated to providing reliable and valuable information and insights regarding leader character. In 2023, Furlong Crossan founded Leader Character Associates, a consulting firm dedicated to the implementation and embedding of leader character in organizations.

For more than a decade, together and separately, the three of us have been engaged in intensive efforts to understand leader character. Based on the findings derived through that effort—findings based on rigorous scientific methods—we have sought to elevate character to its rightful place alongside competencies and commitment.

The strategic roadmap

We have been helped in that work by both practitioners and academics from around the world, and our shared effort has been highly successful.

Today, we can not only define and assess leader character; we can also confidently prescribe ways to develop it within individuals and instill it in complex organizational settings. Based on our interactions with organizations in the public, private, and not-for-profit sectors around the world, we can offer practical roadmaps for embedding leader character in such areas as strategy development;

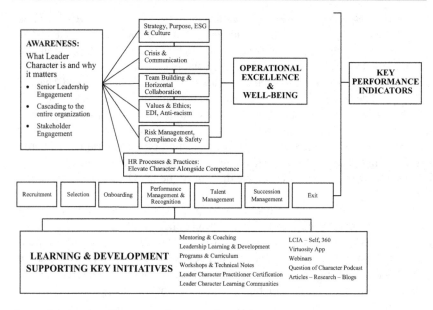

Figure 0.1 Leader Character Strategic Roadmap

manifesting purpose; culture-building; executive recruitment and development; equity, diversity, and inclusion (EDI) initiatives; risk management, and other key corporate activities. The result of these implementations is *sustained organizational excellence.*

In other words, leader character makes the transition from a nice-to-have to a *need-to-have.*

We capture the context of these insights in the leader character Strategic Roadmap, shown in Figure 1.1.

Based on the conceptual flow of this roadmap, we have offered courses in leader character at the Ivey Business School to hundreds of senior executives in recent years: in person at Ivey and through virtual classrooms and offices that reach audiences worldwide. Through those sessions and other engagements with practitioners, we have continually tested our leader character framework and the roadmap that captures it. Again, the work is iterative, systematic, and rigorous.

That work continues today. The leader character framework *works*, and it continues to get sharper and clearer.

What you will find here

Many of the chapters in *The Character Compass* correspond directly to the strategic roadmap. You will note that the roadmap progresses from *awareness* (on the left) to *operational excellence and well-being* (on the right) through the development and tracking of key performance indicators. The roadmap captures the major functions of complex organizations in relation to leader character, explored in depth in *The Character Compass*. Similarly, from left to right, our chapters progress from a central focus on the individual to an increasing focus on the organizational—although as we hasten to underscore here and in later chapters, individual character always underlies organizational character.

Our opening chapters focus on *the anatomy of character:* in terms of character, the "what." What exactly are we talking about when we refer to leader character? We review the eleven dimensions of leader character, explaining the careful scholarship that underpins it, and illustrating how—when tested in real world situations—leader character delivers improved leadership judgment, outcomes, and well-being in leaders and in those around them.

Our middle chapters explore *character development*. This is the "how," which should be useful to all readers but should be of particular interest to readers familiar with our previous work, including *Developing Leadership Character*. Our main focus in this section of the book is prescription for the *individual*. How does the leader (or aspiring leader at any level) assess and develop leader character? Can leader character be reinforced through deliberate practice, exercise, and the development of good habits? Again, our answer is an emphatic "yes."

One important emphasis here is how leader character benefits the individual, especially in terms of *well-being*. No matter what kind of organization you work for—big or small, new or old, public sector, for profit, or not-for-profit—you will benefit personally from practicing and embodying leader character.[12] The same holds true for your *level* within your organization. Why? Because developing character helps you *thrive*. It's good for your physical and mental health as well as your professional advancement. It supports you in your current role and prepares you for your next role.

In our later chapters, we concentrate on *the application of character*, putting an increased emphasis on implementation in the organizational setting. Using real-world examples of success, we demonstrate how leader character can be embedded and put to work in all types of organizations—countering toxic cultural elements and promoting mental health and individual development.

Our goals and yours

Your authors are motivated, inspired, and driven by the major events of our day. Our research into leader character initially was sparked in part by the global financial crisis of 2008. It intensified through the Great Recession that followed and multiple converging societal forces in those challenging years—including climate change, the various movements to address long-standing social injustices, an increased focus on purpose-driven organizations, the COVID-19 pandemic, political polarization, and increasingly risky geopolitical tensions—encouraged us to redouble our efforts.

That COVID-19 point deserves explanation. In our eyes, the pandemic, in particular, starkly displayed the character of leaders, which in turn has helped determine the success or failure of those leaders.[13] This is certainly true in the political realm: compare the leadership and outcomes in New Zealand with those in, say, Brazil. But it's also very much the case in the world of business and other organizations. Leaders either succeed or fail at helping their organizations navigate troubled waters. The dramatic differences in outcome are less about a failure of competencies or commitment and more the result of a failure of *character*.

We are determined to do our part to help head off large-scale catastrophes in the future. We do not accept that the failures of leadership in the last decade or so are the natural order of things and therefore must be repeated. Far from it! We want to provide our readers with a character-based framework that provides the language, tools, processes, and confidence they will need to navigate today's turbulent waters and those that lie ahead. At the same time, we want to help organizations stop instigating trauma in the workplace and instead start rooting it out. We want to help them achieve the kind of accountability that they say they're searching for. We want to help them avoid putting good apples in bad barrels.

Toward all of these ends, we want to provide a better compass. *The Character Compass* summarizes our current thinking about how that might be done.

Why should you invest time and energy in *The Character Compass*? The first reason is to have richer and deeper relationships with others, to enjoy the benefits of more effective decision-making and better outcomes both at work and at home, and to reap the benefits of improved mental and physical well-being. In short, by developing leader character, you can help yourself and your family, organization, community, society, and perhaps even our world flourish.

And the second reason is because, as we emphasized earlier, our world has profoundly and irrevocably changed. We need to un-anchor our bias toward the primacy of competencies and commitment. Now we need to embrace the ascendency of character, in part because "character helps leaders engage their competencies."[14] Arguably, character can and should be ranked above the other two Cs in terms of the priorities of the moment.

Ahab's fatal pride—which was only one measure of his lack of leader character, by the way—was a threat only to himself and his 43 shipmates.[15] Today, when the world's richest man can buy a social network that reaches 400 million users monthly, the stakes are far higher.[16]

Today, more than ever, we need *The Character Compass*.

Notes

1 Apologies to Herman Melville for this much-simplified and shortened version of Chapter 124, "The Needle," of the magnificent *Moby Dick*.
2 For a number of reasons, Ahab's invention might have worked as a magnet but was probably useless as a compass. See, for example, https://eos.org/geofizz/was-ahab-truly-lord-of-the-level-loadstone, accessed March 13, 2023.

3 For example, the Black–Scholes equation, useful for pricing contracts that had not yet expired, became so abused that it earned the nickname the "Black Hole equation." See www.theguardian.com/science/2012/feb/12/black-scholes-equation-credit-crunch, accessed March 13, 2023.

4 More than half of the employees responding to a recent survey believe that CEOs should speak out on issues that they feel strongly about, and more than half of consumers feel that brands should be visibly involved social issues. See Paul Argenti's article in the October 16, 2020, edition of *Harvard Business Review,* online at https://hbr.org/2020/10/when-should-your-company-speak-up-about-a-social-issue, accessed March 13, 2023.

5 In some cases, failure may be the secret to business success. A 2014 Stanford University/University of Michigan study suggested that entrepreneurs who fail more than once ultimately tend to be more successful than their peers. See for a short write-up www.forbes.com/sites/northwesternmutual/2015/07/14/failure-the-secret-to-business-success/?sh=cfd80cc43a0f, accessed March 13, 2023.

6 Much has been written about the leadership of Michel McCain during the listeriosis crisis. Two illustrative articles include www.theglobeandmail.com/report-on-business/the-testing-of-michael-mccain/article598005/ and www.cbc.ca/news/canada/how-should-a-company-manage-a-meat-recall-crisis-1.1248421, both accessed March 13, 2023.

7 See Marty Parker's opinion piece in the December 10, 2009, issue of the *National Post,* online at https://nationalpost.com/news/values-based-leadership-michael-mccain-at-maple-leaf-foods, accessed March 13, 2023.

8 The article, "Palin's move shocks G.O.P. and leaves future unclear," online at www.nytimes.com/2009/07/04/us/politics/04palin.html, accessed March 13, 2023.

9 We will return to this topic in greater depth in subsequent chapters.

10 See, for example, the article "The entanglement of leader character and leader competence and its impact on performance" by Rachel E. Sturm, Dusya Vera, and Mary Crossan, online at https://daneshyari.com/article/preview/5035254.pdf.

11 The comments came in a 2001 speech to students at the University of Georgia, a transcript of which is online at www.nasdaq.com/articles/warren-buffett-speech-university-georgia-students-part-1-archive-2001-2013-04-21, accessed March 13, 2023.

12 See, for example, the podcast "Can Leader Character and CBT work together to foster well being?" hosted by Bill Furlong and Mary Crossan at www.questionofcharacter.com/episodes/episode-01-leader-character-101a-r9rxc-3r552-3y9df-baf3j-4zexg-j8bst-zf47e-hl7pl, accessed March 13, 2023. Further, Gerard Seijts, Lucas Monzani, Hayden Woodley, and Gouri Mohan published a study that showed that character has a direct effect on the subjective well-being of students and an indirect effect through the perceived stressfulness of life events. Their results imply that it is essential for faculty and students at academic institutions to fully appreciate the importance of character for effective functioning and to develop the various character dimensions needed to address adverse personal, social, and environmental situations in a positive fashion.

13 An example of how character helped people working through the COVID-19 pandemic is provided by Gerard Seijts and Kimberley Milani. In their article "The myriad ways in which COVID-19 revealed character," the authors illustrate the dimensions of character with concrete examples of the behaviors that leaders and citizens alike manifested during the pandemic. The article is available online at www.sciencedirect.com/science/article/pii/S0090261620300176?via%3Dihub.

14 The quote is from the article "The entanglement of leader character and leader competence and its impact on performance," by Rachel E. Sturm, Dusya Vera, and Mary Crossan, online at https://daneshyari.com/article/preview/5035254.pdf.

15 Melville was inconsistent on this point, at one point mentioning a crew of 44 but at several other times referring to a crew of 30. With the latter number, he may have been making an analogy to the then 30 states in the U.S. See https://insearchofmoby-dick.wordpress.com/2017/02/18/crewmembers-of-the-pequod/, accessed March 13, 2023.

16 As of January 2022. See the statistics, including the very interesting breakdown of Twitter users by country, online at https://backlinko.com/twitter-users accessed, March 13, 2023.

Chapter 1

The case for character

In retrospect, marketing should have been in closer touch with engineering—*much* closer.

By January 2014, Volkswagen had been an advertiser in the US National Football League's Super Bowl for four years running, with those ads already having established the company as the "most shared" brand of all time, meaning that more online consumers had shared VW's ads with their friends than any other company's.[1] Now, VW was coming back for its fifth appearance during the upcoming game, scheduled for February 2.[2] The spot was titled "Wings," and its premise was whimsical: whenever a VW's odometer broke the 100,000-mile mark, an engineer back in Germany earned his wings, literally.[3] The ad featured white-coated engineers in various factory settings with white angel wings erupting out of the backs of their lab coats, mostly at inopportune moments, such as on an elevator or in a wind tunnel.[4]

"Wings" was cheeky and funny, harking back to the offbeat style of earlier VW campaigns, and it was fairly well received. According to market research, it performed better than rival Chevrolet's ad but not as well as Kia's or Jaguar's—and only about a tenth as well as Budweiser's treacly "Puppy Love," which came in number one in the postgame viewer rankings.[5] But "Wings" successfully projected the image of a squeaky-clean cadre of engineers turning into angels, one by one, in a squeaky-clean factory.

The reality was dramatically different. *That* story begins several years earlier—in 2011—when VW CEO Martin Winterkorn publicly announced an ambitious goal that his company had embraced back in 2008, which was to become the world's largest automaker by 2018.[6] To get there, VW adopted a risky, outlying strategy—producing high-performance diesel cars rather than the hybrid-electric vehicles then being pushed by industry-leading Toyota. "High performance" had to mean not only drivability, of course, but also good mileage and low emissions. By all accounts, Winterkorn *leaned hard* on the strategy. And leaning hard came naturally to him: colleagues recall him as an authoritarian who purposely fostered a climate of fear in his "no-failure" organization.[7]

DOI: 10.4324/9781003341215-2

But corporate fear of failure notwithstanding, Winterkorn's strategy proved unworkable, especially when it came to hitting the increasingly tough emissions standards then being imposed in the US. So rather than embrace an available pollution-control technology produced by archrival Mercedes-Benz—which presumably would have been viewed internally as a corporate failure—some of those white-coated VW engineers decided to cheat. They designed and installed what were known as "defeat devices" in Jetta, Passat, and Audi diesels intended for sale in the American market—essentially, a software subroutine that would help the cars perform extremely well on the pollution test stand but also disguise the very high levels of nitrogen oxide that those same cars emitted under normal driving conditions.[8]

The cheat was discovered almost by accident in 2013 by a nonprofit testing group, which forwarded its findings to regulators in California, who in turn alerted the Environmental Protection Agency in Washington. When confronted by these growing legions of regulators with probing questions and negative results, VW stalled and lied for many, many months—including, ironically, during the year and a half that followed the airing of "Wings." Constantly and aggressively, VW disputed the regulators' findings and cast aspersions on their collective competence. Finally, in early September 2015, the company's engineers were forced to admit not only that they had cheated, but also that the scheme dated all the way back to 2009: the year that VW introduced into the US its "clean diesel" technology, which it billed at the time as a major environmentally friendly breakthrough. In other words, Winterkorn's unworkable strategy of 2008 almost immediately had led to a far-ranging, systemic, and purposeful fraud within the company, ultimately perpetrated through the sale of some 11 million faulty cars around the world.

Winterkorn first apologized and then—still claiming that he had no knowledge of the defeat-device scheme—resigned. "I am not aware of any wrongdoing on my part," he asserted, adding nevertheless that "Volkswagen needs a fresh start."[9] But others *did* see wrongdoing on his part, with authorities in both the US and Germany indicting him and four other VW executives on multiple counts of fraud. The company, too, was punished, ultimately having to pony up an astounding *$35 billion* in retrofits, legal fees, fines, and settlements.[10]

In retrospect, it's a miserable story, characterized by poor decision-making over many years. What if VW hadn't adopted Winterkorn's aggressive strategy in the first place—or at least had modified it sufficiently to make an honest success possible? What if the company had swallowed its pride, licensed the proven Mercedes-Benz pollution-control technology or some similar solution, and sidestepped the whole problem? What if early on, VW's leaders had accepted the inevitable—that is, owning up to the deception—and thereby minimized the damages to the company, its dealer network, its customers, and the environment?

In a later chapter, we'll talk about what we call "micro-moments"—those decision points along the way that represent critical nodes in the decision tree of judgment. There were many such micro-moments during the half decade in which the VW cheating scandal took root and unfolded. At all too many of those micro-moments—at all too many forks along that critical path of judgment—the company took the wrong turn. A phenomenon that we call "character contagion" set in, with more and more colleagues signing on to the fraud.

As we'll explain, character contagion can work either for the good or for the bad. In VW's case, it worked aggressively for the bad. And because character contagion serves as a prime determinant of organizational culture, VW's larger culture became seriously corrupted. For the company, its dealerships, and its shareholders, the results of negative character contagion were disastrous.

So now, as a sort of antidote to that disheartening story, let's look at a case of *positive* character contagion.

Turning an entire nation around

Rolihlahla Mandela was born in 1918 into the Madiba clan, in a village in south-eastern South Africa.[11] While in grade school, in keeping with the custom of the time, he acquired a Christian name: Nelson.

The youthful Nelson Mandela received a good education with no notable bumps along the road—that is, until he was expelled from the University College of Fort Hare for participating in a student protest against apartheid—South Africa's officially sanctioned separation of the races and de facto subjugation of the majority Black population. It turned out that the protest was a harbinger of things to come. In 1944, a year after finishing college, Mandela joined the activist African National Congress party. As the ANC grew more radical in the 1950s, Mandela gained an ever-higher profile—and inevitably attracted the attention of the racist national government. He was first arrested in 1955 and again in 1962. Two years later, at age 46, he was sentenced to life imprisonment in the prison camp on notorious Robben Island.

Ultimately, Mandela spent 18 years there. Because he was perceived as a leader of a revolutionary movement, he was singled out for abuse by a succession of head wardens. Gradually, though, a changing world was catching up with Nelson Mandela. In 1982, he was transferred to Pollsmoor Prison in Cape Town. Over the next six years, the harshest conditions of his imprisonment were gradually relaxed—in part because the government very much needed a prominent member of the ANC with whom it could negotiate. Mandela played that role effectively, and on February 11, 1990, his 27 years of imprisonment finally ended.

Then began the task of rebuilding a nation amidst rising tensions and ever-increasing levels of violence between and within the races. Sitting across the table from South African President F. W. de Klerk, Mandela participated in the talks that led to the end of white minority rule. The deal was struck, and in 1993, Mandela and de Klerk shared the Nobel Peace Prize for heading off what could have degenerated into a catastrophic race-based civil war.

In May 1994, Mandela was inaugurated as South Africa's first democratically elected president. He had initially declined to run for the office, finally agreeing to stand for election on the condition that he would serve only one term if elected. His brief inaugural address included thanks both to the freedom fighters who had prevailed and to the security forces—so long the face of oppression—who had secured the democratic elections that many had believed could never take place.

"None of us acting alone can achieve success," he said toward the end of his remarks. "We must therefore act together as a united people, for national reconciliation, for nation building, for the birth of a new world."[12]

That conviction manifested itself in many ways in the difficult years that followed. On his first day as president—May 11, 1994—Mandela was making his way down the hall to his new office and noticed that room after room was either empty or full of packing materials. With this evidence of a mass evacuation painfully in full view, he called together the remaining staff members, who were almost exclusively white, for an impromptu meeting. After they had assembled, the new president told them that although he had a very busy schedule that day, he wanted to shake hands with each of them, which he proceeded to do.

When he reached one female staffer with a particularly stern-looking face, he stopped and asked, in the somewhat shaky Afrikaans he had learned in prison, "Is jy kwaad vir my?"—"Are you mad at me?" Everyone laughed, including the formerly stone-faced woman.[13] Then he delivered his message: "If you are packing up because you fear that your language, or the color of your skin, or who you worked for before disqualifies you from working here, I am here to tell you: Have no such fear. We look to the future now. We need your help. We want your help. If you would like to stay, you would be doing your country a great service."[14]

Mandela wasn't kidding: he needed all the help he could get. His fledgling democracy had to create entirely new institutions. South Africa—for years an international pariah—now had to re-engage with the global community. Yes, his own enormous stature on the world stage gave him leverage, but it also placed extraordinary demands on him personally. Nevertheless, he insisted on maintaining a relatively small central staff, in part because he wanted to remain open to input from as many outside voices as possible.

So he listened—but at the same time, he was anything but a pushover. As the Mandela archive puts it:

In taking decisions, the president combined readiness to consult his advisors and others on the one hand, with confidence on the other in his opinions he formed that made it often difficult to move him once he had adopted a position. If ultimately he realized that he was not changing people's minds, he might concede, but not easily.[15]

Early in his presidency, Mandela began searching for ways to accelerate racial reconciliation on a national scale. He soon decided to concentrate some of that effort on sports. "Sports has the power to change the world," he wrote. "Sport can create hope where once there was only despair."[16] He started with an unlikely focus: the Springboks national rugby team, which had been banned from the first two Rugby World Cups (1987 and 1991) in condemnation of South Africa's apartheid system, which this team in particular had come to embody.[17] With the collapse of apartheid, the Springboks were allowed to host and compete in the 1995 World Cup—but to many Black South Africans, the team still symbolized racial oppression. Over the objections of many members of his own African National Congress party, Mandela began conferring and collaborating with the team's captain. On a visit to the team's training camp in advance of the World Cup, Mandela made a brief public statement in which he made his larger intentions clear:

> We have adopted these young men as our boys, as our own children, as our own stars. The country is fully behind them. I have never been so proud of our boys as I am now and I hope that pride we all share.[18]

The team made it to the finals against arch-rival New Zealand, held at Johannesburg's Ellis Park on June 24, 1995. After giving the Springboks a pep talk in their locker room before the game, Mandela entered the stadium decked out in the team's traditional green-and-gold cap and jersey—arguably a controversial decision in light of the fact that the team's roster still included only one Black player. But the Springboks had officially embraced a motto of tolerance and unity—"one team; one nation"—and when the mostly white crowd of 80,000 rugby fans spotted their president in green and gold, they began cheering and chanting his name: "Nelson! Nelson! Nelson!"[19]

Against long odds, the Springboks rewarded Mandela's faith in them by providing a storybook ending: a thrilling 15–12 victory over New Zealand. "When the final whistle blew," team captain Francois Pienaar later wrote, "this country changed forever." Mandela led the cheerleading as Pienaar held the championship trophy high—and South Africans of all colors erupted in celebration.[20] In a postgame interview, Pienaar commented that it was a victory "not for 60,000 [rugby fans], but for 43 million South Africans."[21]

"Across South Africa," as one observer commented, "it was clear that Mandela had won."[22] And the positive character contagion that began with a private conversation between two men continued to spread, underscoring the significance of that win. For example, the Springboks began offering coaching clinics to underprivileged youth across the country and providing funding to disadvantaged rugby organizations. A virtuous circle was created: more skilled Black players came up through the ranks, gradually helping to make the Springboks themselves more diverse and increasingly representative of the whole nation.[23]

We'll return to Mandela's character and accomplishments shortly. Meanwhile, it's fair to speculate: what if *all* national leaders around the world tackled issues like health care and social justice and actions based on character? And what if all business leaders behaved that way? How different would our world be today?

Three key questions

We invoke these two very different stories about leaders in their contexts—Winterkorn at Volkswagen, Mandela in South Africa—not only to stake out a broad spectrum of leader character but also to frame three of the core questions that we will answer in this book:

- What is "character"?
- Can you develop character?
- Does character matter?

Let's look at each in turn.

What is "character"?

We begin with the first and most important question: what is character?

One way of answering that question is to state what character does—in other words, its *impacts*. This is what might be called the "peripheral vision" approach to defining character—that is, not looking at it head-on but instead defining it as it manifests itself in the fates of companies, communities, and nations. It's the approach we took in our previous stories about Volkswagen and Nelson Mandela.

Briefly stated, *character is foundational to effective decision-making and functioning*. It shapes a number of things, including what we notice in the context in which we operate; how we engage the world around us; what we reinforce through our rewards and punishments; who we engage in conversation and how we conduct those conversations; what we value; how we interpret feedback; what we choose to act on; how we deal with conflict, disappointment, and setbacks; the goals we set for ourselves; how we communicate; and so forth.[24]

A second way of defining character is to focus on its component parts, which is the central focus of our Chapter 2. This engages our "head-on" vision rather than our peripheral vision. Briefly stated, character is a set of *virtues*—a few of which are *personality traits*—and *values*. At this point, we'll introduce each of these terms and return to work on them harder in the next chapter.

Virtues are central to our analysis and to the prescriptions that we will derive from that analysis. Virtues are patterns of situationally appropriate behaviors— for example, courage and accountability—that are considered to be emblematic of good leadership. The opposite of virtues are vices: unworthy behaviors such as cowardice, arrogance, recklessness, or foolhardiness.

It's important to note that in excess, many virtues become vices. This may seem counterintuitive, but it's true. Courage is admirable, but excessive courage may lead to recklessness. Excessive integrity—a concept that many of our audiences at first have trouble imagining—can lead to a dysfunctional self-righteousness if not supported by sufficient humility. Also somewhat counterintuitive is the fact that excess is *relative to the other dimensions*—which means, for example, that you can only have too much Integrity if you don't have the other dimensions to support it.

The notion of virtues as behaviors (and, by extension, character as impacts) is far from a new concept. "We are what we repeatedly do," Aristotle wrote. "Excellence, then, is not an act, but a habit." Aristotle identified and defined twelve virtues: courage, temperance, generosity, magnificence, magnanimity, right ambition, good temper, friendliness, truthfulness, wit, justice, and practical wisdom. That last virtue, in particular, was deemed necessary by Aristotle to live the "good life" and thereby achieve happiness and well-being. Our framework—again, as explored in depth in Chapter 2—overlaps with Aristotle's in significant ways.

Traits are personality dimensions—patterns of thought, behavior, and emotion—that are relatively stable in individuals across situations and over time.[25] Traits focus on individual differences, and over time, many scholars have focused on what are often called the "Big Five": openness, conscientiousness, extroversion/introversion, agreeableness, and neuroticism. While the personality trait of being an introvert or an extrovert—for example—does not meet the criteria of a virtue, conscientiousness does.

Whereas virtues are something that can and should be developed, traits are considered semi-stable. For example, studies have shown that identical twins share more traits than nonidentical twins—clearly indicating that nature as well as nurture plays a role in trait acquisition.

Values are deep-seated beliefs that influence or guide behaviors. Most values do not meet the criteria of being a virtue, such as valuing health, family, safety, or money, whereas valuing fairness is both a value and a virtue. Values are usually associated with words like "should" and "ought," as in, "Leaders ought to treat everyone with dignity and respect." Values tend to be individual beliefs rather than organizational beliefs. They can change with life stages and also according to the extent to which a particular value has already been achieved. Having values, however, is not the same as having well-developed character.

Looking back to the example of Nelson Mandela, we can see evidence of his character. Certainly, showing his nation a path out of a viciously racist past and into a more just future, thereby avoiding the horrors of a race-based civil war, qualifies on that score. Once in office, moreover, he undertook ambitious and difficult reforms of major branches of his government, including the civil service and security forces. All of these reforms took longer and cost more than anticipated, which tested both Mandela's character and commitment.

At the same time, we should note that the record of Mandela's "character impacts" is mixed. For example, South Africa today is rife with corruption that many say took root during Mandela's presidency. "He was loyal to his comrades to a fault," wrote one insider, "and was therefore blind to some of their misdeeds."[26] More fundamentally, some critics faulted him for being too eager to cater to the white power elite at the expense of the nation's majority. In the same spirit, others argued that his decision to "prioritize tranquility over justice" inevitably meant that serious human rights crimes went unpunished.[27]

What about the component parts of Mandela's character? Looking back years later, Pienaar emphasized two attributes: humility and intellect.[28] One of his former jailers, Christon Brand, pointed to Mandela's "great gift of magnanimity":

His people were being beaten and arrested and detained without charge. Some of them were little more than children. His own wife and daughters were suffering. Yet he was able to produce a smile and a handshake for the very people who were ordering this.[29]

He was courageous and determined. He was an outstanding communicator, arguably because of his strength of character, anchored in a transcendent vision for the future—"the rainbow nation." He tempered his strong sense of justice—fostered both before and during prison—with a compassionate humanity. "He embodied what he proclaimed," declared Bishop Desmond Tutu in a eulogy:

He invited his former jailer to attend his presidential inauguration as a VIP guest, and he invited the man who led the state's case against him at the Rivonia Trial, calling for the imposition of the death penalty, to lunch at his presidential office. . . . He had a unique flair for spectacular, hugely symbolic acts of human greatness that would be gauche if carried out by most others.[30]

But again, using this "components-part" metric, Mandela was far from perfect. By nature and life experience, he was not inclined toward the kind of administrative detail that his infant democracy sorely needed. He was personally vain, insisting on being supplied with a particular hair oil—even in the later, less punitive years of his imprisonment and even after the product stopped being manufactured. But to his credit, he himself took pains to dispel the notion that he was a saint. Toward the end of his life, in a 2013 interview with Oprah Winfrey, he confessed that throughout his rapid ascent to global celebrity, he worried that he was being raised to the position of a "semi-god." He insisted that he hated being cast as the "rare, exceptional, Messianic specimen of the breed" on which a Black-led African government was entirely dependent.[31] He always wanted to be known, he said, as a man with weaknesses, some of which were fundamental.[32]

Mandela died in December 2013. Eight years earlier, he had sat with a *New York Times* reporter to help that writer prepare his obituary. The writer recited the long list of torments that Mandela had suffered at the hands of his jailers and asked the obvious question: How do you keep hatred in check?

"Hating clouds the mind," Mandela replied almost dismissively, as if he thought the answer to the question was obvious. "It gets in the way of strategy. Leaders cannot afford to hate."[33] In other words, at the core of his character was a rare form of *judgment* that allowed him to bring his formidable intellect to bear on his emotions and intuitions.

With Mandela's example in mind, we can probably agree that character is something that we want to cultivate in ourselves. And we can probably agree further that character is something that we want to discover in our leaders. In other words, given the choice, we'd rather be led by someone who is character-rich than by someone who is character-poor.

But is that a realistic expectation?

Can you develop character?

If we want our leaders to be embody and be directed by character, then we only have two choices. We either have to beat the bushes and hope that we find enough character-rich leaders, or we need to find a way to develop character in ourselves and in the people around us.

Is that even possible? Can you develop character? We've all heard the expression that *leaders are born, not made.* Think of all those metaphors borrowed from the natural world that come to bear on this point. *A tiger can't change its stripes. A leopard can't change its spots.*

When it comes to the specific realm of character and its component parts, moreover, we're often told that our personal identities and our psychological makeups are pretty much locked in place by an early age.[34] For example, we are often told that important behaviors may be fully ingrained before we head off to kindergarten. Again looking to the animal kingdom, we hear that *you can't teach an old dog new tricks.*[35] We are presented with seemingly fixed, bimodal, and immutable categories—*introvert* versus *extrovert*, for example— and encouraged to locate ourselves within them: *Am I this, or am I that?* Even some of those who say that we *can* change after childhood assert that as we mature, our developmental processes slow down and become more resistant to change.

All of this would seem to validate the "beating the bushes" prescription posed previously: find your leaders with character where you can because you're certainly not going to develop them. We sometimes encounter this philosophy in our MBA classrooms and even more often in our discussions with participants in our executive programs. During one of those sessions, in the context of a

discussion about character, one executive—who had sat in on some of our related MBA sessions—commented:

> The issue, based on my observations, is that the character of MBA students is
> already deeply formed before entering business school, and then is burnished
> by business school. The MBA students are driven—after all, that's how they
> earned the qualifications to get accepted. They are then driven further by a
> hyper-intense MBA environment. When they graduate, they *continue* to be
> driven. And driven people are unlikely to be reflective and morally aware, at
> least until a life-altering event occurs.

I would also add that I saw clear lies and pandering during MBA class discussions about ethics. People said what they thought would get them the marks. So I,
for one, am less than hopeful about MBA students and their moral awakening.[36]

So, indeed, it appears that tigers can't change their stripes unless they enroll
in an MBA program, in which case they are likely to intensify their existing
stripes—right?

Certainly not! People *can* and *do* change. At the risk of sounding like business educators who are defensive about business education, we begin with the
premise that when it comes to character development, there are three primary
gaps—at least two of which can and should be addressed in the context of an
MBA program and, indeed, education more broadly.[37]

First, many people, including many young people, are simply not aware of
any models of virtues and character strengths. At a minimum, therefore, we need
to expose students to learning opportunities that enable them to uncover these
elements.

Second, many individuals—again including many young people—are unaware of where they stand relative to character development, particularly given
that most haven't spent much (or even any) time reflecting on their character. So
there's an important reflective/diagnostic element to developing character, and
most would agree that an academic community is highly suited to that. Deliberate teaching interventions such as roleplays, collaborative learning techniques,
service-learning opportunities, and self-reflection exercises in the classroom appear to affect character development through increased moral awareness and
moral reasoning.[38]

And third, we (and Aristotle) note that closing the gap between knowing and
doing is a lifelong journey, much of which must occur in context—and hence,
experiencing character development is necessary.

To reiterate, we will always *become* something when it comes to character.
Our character changes for better or worse. Subsequent chapters reveal how we
can intentionally develop character whatever our life circumstances. Look again
to Nelson Mandela's example. "Before I went to jail," he commented in an interview late in his life, "I was a reckless young man. But when I came out, I had,

to a very large extent, I believe, matured."[39] In our terms, his character had developed. He also seemed to see that development process as continuing, noting that his second wife, Graca Machel—whom he married at age 79—had "helped me in that process of maturity."[40]

Bishop Desmond Tutu offered personal reflections at the time of Mandela's death:

> The truth is that the 27 years Madiba, as he was known, spent in the belly of the apartheid beast deepened his compassion and capacity to empathize with others. On top of the lessons about leadership and culture to which he was exposed growing up, and his developing a voice for young people in anti-apartheid politics, prison seemed to add an understanding of the human condition.
>
> Like a most precious diamond formed deep beneath the surface of the Earth, the Madiba who emerged from prison in January 1990 was virtually flawless.

Instead of calling for his pound of flesh, he proclaimed the message of forgiveness and reconciliation, inspiring others by his example to extraordinary acts of nobility of spirit.[41]

Certainly, Mandela would have been uncomfortable with some of Tutu's language—"precious diamond," "virtually flawless," "nobility of spirit." But at the same time, he would have agreed that the extreme hardships he endured gave him an enhanced understanding of the human condition.

Can character be developed? We've already cited Aristotle on the specifics— the component parts, or "front-on" view, of character. But this was only one element in Aristotle's thinking and writing on the subject. For many of the ancient Greeks, including Plato as well as Aristotle, it was not so much that character could be taught but rather that character is something that is *habituated*—that is, acquired through the consistent application of the virtues over the course of one's lifetime.[42] It's like learning any other new skill: only by practicing virtuous acts do we develop character. And as we described in subsequent chapters, linking the science of character to the science of habit development provides the robust foundation for the paradigm of character development.

In addition, Aristotle saw character as something that is not formed on one's own but requires a context: relationships and community. Only through sharing our interests and goals with others—in other words, forging and strengthening the bonds of kinship—can we develop social virtues such as temperance, generosity, and friendliness.[43]

Individuals learn what is right and good by observing good people doing the right thing and then aspiring to become of similar character.[44] Similarly, people are motivated to do good deeds when they see someone else perform a helpful act.[45] Researchers have found that people generally tended to mirror others' generosity across different types of helping behaviors and different types of people in need of help. So we are confident in saying that not only is character something that can be learned, but also, it is the responsibility of *all* of our institutions—including, yes, our educational institutions—to provide an environment that fosters virtuous behavior and in which virtuous behaviors can be observed and discovered.[46]

And we are confident in answering our own question: can you develop character? Yes, you can.

Does character matter?

If we can agree that character can be developed, we next have to address the issue of whether changing our character for the better is simply a nice-to-have or an organizational imperative. Put more bluntly, for people engaged in the daily rough and tumble of business, is there a compelling case for focusing on character?

We say *yes* emphatically. But we also stress up front that it's not easy. "Leaders are not born, they are made," the legendary US football coach Vince Lombardi once observed. "And they are made by hard effort, which is the price we must all pay for success."[47] So once again: for people in business and other complex human organizations, is the hard effort required for character building worth it?

Again, we say the answer is "yes," and on several levels. The first is the *personal* level. When you develop character within yourself, you are very likely to achieve a heightened sense of well-being. You feel better, physically and emotionally, and have more energy. With enhanced well-being, you help unlock your leadership potential.

And let's posit that this heightened sense of well-being extends outward from you, through your interactions with family members and friends. You are a more competent and caring parent. You are a more patient coach of your kid's soccer team. You are more likely to attend and enjoy social events. You are a more effective member of your local school board, director of your favorite nonprofit, or volunteer at the church social. All of this adds up to you exerting a new kind of positive impact on your families, friends, and communities.

If this is all true, then developing character within ourselves is a *highly practical* undertaking. It's not a case of "virtue being its own reward" (although that in and of itself is not a bad thing). It's a case of transforming yourself into a more effective force for good and force for change with near-universal applicability.

And of course, this effectiveness travels with you to the office. With the benefit of enhanced leader character, you are better at entering into business partnerships—probably with better partners!—better at onboarding yourself and others, better at hiring good people, and so on, and so on.

So now let's imagine a corporate (or other) organizational setting that is populated with an abundance of leaders with character on all levels. That company is likely to have less friction, more cross-enterprise collaboration, more innovation, less turnover, increased customer retention (or whatever metrics are most important in that particular context), and better relations with its shareholders and other constituents.[48]

Conversely, that company is less likely to fall prey to judgment-derived disasters. We focused on Volkswagen earlier in the chapter, but VW's downfall was far from unique. Think of the implosions at Enron, Global Financial Crisis, Wells Fargo, Boeing, and so many other companies that fell from grace, dramatically and suddenly. In all those cases, a negative character contagion set in, and sooner or later, a corrupted culture collapsed. A 2010 study at the University of North Carolina at Chapel Hill found that people were more likely to cheat on an exam if the exam room was made slightly darker.[49] We'll take that as a metaphor for negative character contagion: Volkswagen's engineers turned the "character lights" down low.[50]

It's about individuals with character, and it's also about those leaders operating in a context of *positive* character contagion. True, Mandela was an embodiment of strength of character. But he was only able to be effective when his ideas took root in a context: first an open-minded coach, then a team, then 60,000 people in a stadium, then a nation. Again, as we said earlier, in the context of *positive* character contagion.[51]

Can the same phenomenon occur in the for-profit sector? Consider the case of Martin Guitar, based in Nazareth, Pennsylvania. The company faced its first collapse in the 1970s, when a disgruntled workforce briefly unionized. But even after that challenge passed, things got increasingly grim.[52] By 1982, the company was $9 million in debt. Chris Martin—the great-great-great grandson of the founder—took over as CEO in 1986. Annual guitar sales had fallen from 23,000 in the 1970s to 3,000 by the late 1980s. Even more worrisome, the guitars that they *were* selling weren't particularly good—they couldn't be tuned properly—and the company hadn't invested to solve the problem. Financial woes mounted, and appraisers recommended selling the company to salvage some value from the still-illustrious brand. "My dad hobbled the company with a lot of debt," Martin recalls. "Our banks fired us."[53]

The very young CEO called together the workforce and offered a challenge: "I said, 'Look, if it's only 3,000 guitars, we'll try to figure out how to make this business work, and we've got to make damn good guitars because that's what we are.' That resonated with my colleagues."

At the same time, he proposed a deal: "If you guys fix our quality problems, I'll share whatever profits we make with you."

"We knew that if we succeeded in turning this company around and didn't share the fruits of that success," Martin recalls, "the employees would be resentful." The workers accepted the unprecedented deal, and things rapidly turned around. The first profit-sharing checks were so pitifully small—and the company still so financially shaky—that some employees simply taped their un-cashed checks to their workstations. But by the late 1980s, the company had returned to significant profitability, and those profit-sharing checks began to swell. Meanwhile, the company began offering college-tuition reimbursement and committed itself to solving sustainability issues. Martin made a point of introducing himself to all new employees in Nazareth, taking them on factory tours as he talked about the company's traditions. By 2020, Martin was cranking out 130,000 guitars a year.

"I'm not sure how an atomic bomb works," Martin recently reflected. "But I think it starts with an implosion, then an explosion. In a similar way, I forced us to look inward [and focus on guitar-making], and, in the process, I've unleashed a lot of energy."[54]

We reach the same conclusion using different language. Despite all the crush-ing pressures Martin was under, he remained transparent, candid, empathetic, and committed to the cause—and thereby sparked a positive and sustained char-acter contagion.

Think of your company in the same light. Now think bigger, looking toward your supply chains. Would even those structured, highly transactional relation-ships benefit from a large-scale infusion of character? We believe they would, and can, and do. You can probably already identify those vendors and customers whom you trust to *do the right thing* under both normal and abnormal circum-stances. Most likely, they are organizations with strong cultures infused with strength of character.

Now think about the biggest challenges facing our organizations and our so-ciety, and ask the same question on this bigger scale: *would we benefit if those challenges were tackled by people and organizations of character?* This is an-other one of those questions that may best be answered by toggling back to the converse proposition. What if crypto, AI, quantum computing, bioengineering, and social media were dominated by bad actors?[55] Can we afford to have char-acter-poor individuals and corrupted cultures determining how these tools and technologies will get used?

In short, there *is* a case for character—a powerful case. Based on that conclu-sion, what we need now is a reliable set of tools and techniques for observing, assessing, and developing character in people and organizations—a tool kit that is based not on goodwill and wishful thinking but rather in systematic research and rigorous testing in the real world. In *The Character Compass*, and in the universe of organizational experience that lies behind it, that's what we have.

Finally, let's look back to the definition of "Leader Character" that we put forward in the introduction. Leader character, you'll recall, is a defined set of interconnected behaviors that satisfy a set of criteria as being "virtuous"—in other words, behaviors that deliver sustained excellence and well-being. Here, we'll add that we're talking about excellence and well-being that are not only enjoyed by the individual but which also benefit the context within which that individual operates.

Obviously, this definition begs a key question: *which* "defined set of interconnected behaviors"? That's the subject we explore in Chapter 2: the science of character.

Notes

1 The supporting data can be found here: www.marketingcharts.com/industries/automotive-industries-39421, accessed March 13, 2023.

2 See an interview on *The Street* with Vinay Shahani, vice president of marketing at Volkswagen, teeing up the ad a week before the game at www.youtube.com/watch?v=US7LpFXxlpg. Awkward in retrospect!

3 All the featured "angelic" engineers, incidentally, were men.

4 See the ad at www.youtube.com/watch?v=qfctJovhi_o. The angel-transformation "plot" derives, loosely, from the classic movie *It's a Wonderful Life.*

5 "Puppy Love" pushed Budweiser past VW that year as most shared brand. The add can be accessed here; www.youtube.com/watch?v=dlNO2trC-mk.

6 Many of the details in this section are from Danny Hakim's, Aaron M. Kessler's, and Jack Ewing's insightful article in the September 27, 2015, issue of the *New York Times,* online at www.nytimes.com/2015/09/27/business/as-vw-pushed-to-be-no-1-ambitions-fueled-a-scandal.html, accessed March 13, 2023.

7 See Robert Glazer's contemporary opinion piece in the January 8, 2016, edition of *Entrepreneur,* online at www.entrepreneur.com/article/254178, accessed March 13, 2023.

8 The cars spewed out almost *40 times* the amount of NOx allowed by law. See www.nytimes.com/2015/09/27/opinion/sunday/me-and-my-jetta-how-vw-broke-my-heart.html?action=click&module=RelatedCoverage&pgtype=Article&region=Footer, accessed March 13, 2023.

9 Again, www.nytimes.com/2015/09/27/business/as-vw-pushed-to-be-no-1-ambitions-fueled-a-scandal.html.

10 As of this writing, Winterkorn's trial has been repeatedly delayed due to Winterkorn's ill health and the disruptions of the COVID-19 pandemic. See the Reuters account at www.reuters.com/business/autos-transportation/trial-ex-volkswagen-ceo-likely-be-delayed-again-2021-08-25/ accessed March 13, 2023. Winterkorn did agree in June 2021 to pay VW $13 million in damages resulting from the scandal. See www.expatica.com/de/uncategorized/trial-of-former-vw-boss-delayed-again-over-ill-health-331441/, accessed March 13, 2023.

11 This biography is principally derived from the Nelson Mandela Foundation at www.nelsonmandela.org/content/page/biography, and part of it was included in our earlier book, *Developing Leader Character.*

12 The full text is online at the African National Congress's website at www.anc.org.za/show.php?id=3132, accessed March 13, 2023.

13 This anecdote and quote is taken from https://tpy.nelsonmandela.org/pages/part-i-democratic-breakthrough/the-presidency-getting-into-union-buildings/2-1-first-days-in-office-building-trust, accessed March 13, 2023.

14 This paraphrase is taken from Morgan Freeman's powerful rendition of the impromptu speech in the movie *Invictus,* online at www.americanrhetoric.com/MovieSpeeches/moviespeechinvictus2.htm, accessed March 13, 2023.

15 This quote is taken from https://tpy.nelsonmandela.org/pages/part-i-democratic-breakthrough/the-presidency-getting-into-union-buildings/2-3-a-small-office, accessed March 13, 2023.

16 This quote is taken from www.history.com/news/nelson-mandela-1995-rugby-world-cup-south-african-unity, accessed March 13, 2023. He delivered similar words during his iconic speech, "Sport has the power to change the world," which can be accessed here: www.youtube.com/watch?v=y1-7w-bJCtY.

17 This story is told at length in John Carlin's book, *Playing the Enemy,* later adapted by director Clint Eastwood into the movie *Invictus*.

18 This quote is taken from www.history.com/news/nelson-mandela-1995-rugby-world-cup-south-african-unity, accessed March 13, 2023.

19 See the stirring YouTube video featuring this moment and reflections by team members, online at www.youtube.com/watch?v=G7E4KGJFTek.

20 The powerful and emotional scene can be seen online at www.youtube.com/watch?v=2S6YYDbjUu8.

21 This quote is taken from www.bangkokpost.com/sports/1938988/how-mandela-inspired-pienaar-and-springboks-to-conquer-the-world, accessed March 13, 2023.

22 It's hard to overstate the enduring global impact of the event. This comment comes from a 2019 Indian business periodical, online at www.thehindubusinessline.com/news/sports/invictus-how-nelson-mandela-used-rugby-to-unite-south-africa/article29870024.ece, accessed March 13, 2023.

23 We encourage the reader to read the following blog on the Springboks, www.worldrugbyshop.com/blogs/blog/springbok, accessed March 13, 2023.

24 These definitions are derived from our previous work, *Developing Leadership Character*.

25 This material is drawn in large part from an article written by Mary Crossan, Jeffrey Gandz, and Gerard Seijts, "Developing leadership character." *Ivey Business Journal*, January/February 2012, reprint #9B12TA07.

26 This quote is taken from www.nytimes.com/2013/12/06/opinion/the-contradictions-of-mandela.html?searchResultPosition=1, accessed March 13, 2023.

27 See, for example, www.nytimes.com/2013/12/07/world/africa/mandela-politics.html, accessed March 13, 2023. Mandela's former wife, Winnie Madikizela-Mandela, loudly espoused the "betrayal" point of view. See www.standard.co.uk/hp/front/how-nelson-mandela-betrayed-us-says-exwife-winnie-6734116.html, accessed March 13, 2023.

28 Francois Pienaar's reminiscences about the World Cup and Mandela are at www.youtube.com/watch?v=BMMrhZzp3Mw.

29 This quote is taken from the book *Mandela: My Prisoner, My Friend*, by Christo Brand. Thomas Dunne Books, 2014.

30 This quote is taken from the December 6, 2013, eulogy by Desmond Tutu, published in *The Washington Post,* online at www.washingtonpost.com/local/nelson-mandela-a-colossus-of-unimpeachable-moral-character/2013/12/06/0a2cd28a-5ec9-11e3-be07-006c776266ed_story.html, accessed March 13, 2023. The Rivonia Trial to which Tutu refers took place in 1963–64 and resulted with eight defendants, including Mandela, being sentenced to life imprisonment.

31 From the retrospect section of the Mandela archives, online at https://tpy.nelsonmandela.org/pages/part-i-democratic-breakthrough/the-presidency-getting-into-union-buildings/2-5-retrospect, accessed March 13, 2023. The quote is a paraphrase of Mandela's mindset by an aide, Jakes Gerwel.

32 See the segment "Why Nelson Mandela Says He's Only Human," from *The Oprah Winfrey Show*, www.youtube.com/watch?v=t1hZ-z6aoHs.

33 See the obituary online at www.nytimes.com/2013/12/06/world/africa/nelson-man-dela_obit.html, accessed March 13, 2023 The italicized quotes are the obituary writer's paraphrases.

34 For the moment, we'll allow "personality" to stand in as an inadequate substitute for "character."

35 This seems to imply that with good training, puppies might aspire to Leader Character someday, but their untrained parents probably can't.

36 This quote is taken from an award-winning article written by Mary Crossan, Daina Mazutis, Gerard Seijts, and Jeffrey Gandz, "Developing Leadership Character in Business Programs," published in *Academy of Management Learning & Education*, 2013. The article can be accessed through https://journals.aom.org/doi/abs/10.5465/amle.2011.0024a.

37 See "Developing Leadership Character in Business Programs," by Mary Crossan, Daina Mazutis, Gerard Seijts, and Jeffrey Gandz.

38 Relevant articles to support our statement include the following. Comer, D. R., & Vega, G. (2008). Using the PET assessment instrument to help students identify factors that could impede moral behavior. *Journal of Business Ethics*, 77: 129–145. Kish-Gephart, J. J., Harrison, D. A., & Treviño, L. K. (2010). Bad apples, bad cases, and bad barrels: Meta-analytic evidence about sources of unethical decisions at work. *Journal of Applied Psychology*, 95: 1–31. Schmidt, C. D., McAdams, C. R., & Foster, V. (2009). Promoting the moral reasoning of undergraduate business students through a deliberate psychological education-based classroom intervention. *Journal of Moral Education*, 38: 315–334.

39 From the Nelson Mandela Archives, online at https://tpy.nelsonmandela.org/pages/part-vii-personal/18-the-bloom-from-lonely-winter/18-4-what-drew-me, accessed March 13, 2023.

40 From the Nelson Mandela Archives, online at https://tpy.nelsonmandela.org/pages/part-vii-personal/18-the-bloom-from-lonely-winter/18-4-what-drew-me, accessed March 13, 2023.

41 Again, this quote is taken from the December 6, 2013, eulogy by Desmond Tutu, published in *The Washington Post,* online at www.washingtonpost.com/local/nelson-mandela-a-colossus-of-unimpeachable-moral-character/2013/12/06/0a2cd28a-5ec9-11e3-be07-006c776266ed_story.html accessed March 13, 2023.

42 These ideas are taken from Arjoon, S. (2000). Virtue theory as a dynamic theory of business. *Journal of Business Ethics*, 28: 159–178. Irwin, T. (1999). *Aristotle's Nicomachean Ethics* (Translated, with Introduction, Notes, and Glossary). Indianapolis, IN: Hacket Publishing.

43 This idea is taken from Horvath, C. M. (1995). Excellence v. Effectiveness: MacIntyre's critique of business. *Business Ethics Quarterly*, 5: 199–532. Solomon, R. C. (1992). Corporate roles, personal virtues: An Aristotelean approach to business ethics. *Business Ethics Quarterly*, 2: 317–339.

44 These ideas are taken from Hill, A., & Stewart, I. (1999). Character education in business schools: Pedagogical strategies. *Teaching Business Ethics*, 3: 179–193.

45 This idea is based on Jung, H., Seo, E., Han, E., Henderson, M. D., & Patall, E. A. (2020). Prosocial modeling: A meta-analytic review and synthesis. *Psychological Bulletin*, 146: 635–663.

46 These ideas are taken from Crossan, M., Mazutis, D., Seijts, G. H., & Gandz, J. (2013). Developing leadership character in business programs. *Academy of Management Learning and Education*, 2: 285–305. Sadler-Smith, E. (2012). Before virtue: Biology, brain, behavior, and "moral sense." *Business Ethics Quarterly*, 22: 351–376.

47 The excerpt is from "The Speech," Vince Lombardi's stump talk, last delivered by Lombardi in Dayton, Ohio on June 22, 1970. The full text is online at www.pnbhs. school.nz/wp-content/uploads/2015/11/VINCE-LOMBARDI-The-Speech-Leadership.pdf, accessed March 13, 2023.

48 See, for example, "Exploring the relationships between organizational virtuousness and performance," by Kim S. Cameron, David Bright, and Arran Caza, in *American Behavioral Scientist,* online at https://journals.sagepub.com/doi/pdf/10.1177/00027 64203260209?casa_token=rCTn8wQJOwYAAAAA%3AVPmE2GYo_gwkqUm-00WuiPvTYOAsqBNlhz3wpB9YPHMQpMCKe1zKWBrwtIAArIjTZN_V4dTm-vWZ2v&, accessed March 13, 2023.

49 See Joseph Spino's "Character development and business ethics" blog, online at https://blogs.lse.ac.uk/businessreview/2020/08/13/character-development-and-business-ethics/ accessed March 13, 2023.

50 This is also an example—admittedly a bad example—of how our characters aren't carved in stone at birth. If we're corruptible, we're certainly changeable and most likely "improveable."

51 We've emphasized the Springboks/rugby story here because of its dramatic value—but of course, it was only one of many contexts within which Mandela exercised and leveraged his Leader Character.

52 We have pieced together this story from multiple sources. See, for example, https:// guitar.com/features/interviews/the-industry-interview-chris-martin-iv-ceo-of-martin-guitar/; www.captrust.com/a-journey-of-six-generations/; and www.family-businessmagazine.com/grandson-who-amplified-brand-0 as well as conversations with the principals.

53 See the article https://msretailer.com/interview-chris-martin-iv-ceo-cf-martin/, accessed March 13, 2023.

54 See the article www.familybusinessmagazine.com/grandson-who-amplified-brand-0, accessed March 13, 2023.

55 Unfortunately, in the time since we first drafted this chapter, some of those bad actors have stepped forward.

Chapter 2

The science of character

In the first weeks of 2020, a new and deadly disease—first detected in December 2019 in Wuhan, Hubei Province, China, where a cluster of patients began experiencing unexplained shortness of breath and fevers—began racing around the planet. Even before they understood their enemy, governments began scrambling to fight back.[1]

Unfortunately, the epidemic moved far faster than those governments.

The disease didn't even get its own name—"COVID-19," from the World Health Organization—until February 11. Not until a month later, on March 11, did WHO declare COVID-19 an epidemic. Two days after that, US President Donald Trump declared a nationwide emergency. And a week later, on March 20, 2020, the Canadian and U.S. governments announced they had reached a temporary agreement to close their shared border in a "collaborative and reciprocal" effort to limit the spread of the COVID-19 virus.[2]

The agreement covered all nonessential air, ferry, rail, and land travel across the international border—the longest in the world at 5,525 miles, or 8,891km. This was, to put it mildly, a big deal. Every day, under normal circumstances, an average of more than 300,000 people and approximately $1.6 billion of goods crossed that border at 8 airports, 13 seaports, 27 rail crossings, and 117 land crossings. As a joint statement issued by the US and Canadian governments put it:

> The United States and Canada recognize it is critical we preserve supply chains between both countries. These supply chains ensure that food, fuel, and life-saving medicines reach people on both sides of the border. Supply chains, including trucking, will not be impacted by this new measure. Americans and Canadians also cross the land border every day to do essential work or for other urgent or essential reasons, and that travel will not be impacted.[3]

In other words, the temporary closure agreement—to be implemented within 24 hours—was fairly brimming over with exceptions, exemptions, and conditions, including the "essential/nonessential" distinction, all of which would

DOI: 10.4324/9781003341215-3

require exceptional yet consistent judgment on the part of thousands of border officials.[4]

On the Canadian side of the border, that judgment would be exercised by the Canada Border Services Agency (CBSA), which in the course of its normal duties enforces more than 90 acts and regulations that are intended to facilitate the flow of legitimate travelers and trade between Canada and the rest of the world. CBSA employs approximately 14,000 staff, including more than 6,500 uniformed (and armed) CBSA officers, who provide services at more than 1,200 service locations across Canada, within the US, and around the world. It is the second largest law enforcement agency in Canada.

In the years preceding March 2020, CBSA had gone through some difficult times. Budget cuts and freezes had hurt morale. A we/they divide had opened between the uniformed frontline officers and the (more numerous) back-office staff who supported them. The training that had been made available to the frontline leadership was generally conceded to be inadequate, and it wasn't clear whether those leaders had the skills necessary to address a range of workplace-based cultural issues that had begun to emerge. John Ossowski—a career Canadian public servant who took over as president of CBSA in 2016—was concerned about that looming challenge, which called for enhanced judgment, teamwork, and resilience. Having worked with Ivey faculty members on similar challenges in several of his prior government postings, he now explored ways to use leader character to start reshaping the culture at CBSA.

Ossowski began with his executive team and built outward to the superintendents in charge of the uniformed officers. The focus of the training was Leadership Character, using both an individual and organizational lens. Over time, nearly every major function of the CBSA came under scrutiny through this lens: recruitment and selection, performance management, training, recognition, leadership development, and so on. "Character is really embedded in everything we do," he commented in a recent interview. "I bet a day doesn't go by that we don't talk about it, in some way or another."[5]

Over the next few years leading up to March 20, 2020, recalled Ossowski, the focus on leader character helped his agency's leaders develop their judgment and ability to function as a coherent team—all of which paid off in the difficult weeks and months following the closure of the border:

> I firmly believe that the investments that we made before the pandemic gave us resilience, in terms of how we've managed through all of the ambiguity, and all the attention on us—sometimes negative—in terms of how we were managing things.
>
> There's a lot of armchair quarterbacks out there with opinions about how we should have done things differently. And you know what? That's fine. There was no road map for doing anything like this. It truly was a black swan event.

But in terms of the strength of the team and the commitment of the team, I think some of the investments that we started to make, and continue to make, in terms of choosing the right leaders, and supporting those people, have served us well. Including myself! I mean, I've gotten a lot of strength from the team that we've created here. I think I've got the best team in government, quite frankly. And that's only because we've had the courage to sort of go through a self-examination process—sometimes together and sometimes individually—that we're in that sweet spot.

Early in 2022, Canada's top public safety minister, Marco Mendicino, sent so-called "mandate letters" to four federal agencies tasked with assuring public safety: the Royal Canadian Mounted Police, the Correctional Service of Canada, the Canadian Security Intelligence Service, and the CBSA. Those mandates—drawn up by the Prime Minister to give policy guidance to recently appointed Cabinet ministers—may have been shaped, in part, by a class-action lawsuit that had been brought recently by more than 1,000 black federal workers claiming that the government and its agencies were institutionally racist. The agencies that Mendicino oversaw had come under increasing pressure in recent years from pandemic-related concerns and demands for enhanced national security, many of which had the effect of throwing up new barriers in front of newcomers and members of minority groups.[6] Even under these difficult circumstances, however, those agencies had to own the challenge of inclusion.

Although the mandate letter received by John Ossowski at the CBSA focused mainly on the need to further upgrade Canada's ports of entry—to combat illegal immigration and the smuggling of drugs and firearms—Ossowski took to heart Mendicino's larger message: that he and his CBSA team had to come up with benchmarks aimed at combating institutional racism, misogyny, and unconscious bias. It was a challenge he willingly accepted—in part because, as noted previously, CBSA had already been working hard on the challenge of culture change for several years.

One thing that those prior years of hard work had already taught Ossowski was that none of this would be easy. He was the leader of the second-biggest law enforcement agency in Canada and wasn't surprised when he encountered traditional, even rigid, points of view. But he was determined to give his managers and frontline officers the tools they need—even when they didn't always want to pick up and wield those tools:

The language [of Leader Character] transcends the different cultural backgrounds the organization might have, right? These [dimensions] are universal attributes. It doesn't matter what your heritage is, or what culture you might have come from. And the neutrality of the language advances the accessibility of the ideas, and help make them something that everyone can buy into.

I'm currently unpacking that a little bit with my team. We're really focusing on bringing that out. I'm very lucky to have a very diverse workforce—but we've found that not everybody wants to lead. Why? I don't know that we've been supporting their leadership potential, right? So that's another piece that I'd like to explore with my team. If this [Leader Character] language really is cross-cultural, how can we take advantage of that?

In Chapter 8, we'll return to the CBSA and its efforts to promote equity, diversity, and inclusion, in part by using the leader character framework to effect cultural change. For now, though, let's pin down the elements of that framework. What are its roots, how was it developed, and what does it look like today?

The roots of Leader Character

On a gloomy morning in 2009, we—two of this book's authors along with several other academic colleagues—were running a focus group in an elegant oak-paneled board room in London. Taking part in our meeting that day was a group of about 25 high-powered C-suite executives, mostly from the financial services sector.

The mood in the room was even gloomier than the London weather. Everyone was still trying to come to grips with the recent near total collapse of the global financial system. This meeting was one of a series we were holding with more than 450 senior executives around the world in the aftermath of the 2008 crisis. At each gathering, we kicked off with the same question: *what went wrong?*

On this occasion, like many others, the group answered the question by talking through the usual culprits: overreliance on complex and unrealistic financial models, perverse compensation systems, flawed governance and risk-management frameworks, or a perfect-storm combination of all them. But in this and almost every other focus group we ran, the conversation soon turned in a direction that we eventually learned to expect. Without prompting from us, our participants began pointing to a factor that they considered most important of all: the *character* of the leaders involved in the global debacle. Invariably, someone would express the conviction that at crucial moments in the unfolding economic catastrophe, different decisions—*better* decisions, by which they meant decisions that exhibited stronger character—might have changed the course of the crisis for the better and might have averted disaster.

But that consensus turned out to be both fragile and shallow. While almost all of these executives agreed that something called "character" mattered— and mattered a great deal—they rarely reached agreement on how it could be defined. Lacking that definition, they wondered aloud whether it could be assessed, developed, and implemented in organizations. Some were honest (and brave) enough to express skepticism about whether stronger character would lead naturally to better performance or whether it might even lead to *worse* performance. As one asked pointedly, "Isn't character like operating with one hand behind your back?"

And that was only one good question among many. In the wake of those meetings, we began working to "pin character down"—to make it less elusive, more rigorous in the sense of scientific testing, and more practically applicable. We adopted what we referred to as an "engaged scholarship" approach, combining a historical review with both quantitative and qualitative analyses and involving more than 2,500 executives from the public, private, and not-for-profit sectors. Our ultimate goal became clearly defined: *to forge a bridge between the research foundations of character and the application of character in leadership practice.*

Of course, we weren't the first to try to bring notions of character into the marketplace. More than two millennia ago, Aristotle declared "character" to be a virtuous set of habits. What we saw in his definition was a prescription for cultivating certain behaviors through repetitive action—that is, habits. If you consistently and intentionally *act* in virtuous ways, Aristotle was saying, you will *be* virtuous.

But of course, it begged the question: *which* virtuous behaviors? As we noted in Chapter 1, Aristotle pointed to *courage, temperance, generosity, magnificence, magnanimity, right ambition, good temper, friendliness, truthfulness, wit, justice*, and *practical wisdom*. This is a good list, which people have been trying to improve upon ever since. In 2004, for example, psychologists Christopher Peterson and Martin Seligman published *Character Strengths and Virtues*, which they characterized as a "handbook and classification" of the subject.[7] Their goal was, in part, to provide a sort of positive-side antidote to the American Psychiatric Association's *Diagnostic and Statistical Manual of Mental Disorders*: the "bible" that medical professionals consult to identify, understand, and treat upward of 300 psychopathologies.

Toward that end, Peterson and Seligman examined philosophical and religious traditions in China (Confucianism, Taoism), South Asia (Buddhism, Hinduism), and the West (Athenian philosophy, Judaism, Christianity, and Islam) to identify virtues and character strengths that facilitate moral behavior and well-being.[8] Their research ultimately identified six universal virtues—transcendence, temperance, practical wisdom, humanity, courage, and justice—and operationalized them through 24 character behaviors that transcend culture: a very useful attribute for work, like ours, that aspires to have broad application.[9] In essence, Peterson and Seligman helped translate character from the fields of theology and philosophy to psychology.

So certainly, our research took this ambitious work and other laudable efforts into account. But we were determined to close the gap between strong theoretical work and the application of that work in the kind of real-world marketplace that Aristotle was aiming at. We were trying to transport character from theology, philosophy, and psychology to individual and organizational leadership education and practice. We wanted to produce something that would be useful not only to individuals but also to contemporary organizations in the public, private, and not-for-profit sectors. Toward those ends, using an engaged scholarship approach to bridge theory and practice, we began the careful work of identifying terminology that spoke more effectively to today's organizational leaders. "Virtues" became dimensions, for example; "character strengths" became elements (recognizing they may not be strengths); and "wisdom" became "judgment," for example.

Based on more than a decade of research as well as extensive experience consulting in major organizations, we believe the evidence is now clear: character can be defined, assessed, developed, and applied *in organizations*, enabling them to arrive at better decisions and sustained excellence.

To condense and slightly restate the definitions offered in Chapter 1, character is an interconnected set of dimensions and elements that are foundational to effective decision-making and functioning. And to answer that question raised by those skeptics in our long-ago focus group, yes, *strong character is an advantage for leaders and organizations* and certainly not a handicap. Not incidentally, it also leads to enhanced well-being of individual leaders—a subject to which we will return in later chapters.

The framework

Our work and our definitions ultimately led to a framework for leader character, one that is based on ten separate dimensions that support an eleventh— *judgment*, which is our rough equivalent of Aristotle's practical wisdom.

Here we will present the framework in two ways. First, in Figure 2.1, we share what might be called a *structural* view, which shows the dimensions of the framework in their interactive relationships with each other. (Don't focus at this point on the small type within the circles—the *elements* that comprise the dimensions—to which we'll return shortly.) All of the dimensions in the outer ring influence, and are influenced by, judgment. They also influence each other in combinations of two or more (although we've left out all of those many additional cross-cutting arrows for the sake of legibility!).

Now we'll define and expand upon these 11 dimensions in the form of a table, Figure 2.2, which is more or less self-explanatory. We encourage you to read and consider these expanded definitions—this time including a prose explanation of the elements—which reflect the considered input of a great many practitioners in real-world organizations.[10] Note that we put "judgment" at the top of the list, representing its central position in the leader character framework:

Now let's consider the next step in our analysis, which is consistent with Aristotle's thinking: *dimensions can become vices in either deficiency or excess.* Consider Figure 2.3[11]

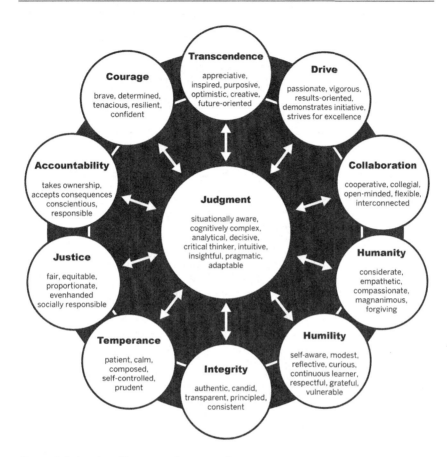

Figure 2.1 Leader Character Framework

Figure 2.3 introduces the next important step in our analysis. "Excess" is not about simply having too much of a single dimension. As our structural model (Figure 2.1) implies, the dimensions of character must be considered *in relationship with each other*. Excess, then, is having too much of one dimension relative to other dimensions that you have too little of and which need to be in balance. Courage, for example, needs to be balanced (constrained) by Temperance to avoid tipping into recklessness. At the same time, Courage needs to be fortified (supported) by Justice and Accountability to avoid slipping back to deficiency. An appropriately Courageous leader supported by a strong sense of Justice and Accountability but constrained appropriately by Temperance is not afraid to speak up and take action even in a difficult situation. This leader speaks and acts in a measured manner that avoids inflaming the difficult situation further.

Maybe an illustration would be useful, at this point. Are there industries in which participants engage in a purposeful underweighting or overweighting of

Dimension	Definition
Judgment	Makes sound decisions in a timely manner based on relevant information and critical analysis of facts. Appreciates the broader context when reaching decisions. Shows flexibility when confronted with new information or situations. Has an implicit sense of the best way to proceed. Can see into the heart of challenging issues. Can reason effectively in uncertain or ambiguous situations.
Courage	Does the right thing even though it may be unpopular, actively discouraged, and/or result in a negative outcome for him/her. Shows an unrelenting determination, confidence, and perseverance in confronting difficult situations. Rebounds quickly from setbacks.
Drive	Strives for excellence, has a strong desire to succeed, tackles problems with a sense of urgency, approaches challenges with energy and passion.
Collaboration	Values and actively supports development and maintenance of positive relationships among people. Encourages open dialogue and does not react defensively when challenged. Is able to connect with others at a fundamental level, in a way that fosters the productive sharing of ideas. Recognizes that what happens to someone, somewhere, can affect all.
Integrity	Holds oneself to a high moral standard and behaves consistently with ethical standards, even in difficult situations. Is seen by others as behaving in a way that is consistent with their personal values and beliefs. Behaves consistently with organizational policies and practices.
Temperance	Conducts oneself in a calm, composed manner. Maintains the ability to think clearly and respond reasonably in tense situations. Completes work and solves problems in a thoughtful, careful manner. Resists excesses and stays grounded.
Accountability	Willingly accepts responsibility for decisions and actions. Is willing to step up and take ownership of challenging issues. Reliably delivers on expectations. Can be counted on in tough situations.
Justice	Strives to ensure that individuals are treated fairly and that consequences (positive or negative) are commensurate with contributions. Remains objective and keeps personal biases to a minimum when making decisions. Provides others with the opportunity to voice their opinions on processes and procedures. Provides timely, specific, and candid explanations for decisions. Seeks to redress wrongdoings inside and outside the organization.
Humility	Lets accomplishments speak for themselves, acknowledges limitations, understands the importance of thoughtful examination of one's own opinions and ideas and embraces opportunities for personal growth and development. Does not consider oneself to be more important or special than others, is respectful of others, and understands and appreciates others strengths and contributions.

Figure 2.2 The Definitions of the Dimensions

Dimension	Definition
Humanity	Demonstrates genuine concern and care for others, and can appreciate and identify with others values, feelings, and beliefs. Has a capacity to forgive and not hold grudges. Understands that people are fallible and offers opportunities for individuals to learn from their mistakes.
Transcendence	Draws inspiration from excellence or appreciation of beauty in such areas as sports, music, arts, and design. Sees possibility where others cannot. Has a very expansive view of things both in terms of taking into account the long term and broad factors. Demonstrates a sense of purpose in life.

Figure 2.2 (Continued)

Deficient Vice	Virtue	Excess Vice
Accountability		
Deflects	Takes Ownership	Cannot delegate
Unaccepting of consequences	Accepts Consequences	Burdened
Negligent	Conscientious	Obsessive
Irresponsible	Responsible	Controlling
Courage		
Cowardice	Brave	Reckless
Hesitant	Determined	Bull-headed
Yielding	Tenacious	Stubborn
Fragile	Resilient	Overly compensating
Unassured	Confident	Arrogant
Transcendence		
Unthankful	Appreciative	Awe-struck
Uninspired	Inspired	Over-stimulated
Directionless	Purposive	Fixated
Short-sighted	Future-oriented	Missing the present
Pessimistic	Optimistic	Delusional
Unimaginative	Creative	Untethered
Drive		
Apathetic	Passionate	Fanatical
Lethargic	Vigorous	Forceful
Aimless	Results-oriented	Tunnel-vision
Waits for direction	Demonstrates Initiative	Dictatorial
Mediocrity	Strives for Excellence	Strives for perfection
Collaboration		
Self-centered	Cooperative	Conflict-avoider
Confrontational	Collegial	People-pleaser

Figure 2.3 The Leader Character Dimensions in Their Virtue and Vice States

Deficient Vice	Virtue	Excess Vice
Narrow-minded	Open-minded	Abstract
Inflexible	Flexible	Directionless
Disconnected	Interconnected	Cannot discern boundaries

Humanity

Deficient Vice	Virtue	Excess Vice
Oblivious to others needs	Considerate	Overly focused on others
Unrelatable	Empathetic	Overwhelmed by feelings
Uncaring	Compassionate	Unable to regulate emotions
Aloof	Magnanimous	Over-bearing
Vindictive	Forgiving	Exploitable

Humility

Deficient Vice	Virtue	Excess Vice
Unaware	Self-aware	Self-conscious
Braggard	Modest	Self-effacing
Unreflective	Reflective	Ruminating
Disinterested	Curious	Transfixed
Fixed Mindset	Continuous Learner	Lacking focus
Disrespectful	Respectful	Fawning
Ungrateful	Grateful	Overwhelmed
Protective	Vulnerable	Over-exposed

Integrity

Deficient Vice	Virtue	Excess Vice
Fake	Authentic	Uncompromising
Untruthful	Candid	Belligerent
Manipulative	Transparent	Indiscriminate
Unprincipled	Principled	Dogmatic
Inconsistent	Consistent	Rigid

Temperance

Deficient Vice	Virtue	Excess Vice
Impatient	Patient	Overly accepting
Anxious	Calm	Indifferent
Agitated	Composed	Detached
Rash	Self-controlled	Overly regulating
Inattentive	Prudent	Overly cautious

Justice

Deficient Vice	Virtue	Excess Vice
Unfair	Fair	"One size fits all"
Inequitable	Equitable	No recognition of exceptions
Disproportionate	Proportionate	Micromanage proportionality
Biased	Even-handed	No recognition of differences
Narrow concerns	Socially Responsible	Paralyzed by complexity

Figure 2.3 (Continued)

Deficient Vice	Virtue	Excess Vice
Judgment		
Oblivious	Situationally Aware	Over valuing each situation
Simplistic	Cognitively Complex	Complicating
Lacking logic	Analytical	Over-analyzing
Indecisive	Decisive	Impulsive
Lazy thinking	Critical Thinker	Overly critical
Lacking instinct	Intuitive	Lacking reason
Ignorant	Insightful	Cunning
Unrealistic	Pragmatic	Overly practical
Stagnant	Adaptable	Overly malleable

Figure 2.3 (Continued)

character dimensions to achieve a particular end? For the sake of argument, let's nominate the world of professional sports, which in at least some circumstances focuses on *winning at all costs*. We'll define the path to that outcome as some combination of Courage and Drive. To the extent that "winning is everything," then you can't have too much of Courage and Drive, right?

The question needs to be answered on several levels: organizational, team, and individual. Coaches tend to represent the character of their organization. Poor leadership cascades downward and can lead both coaches and their players to engage in behaviors that over time work against themselves. This can compromise individual judgment—and ultimately inhibit the performance of the player, the coach, and the team.

In January 2011, during off-season training, 13 members of the University of Iowa's football team were hospitalized following a timed workout consisting of 100 squats. They were suffering from rhabdomyolysis: an ailment caused by intense physical exertion. All of the players recovered, and the coaching staff agreed not to repeat that particular drill—but clearly, unchecked Courage and Drive (and bad coaching) can put you in the hospital.[12]

In terms of the individual, yes, unchecked Courage and Drive may yield the kind and level of short-term performance that's desired—but in excess, they may be unsustainable. The great basketball players, for example, are those who not only hit three-pointers reliably but who also are willing and able to set a pick, grab rebounds, and pass to the open player. "We have never had the league's top scorer," legendary Boston Celtics coach Red Auerbach once said of the most sustained winning dynasty in NBA history. "In fact, we won seven league championships without placing even one among the league's top ten scorers." This was a reflection of a larger and deliberate strategy. When Auerbach recruited, he looked for the young player who was "great yet never stopped being nice"—an

Auerbachian summary that we'll take as a workable definition of an athlete whose Leader Character dimensions are in reasonable balance.[13]

The fact is, unchecked Courage and Drive can be both spectacular and insufficient. In 1961–1962, the Philadelphia Warriors' Wilt Chamberlain enjoyed a truly astounding season, leading the league with an NBA record 50.4 points per game. In one of those games, he scored 100 points—a feat that has never been repeated in professional basketball—and scored more than 4,000 points that season, another total that no other player has ever approached. But to average 50 points per game, let alone 100, you have to freeze your teammates out of the action and do almost all the shooting yourself. Over the course of a long season, that strategy doesn't work. In that same year, the Warriors finished second behind Red Auerbach's Celtics—led by center Bill Russell, who won the league's Most Valuable Player award that year despite scoring an average of "only" 18.9 points per game.[14]

Looking to another sport, cyclist Lance Armstrong—seven-time Tour de France winner who was discovered to have used performance-enhancing drugs and also to have pressured his teammates to use them—confessed to having what he called a "flawed character":

> My ruthless desire to win at all costs served me well on the bike but the level it went to, for whatever reason, is a flaw. That desire, that attitude, that arrogance.[15]

Once we agree that character can be defined by the 11 dimensions and elements defined and discussed in Figures 2.1, 2.2, and 2.3, three key points naturally follow:

- *Character is a habit of being that is objectively observable.* This suggests that—as indicated in Chapter 1—it can be assessed and developed scientifically, like other human behaviors, and developed through the purposeful adoption of appropriate habits. Again, these are recurrent themes in later chapters.
- *What could be a virtue often operates as a vice.* This is a main takeaway from Figure 2.3, and for many individuals and organizations; it is both a wake-up call and a paradigm shift. Perhaps it sounds counterintuitive that someone could have "too much integrity." But indeed, you can. A leader with strong Integrity that is not counterbalanced by Humility and Humanity can be dogmatic and abrasive, even arrogant.
- As Aristotle said so long ago, *one becomes virtuous only by acting virtuously.* Our decisions and actions, especially in difficult or crucial moments, manifest character. We've already stressed the importance of *habit.* How we habitually make decisions—what we think about in crucial moments, what considerations we reference—determines our actions and whether they exhibit character. This works in both good and bad directions, of course, but let's focus on the good. The decision and actions to which we are inclined then form patterns and build capabilities, which influence future actions and decisions. And just as physical exercise builds muscle strength, so character

strength develops though intelligent and disciplined repetition. And you have to do it yourself. As one of our colleagues remarked, *You can't get fit watching someone else exercise.*

Looking back to Figures 2.1, 2.2, and 2.3, we should stress again that these three figures and their contents didn't begin as theory and work their way into the reality of the marketplace. They represent a summation of our work conducted over more than a decade, and they have been validated through surveys of thousands of leaders across sectors and in industries around the world—in organizations ranging from international banks to public-sector organizations, police, military and border-protection services, pro sports teams, and many more. Those leaders whom we have interviewed and surveyed broadly agree that *achieving balance among these framework dimensions leads to successful leadership outcomes.*

Collectively, we've made real progress from those dark days of the Great Economic Meltdown, when—in our collective opinion—even an actionable definition of "character" was lacking. But there's still more hard work to be done. For example, looking at the board level, we recently conducted a study of some 800 members of the boards of directors of major for-profit, not-for-profit, and public-sector organizations.[16] To state our findings simply, directors agreed or strongly agreed that the character of a CEO has a tremendous impact on the effectiveness of a board and that the board should assess and evaluate the character of the CEO. At the same time, a majority of respondents disagreed or strongly disagreed that boards spend sufficient time assessing a potential director's character before asking them to join a board.

Again, there is more work to be done, which we will cover specifically with respect to boards in Chapter 9.

The critical role of judgment

We've stressed that judgment is at the core of our leader character framework, as represented in Figure 2.1. Let's dig deeper into that point.

The world needs leaders with good judgment—or, in Aristotle's phrase, practical wisdom—to address pressing issues that present themselves in highly volatile, uncertain, complex, and ambiguous contexts. Other researchers in our field have focused on this point and on the importance of *context* to the exercise of judgment. In their book *Practical Wisdom: The Right Way to Do the Right Thing*, for example, academics Barry Schwartz and Kenneth Sharpe define practical wisdom as "the right way to do the right thing in a particular circumstance, with a particular person, at a particular time."[17] In our own terminology, the world needs leaders who are able to activate each of the eleven dimensions of character at the right time and in the right amount to guide their decision-making and call forth the right behaviors.

It's instructive to think through how each character dimension comes into play when leaders are presented with unprecedented challenges. For example, imagine how citizens might feel if a leader failed to exhibit Humanity while sharing critical, hard-hitting information with the public. If individuals perceived a lack of compassion for, and understanding of, their personal hardships, they wouldn't feel much of a sense of connection to and trust in that leader, nor would they be likely to have much confidence in the measures to tackle challenges announced. Their anxiety might well increase while their resiliency decreased.

Let's look at a real-world example of the converse situation. In the midst of the COVID-19 pandemic, Doug Ford—then the premier of Ontario, Canada, and a sometimes controversial figure—received praise from members of almost all political groups for the way he ran the province's daily press conferences. Observers noted the deep empathy (an element of Humanity) he conveyed for the public he served, especially when he delivered the grim message that between 3,000 and 15,000 Ontarians might well die from the pandemic over the following 18 to 24 months.[18] To the surprise of many of his critics, he exhibited transparency and candor (both elements of Integrity) in his briefings, evidently in the belief that the possession of knowledge—even unwelcome knowledge—was better than living with fear of the unknown. By infusing his messages with Humanity and Integrity, Ford helped keep trust in government agencies alive—a very tall order given the trust deficit that then existed in many jurisdictions.[19]

Both in civic and organizational life, truly great leaders demonstrate strength along each of the character dimensions. Those strengths combine into good judgment and are called upon when that judgment is exercised. In other words, great leaders use their judgment to call upon and deploy the character dimensions to suit any particular situation.

As noted, judgment is the most complicated of our dimensions. It requires the skillful analysis of a complex situation to grasp the essence of the challenges they are facing and the employment of logical reasoning to determine the requisite action. It further requires that leaders be situationally aware—that is, attuned to *context*—and demonstrate a nuanced appreciation for circumstances requiring unique approaches.

Leaders must use their judgment to deal with what academics and design theorists Horst Rittel and Melvin Webber defined many years ago as "wicked problems"—that is, challenges that are unique, have multiple causes, aren't easily described, and don't have "right" answers.[20]

Austrian Chancellor Sebastian Kurz provided a compelling illustration of this in March 2020, when he discussed European efforts to head off a paralysis of public health systems. Many people readily observed that COVID-19 was disproportionately affecting (and killing) the elderly; far fewer were noticing—or at least saying out loud—that the disease constituted an economic assault on younger generations. Kurz used his well-tuned judgment to find a way to make the latter point without leaving behind the beleaguered elderly. "You have to consider carefully when to adopt these measures," he cautioned—specifically referencing the COVID-associated economic damage—"because a national economy cannot handle this over too long a period."[21]

In the business world, the advent of "fast fashion" has created a wicked problem that to a large extent still awaits resolution through judgment. As a study by researchers at Georgetown University's Walsh School of Foreign Service details the growing trend of producing more and more fashion collections annually, essentially by producing cheap clothing in the global South for sale—and relatively quick disposal—in the global north continues to intensify.[22] The result is, yes, stylish consumers but also environmental degradation. It's been estimated that the clothing industry alone is responsible for 8 percent of global warming. Almost 100 percent of clothing is made with environmentally costly virgin material, and something like 73 percent of used clothes go into landfills around the world.

Meanwhile, fast fashion translates into the increased exploitation of textile workers in the developing world. Minimum wages in China, Turkey, Bangladesh, and India average about $100 per month—when those wages are actually paid. Working conditions can range from unhealthful to lethal. In 2013, for example, 1,134 textile workers were killed when an eight-story factory building in Dhaka, Bangladesh, collapsed without warning.[23]

By definition, there are no easy answers. But clearly, business leaders can call on judgment to rein in the excesses inherent in fast fashion without unduly punishing the involved constituencies. For example, companies like Tommy Hilfiger Global and Inditex (parent company of Zara) are moving beyond vague "green" claims and exploring ways to create a "circular" textile economy—while still finding ways to satisfy their customers.[24]

But again, when dealing with wicked problems, there are no simple solutions. In the abstract, should we move from synthetic fabrics like polyester to, for example, cotton? Yes and no. Something like 2.4 percent of the world's crop land is devoted to cotton, but that crop demands 24 percent of all insecticides and 11 percent of all pesticides sold globally each year. Organic cotton is far more benign, of course—but because it's more expensive, it only accounts for about 1 percent of the world's cotton supply.[25]

Judgment—fueled by Drive and Accountability, among other dimensions—needs to come into play.

Character and context

By now, you've noticed our repeated emphasis on *context*. Up to this point, we've made the point that character is measured, in part, by the degree to which the leader is able to respond effectively to a changing or challenging world. Now we want to approach context from a different but complementary angle. We want to argue that leader character can be a vital tool in *shaping and remaking context*.

Context has often been cast as an almost overwhelming challenge for leaders. We've already explored the Volkswagen cheating scandal, which grew out of both a corrupting industry context and a corrupt corporate culture. And of course, that story is far from unique. Think back to the terrible stories that emerged from Enron, WorldCom, Arthur Andersen, and other companies that were at the center of the scandals of the 1990s and early 2000s. The excuses we heard from those leaders (and subordinates) who got swept up in those trainwrecks ranged from "I was only following orders" to "I was seduced by a culture that turned out to be corrupt" to "We had to do it to remain competitive because everyone else was doing it."

Enron's president Jeffrey Skilling, for example, used several of those excuses. Referring to CEO of Enron Power Corporation Rebecca Mark—who spent billions on power-plant construction outside the US—and high-rolling CFO Andrew Fastow, Skilling commented, "Rebecca poured gasoline all over the balance sheet, and Andy lit the fuse." Skilling told associates that he relied on the professionals around his to keep things on course: "Show me one fucking transaction that the accountants and the attorneys didn't sign off on."[26]

Not exactly a voice of penitence or—we would argue—of character. At Enron, a corrupt context assured the corruption of character.

And here's a sad truth: *in a contest between context and character, context often wins.* Why? One answer seems to reside in human nature. As the famous 1971 Stanford Prison Experiment amply demonstrated, otherwise "moral" people can be led into immoral acts if their context provides them with sufficiently corrupt psychological and social incentives.[27] The same basic conclusion was reached by Stanley Milgram in his earlier Yale studies, in which participants—under the pressure of context—reluctantly administered (simulated) electrical shocks to subjects and gradually increased those shocks to "fatal" levels.[28] Evidently, there is something within us that, at least under certain circumstances, can be amplified by context and thereby make us susceptible to corrupt leadership.

Combining this human tendency with the excuses for character-deficient behaviors listed previously—including "We had to do it to remain competitive because everyone else was doing it"—explains some of the sadder chapters in recent corporate experience. For a compelling example, one needs to look no further than the US airline industry, dominated by the world's largest aircraft manufacturer: Boeing. As we'll see in Chapter 8, the internal messages and emails that emerged in the wake of the Boeing 737 Max scandal—that erupted after two 737s crashed in 2018 and 2019, killing a total of 346 passengers—strongly suggest that an excess of Drive combined with deficiencies in Accountability and judgment was responsible for the disaster.[29] Character drives culture, a subject to which we will return in later chapters.

Since our goal here is not to demoralize our readers, let's look to the positive. leader character can be a powerful tool in shaping and remaking context—but only if people understand the concept and are taught how to apply it in organizational settings. As the prime developers of the leader character concept, we have felt some responsibility for creating educational opportunities to make it accessible and useful to practitioners. Toward that end, we have developed a 13-day curriculum—the leader character Practitioner Certification Program—whereby leaders at multiple levels and academics can become immersed in the whys and hows of leader character and bring those lessons back to their organizations.[30] To date, several cohorts have been certified under the auspices of the Ian O. Ihnatowycz Institute for Leadership: a modest beginning, certainly, but one that because of its "train the trainers" orientation is likely have an ever-broadening impact. Collectively, we need to work against the twin deficits of human nature and character-deprived management education—a big but welcome challenge!

Does character pay?

Implicit in the previous discussion is the notion that developing leader character requires investment—either by the individual, the organization, or both. We therefore should conclude this chapter on the science of character by looking at relevant data and asking the obvious question: *is that investment worth it?* What do the relevant research studies and real-world experiences tell us?

One affirmative response is essentially anecdotal. Referring back to the example of John Ossowski and the CBSA cited at the beginning of the chapter, yes, says Ossowski, *it's worth it.*[31] Others who have experienced the leader character framework at work in the marketplace tell us the same thing.

Where might it be found in that marketplace? One place is in the performance-review cycle. Effective leaders should be able to activate communication and problem-solving skills during performance-management conversations to coach and counsel employees. The quality or effectiveness of such conversations are enhanced when Leader Character dimensions and elements such as empathy, compassion, justice, patience, and resilience are activated.[32]

Another affirmative answer, this one more quantitative in nature, casts character as a kind of catalyst. Some researchers have concluded that, simply stated, *character helps activate competence.* While "entanglement" often carries a negative connotation, these researchers argue that a high degree of entanglement between character and competence tends to lead to extraordinary performance over time.[33]

While there is some evidence that relates particular dimensions of leader character to individual, team, and organizational performance, studies linking the *interconnected* set of leader character dimensions described previously have been sadly lacking—at least until very recently. Two of this book's authors have recently published the first empirical examination of how leader character as an interconnected framework contributes to positive organizational outcomes.[34] We studied 188 leader/employee relationships in 22 offices of a large Canadian public organization and, based on that work, reached two conclusions.

First, taking all 11 dimensions of leader character into consideration explained positive employee or performance outcomes—subjective well-being, resilience, organizational commitment, and work engagement—better than considering the isolated dimensions alone. Second, two dimensions in particular—judgment and Drive—were linked to these positive outcomes. And as we've seen, judgment is informed by the other 10 dimensions, which presumably reinforces even their indirect impact.

Research by the consulting firm of KRW International provides a more direct answer to the question of a "return on character."[35] Founding partner Fred Kiel and his KRW colleagues conducted a seven-year study of 84 CEOs, their executive staffs, and their employees. The question they had posed and were trying to answer was essentially the same as the one we asked previously: can a leader's character really contribute to an organization's bottom line?

Several factors beyond character were considered at the same time. The KRW study concluded that, for example, neither the age nor the tenure of the CEOs under study contributed measurably to their organizations' bottom lines—but character did. As Kiel explained in an interview:[36]

> We studied the extremes—the top-end "strong character" leaders—and compared them to "weak character" leaders. We called the top group Virtuoso Leaders, and the bottom group Self-Focused Leaders, for obvious reasons. We were astounded to discover that Virtuoso CEOs brought in nearly five times greater return on assets. In addition, they enjoyed a 26 per cent higher level of workforce engagement, and their corporate risk profile was much lower.

Even if one were to discount those numbers based on one methodological or definitional ground or another, they are still astounding: a *five-times-greater* ROA when what we would call leader character was in play and engagement measures that were substantially above average.

Kiel's team also examined how the CEOs they were studying assessed themselves in terms of character. Curiously, KWA's "Virtuoso Leaders" rated themselves slightly lower than their employees rated them on the character scale, while the Self-Focused Leaders rated themselves 30 points *higher* than their employees rated them—and higher than their Virtuoso counterparts rated themselves![37]

This is another aspect of human nature that comes into play: we're not very good at assessing ourselves. Unfortunately, the evidence for this assertion is abundant: 65 percent of Americans, for example, believe they are above average in intelligence.[38] Eight out of ten male drivers in the US say that they're above-average drivers.[39] A *Scientific American* article refers to this phenomenon as the "Superiority Illusion" and suggests that it might have a biological basis.[40]

All of which provides us with a helpful transition to Chapter 3, in which we focus on how you can apply the leader character framework to yourself and determine your *actual* strengths and weaknesses in this important realm.

Notes

1   Some of these dates come from a Centers for Disease Control and Prevention time-line, online at www.cdc.gov/museum/timeline/covid19.html#Early-2020, accessed March 13, 2023.
2   The shutdown wasn't unprecedented. At 10:05 a.m. on September 11, 2001, the White House unilaterally sealed the border—completely—in the wake of the terrorist attacks in New York City and Washington D.C. The chaotic aftermath of this shutdown led to the establishment of bilateral protocols for future emergencies, of which COVID-19 was the first. See the CBC's explanation at www.cbc.ca/news/

world/coronavirus-covid-19-border-canada-united-states-trade-1.5503192, accessed March 13, 2023.

3 From the U.S. Department of Homeland Security's website, online at www.dhs.gov/news/2020/03/20/joint-statement-us-canada-joint-initiative-temporary-restriction-travelers-crossing, accessed March 13, 2023. Actually, the Canadian government first raised the prospect of a limited border closure, to which the U.S. government responded positively. See www.cbc.ca/news/politics/trump-trudeau-covid-19-coronavirus-pandemic-border-1.5502192, accessed March 13, 2023.

4 And it's worth remembering that at that juncture, the disease wasn't well understood, and border officials couldn't be sure they weren't exposing themselves and their families to risk.

5 This and subsequent Ossowski quotes are from episode 12 of the podcast by Bill Furlong and Mary Crossan, *Leading with Character: A Conversation with John Ossowski, President of the CBSA*, online at www.questionofcharacter.com/episodes/episode-01-leader-character-101a-r9rxc-3r552-3y9df-baf3j-4zexg-j8bst-zf47e-hl7pl-egkzt, accessed March 13, 2023.

6 See, for example, the summary article by Jack Aldane in the June 1, 2022, edition of *Global Government Forum*, online at www.globalgovernmentforum.com/canadas-public-safety-agencies-told-to-stamp-out-institutional-racism-and-discrimination/, accessed March 13, 2023.

7 The full citation of the book is as follows: Peterson, C., & Seligman, M. E. P. (2004). *Character Strengths and Virtues: A Handbook and Classification*. New York, NY: Oxford University Press.

8 From Dahlsgaard, K., Peterson, C., & Seligman, M. E. (2005). Shared virtue: The convergence of valued human strengths across culture and history. *Review of General Psychology*, 9: 203–213.

9 The 10 criteria Peterson and Seligman chose for their character strengths include that the elements be: fulfilling; intrinsically valuable; non-rivalrous; not the opposite of a desirable trait; trait-like or habitual patterns that are relatively stable over time; not a combination of the other character strengths; personified by people made famous through story, song, etc.; absent in some individuals; and nurtured by societal norms and institutions. We also note that in our research, we did *not* invoke Peterson and Seligman's criterion that the character strength be observable in child prodigies, given that 1) they themselves noted that it was not applicable to all character strengths and 2) given our focus on the context of leadership in organizations, we deemed this criterion to be tangential.

10 Also significant are the many words that *don't* show up here. Certain candidates—such as "love," "humor," and "spirituality"—generated a pushback from many of our practitioners, who felt that these terms might undermine the perceived relevance of our framework to leadership in organizations.

11 This figure is taken from the following book chapter: Crossan, C., & Crossan, M. M. (2023). The practice of developing leader character to elevate judgment. In T. Newstead & R. Riggio (Eds.), *Virtues and Leadership: Understanding and Practicing Good Leadership*. New York, NY: Taylor and Francis Group.

12 This episode is captured in the online article www.thegazette.com/news/athletes-push-their-limits-but-how-much-is-too-much/, accessed March 13, 2023.

13 See the ESPN Red Auerbach biography at www.espn.com/classic/biography/s/auerbach_red.html accessed March 13, 2023. Notably, Auerbach is also credited with inventing the "role player," who was willing to sacrifice personal stardom in favor of team success.

14 See the Wikipedia write-up of the Warriors' season online at https://en.wikipedia.org/wiki/1961%E2%80%9362_Philadelphia_Warriors_season, accessed March 13, 2023. Chamberlain's phenomenal season is summarized online by *The Sporting*

News at www.sportingnews.com/us/nba/news/wilt-chamberlain-unbreakable-nba-re cords/1dprc2fnzo0mx15dkx9g9ptzn6, accessed March 13, 2023.

15 From Lance Armstrong's 2013 tell-all interview with Oprah Winfrey, online at www. bbc.com/sport/cycling/21065539, accessed March 13, 2023.

16 See the 2019 article "Leader character in board governance," by Gerard Seijts, Aly son Byrne, Mary Crossan, and Jeffrey Gandz, published in the *Journal of Manage ment and Governance*, 23: 227–258.

17 The full citation of the book is as follows: Schwartz, B., & Sharpe, K. (2010). *Practi cal Wisdom: The Right Way to do the Right Thing*. New York, NY: Penguin.

18 Unfortunately, Ford was right on the high side. As of this writing, some 16,000 Ontarians have died. See www.statista.com/statistics/1107079/covid19-deaths-by province-territory-canada/.

19 This was tracked, for example, by the 2020 Edelman Trust Barometer: Canada. The full report can be read on www.edelman.ca/trust-barometer/trust-barometer-2020, accessed March 13, 2023.

20 There are many more aspects to the definition of "wicked problems." See Horst W. Rittel's and Melvin M. Webber's 1973 article "Dilemmas in a general theory of plan ning," published in *Policy Sciences*, 4: 155–169; and see also Stony Brook Univer sity's interesting explanation at www.stonybrook.edu/commcms/wicked-problem/ about/What-is-a-wicked-problem, accessed March 13, 2023.

21 This anecdote and quotes were taken from the article "Coronavirus: More countries will adopt Italy's measures, says Austrian leader," which appeared in *The Guardian*, 2020, March 8; www.theguardian.com/world/2020/mar/08/coronavirus-more countries-will-adopt-italys-measures-says-austrian-leader, accessed March 13, 2023.

22 This study is described in a 2021 article by Kirsi Niinimäki at https://gjia.george town.edu/2021/08/30/from-fast-to-slow-how-to-construct-a-better-balance-in-the fashion-system/, accessed March 13, 2023.

23 These statistics are from the Zero Waste Memoirs website at https://zerowastemem oirs.com/disadvantages-of-fast-fashion/, accessed March 13, 2023.

24 See, for example, the interview with CEO Martijn Hagman in the March 4, 2022, edition of *Gulf Business*, online at https://gulfbusiness.com/martijn-hagman-ceo tommy-hilfiger-global-and-pvh-europe-discusses-inclusivity-and-sustainability-in fashion/ accessed, March 13, 2023.

25 See the documentary "For the love of fashion," narrated by Alexandra Cousteau for the National Geographic Channel, described online at www.c-and-a.com/uk/en/cor porate/company/newsroom/featured-stories/2016/for-the-love-of-fashion/ accessed, March 13, 2013.

26 From a March 8, 2004, *Fortune* article, online at https://archive.fortune.com/maga zines/fortune/fortune_archive/2004/03/08/363679/index.htm.

27 Researcher Philip Zimbardo summarized his Stanford prison experiment and subse quent examples of moral people committing immoral acts in his 2007 book, *The Luci fer Effect: Understanding How Good People Turn Evil*, published by Random House, New York. We should note that scholars including but not limited to Alex Haslam, Jay van Bavel, and Stephen Reicher encourage us to rethink the infamous Stanford Prison Experiment; see, for example, https://blogs.scientificamerican.com/observations/re thinking-the-infamous-stanford-prison-experiment/, accessed March 13, 2023.

28 Not coincidentally, Milgram's experiments ran currently with the trial of Nazi war criminal Adolf Eichmann—who famously claimed that he couldn't be held account able for genocide because he was only following his orders.

29 See, for example, www.cbc.ca/news/business/boeing-fifth-estate-costs-safety 1.5426571, accessed March 13, 2023. We'll return to the Boeing story in detail in Chapters 7 and 8.

30 Details about the program can be found online at www.ivey.uwo.ca/leadership/for-leaders/professional-development-consulting/leader-character-practitioner-certification-program/.

31 And the deep-voiced Ossowski is six feet, five inches tall. When he declares something, people tend to *listen*.

32 This example is taken from a 2018 article by Gerard Seijts and Jeffrey Gandz: "Transformational change and leader character," *Business Horizons*, 61: 239–249. A similar argument is made by Kim Scott in her 2017 book *Radical candor: Be a kick-ass boss without losing your humanity*, published by St. Martin's Press, New York.

33 See, for example, the article by Rachel E. Sturm, Mary Crossan, and Dusya Vera in the December 2017 issue of *The Leadership Quarterly* (and cited in Chapter 1).

34 The full set of results can be found in Monzani, L., Seijts, G., & Crossan, M. (2021). Character matters: The network structure of leader character and its relation to follower positive outcomes. *PLoS ONE*, 16(9): e0255940. https://doi.org/10.1371/journal.pone.0255940 accessed March 13, 2023.

35 See "Questions for Fred Kiel" in the fall 2015 issue of the University of Toronto's *The Leading Edge* publication, online at www.rotman.utoronto.ca/Connect/Rotman-MAG/IdeaExchange/Page3/Fred-Kiel, accessed March 13, 2023. Kiel, an executive coach, is the author of *Return on Character*, Harvard Business Review Press, 2015. He passed away in October 2022.

36 See "Questions for Fred Kiel."

37 Meanwhile, a growing number of empirical studies underscore that self-awareness is associated with effective leadership. Examples of these studies include the following: Church, A. H. (1997). Managerial self-awareness in high-performing individuals in organizations. *Journal of Applied Psychology*, 82: 281–292. Sosik, J. J., & Megerian, L. E. (1999). Understanding leader emotional intelligence and performance: The role of self-other agreement on transformational leadership perceptions. *Group & Organization Management*, 24: 367–390. Further, the lack of self-awareness is related to derailment. Examples of relevant studies include: Gentry, W. A., Ekelund, B. Z., Hannum, K. M., & de Jong, A. (2007). A study of the discrepancy between self- and observer-ratings on managerial derailment characteristics of European managers. *European Journal of Work and Organizational Psychology*, 16: 295–325. Hogan, R., & Hogan, J. (2001). Assessing leadership: A view from the dark side. *International Journal of Selection and Assessment*, 9(1–2): 40–51. Research on leader derailment has revealed a host of derailment factors, including behaviors that are character-based, such as arrogance and the absence of self-awareness (thus reducing humility), being argumentative (thus reducing temperance), lack of empathy (thus reducing humanity), and being detached or unable to establish and maintain healthy, respectful, and long-term relationships with other people (thus reducing collaboration). Hogan and Hogan (2001) outlined two consequences of such dysfunctional dispositions. First, the person is generally unable to learn from past experiences. Consequently, the person repeatedly engages in the same self-defeating behavior. Second, such behaviors erode trust, which in turn undermines one's ability to build the kind of high-performing team needed to tackle tough challenges.

38 See the 2018 PLoS One article that reported these statistics, online at www.ncbi.nlm.nih.gov/pmc/articles/PMC6029792/, accessed March 13, 2023.

39 See the 2018 article, online at www.businessinsider.com/americans-are-overconfident-in-their-driving-skills-2018-1, accessed March 13, 2023.

40 See the April 1, 2013 edition of *Scientific American*, online at https://blogs.scientificamerican.com/scicurious-brain/the-superiority-illusion-where-everyone-is-above-average/, accessed March 13, 2023.

Chapter 3

What's your Achilles' heel?

It was a tale of two companies under the same roof: one with character and one without.

Theranos was a privately held health-care and life-sciences company based in Palo Alto, California. Its stated mission was to revolutionize medical lab testing through innovative methods for drawing and testing blood and interpreting the results of those tests.[1] The company was founded in 2003 by a 19-year-old Stanford University dropout named Elizabeth Holmes, who leveraged family connections to raise $6 million from high-profile investors by the end of 2004.[2] Quickly emerging as one of Silicon Valley's most conspicuous "unicorn" start-ups, Theranos was valued at something like $9 billion by 2014.[3] Holmes became a high-tech celebrity, appearing on the covers of *Fortune* and *Forbes*. The media loved her Steve Jobs–like discipline and unconventionality and hyped her as the world's youngest self-made female billionaire, with a net worth approaching $4.5 billion.

But behind the scenes, another story was unfolding. The company—under the direction of Holmes and its president and COO, Ramesh "Sunny" Balwani—was engaging in two multimillion-dollar wire frauds: one aimed at bilking investors and the other designed to scam doctors and patients.

The former scheme involved fraudulent claims about a supposedly revolutionary and proprietary testing technology that Holmes and Balwani variously referred to as the Edison, the TSPU (Theranos Sample Processing Unit), or the "miniLab." This new technology, it was claimed, could use a small amount of blood from a finger prick to perform a wide range of tests and then analyze those tests far more quickly and cheaply than any competing technologies. But none of this was true: when the company conducted tests, it simply used analyzers produced by its competitors and claimed that Edison was at work. Holmes and Balwani nevertheless doubled down, telling investors that Theranos would generate $100 million in revenues in 2014—and thereby reach breakeven—and $1 billion in 2015. In fact, there was no way their company could come close to hitting those targets.

In terms of defrauding doctors and patients, even though Theranos insiders knew that TSPU (or "Edison," or "miniLab") couldn't produce accurate, fast, and cheap blood-test results, the company heavily advertised its testing products

DOI: 10.4324/9781003341215-4

to Walgreens customers in California and Arizona.[4] Throughout this rapid rise, it should be noted, the Theranos board—which included two former US secretaries of state (Henry Kissinger and Holmes family friend George Shultz), among other notables—walked in lockstep with their executives. For example, when a US Army lieutenant colonel, David Shoemaker, objected to a plan for deploying the still-unproven Edison on a grand scale in the military, Shoemaker found himself doing battle with highly respected former four-star general and board member James Mattis.[5]

But whispers and doubts were starting to gain momentum. By late 2015, both the *Wall Street Journal* and federal investigators were digging into Theranos, and in March 2018, the company, Holmes, and Balwani were charged with "massive fraud" by the US Securities and Exchange Commission, followed by wire-fraud charges from a federal grand jury. Holmes was convicted on several of the investor-focused wire-fraud counts in January 2022, and six months later, Balwani—tried separately—was found guilty on two counts of conspiracy and ten counts of wire fraud.[6]

But what about that other company—the Theranos *with* character? This version of the company only shows up in dribs and drabs and in short chapters that often came to abrupt and sometimes dramatic ends. In November 2006, for example, the company's CFO was fired after he questioned the reliability of Theranos' technology and the company's honesty.[7] Seth Michelson, chief scientific officer at Theranos, resigned in 2010 for essentially the same reasons. In the spring of 2013, the company's chief scientist, Ian Gibbons, expressed concerns about the Theranos blood-testing technology and was summoned to a meeting in Holmes' office; before that meeting could take place, Gibbons committed suicide.[8]

But the first real cracks in the dam appeared in 2015, when newly arrived employee Tyler Shultz—coincidentally, a grandson of board member George Shultz—made a startling discovery, informed in part by his many hours in college laboratories: *there was nothing that Edison could do that he couldn't do with a pipette in his own hand.* And worse, Theranos was conducting its all-important quality-control safety audits on commercially available lab equipment rather than on its own equipment. "It was clear," he later told National Public Radio, "that there was an open secret within Theranos that this technology simply didn't exist."[9]

Shultz first took his concerns to Holmes and other senior leaders in the company but was met with a wall of denials and skepticism. He tried to explain to his grandfather what was going on, only to be brushed off. A long email that he sent to Holmes, detailing the company's apparent shortcomings, provoked an angry reply from Sunny Balwani. As Shultz recalls:

He essentially was just saying that I was arrogant, ignorant, patronizing, and reckless, with no understanding of math, science, or basic statistics, and that if I had any other last name, I would already have been held accountable to the strongest extent.[10]

Family members advised him to resign and publicly say only that he was leaving Theranos to enroll in a PhD program. He did quit the company in frustration, offering no explanation for his departure. That might have been the end of the story—except that he was approached by *Wall Street Journal* reporter John Carreyrou, who asked if he wanted to chat about practices in the company's laboratories.

And so a whistleblower was born. But Shultz had only been with the company less than a year before his departure, and Carreyrou needed corroboration. He soon got it from several of Shultz's colleagues, including lab director Adam Rosendorff and technician Erika Cheung. "That was absolutely critical," Carreyrou recalled.

Shultz's whistleblower role put him in direct conflict with his grandfather, who refused to believe that Theranos and CEO Holmes were engaged in less than honorable activities and also refused to apologize to his grandson when the truth eventually came out. But the worst was still to come. For the better part of two years, the younger Shultz was harassed by lawyers and private investigators hired by the company. He and his family spent something like $400,000 fighting off Theranos' various legal actions against him.[11]

Erika Cheung, another of the Theranos whistleblowers, went through a very similar experience. Like Shultz, she had extensive experience in labs, and she quickly realized that Edison didn't work. She approached Sunny Balwani and conveyed her mounting concerns. His response, she recalls, was not encouraging:

He said, "What makes you think you're qualified to make those calls? You need to do the job I pay you to do, which is process patient samples, and that's it." For me, just that type of response was an indicator of this person's character. You just intuitively know, "Oh. These people know what's going on, but they're not doing anything about it."

It was really at that moment, my world kind of crumbled, right? Because here I am, sleeping in my car, working 16 hours a day—doing all this crazy stuff because I have this belief that we're all in alignment about the mission that we're trying to accomplish, and actually, there's something else going on.[12]

She decided that she couldn't just stand by and let the inevitable train wreck happen. She collected reams of damning quality-control data, quit the company, and began her own conversations with Carreyrou—and eventually, with state and federal regulators.

At Holmes' trial, Cheung took the stand for three days, detailing the failings of that equipment and the results it produced.[13] Tyler Shultz—who was not called as a witness—attended the closing arguments of the trial, sitting in the courthouse's overflow room in a makeshift disguise to avoid drawing unwanted attention. Weeks later, when the "guilty" verdict came in, he shared a champagne toast with his family and friends.[14]

Shortly thereafter, as the CEO of his own biotech company—Flux Biosciences, Inc.—Shultz found himself making pitches to investors just as Holmes had done years earlier. Pitching proved a sobering experience, once again with a subplot of character. "I'm under pressure to exaggerate technology claims," he told NPR, "exaggerate revenue projection claims. Sometimes investors will straight-up tell you, you need to double, quadruple, or 10x any revenue projection you think is realistic."

"I could see how this environment could create an Elizabeth Holmes," he concluded. As we've already pointed out, when it comes to character, *context* is critical. If you begin the game with crippled judgement—as seems to be the case with Elizabeth Holmes—that character imbalance can become more and more crippling as the competitive pressures on you intensify. The slippery slope plunges downward in front of you.

Lessons to be learned

Again, Shultz's comment points us toward our first lesson from the Theranos disaster: it took place within a *context*. Whatever character flaws Holmes, Balwani, and other senior company leaders possessed going into the game—a subject to which we'll return shortly—those flaws were greatly reinforced and magnified by the hypercompetitive setting of venture capital in the Valley, which set the standard for the larger global VC community. When a potential investor advises you to *increase that likely revenue projection tenfold* and you really need the money, what will you do? Will you exercise character and stick to your principles (Integrity, Courage, and Accountability), or will you give in to the pressure, cross the line, and do things that you know are wrong?

Easier said than done, certainly. You've worked hard, taken risks, and honestly believe in your cause. (This may well describe Elizabeth Holmes in the very early days of Theranos.) The person who walks away from a large sum of money at that point is understandably rare.

A second lesson focuses more on competence but quickly shades into character. Even before joining the company, Erika Cheung noticed that the Theranos board of directors consisted mainly of ex-politicians and military personnel—rather than, say, doctors, other qualified medical personnel, and health-care sector professionals—and inferred that there must be a prospecting or fundraising rationale for this odd board lineup. Tyler Shultz was blunter in his assessment: "The board didn't really have any power. It was kind of like a fake board."[15]

Shultz also lamented about the divide at Theranos between what he called the "carpeted world" and the "tiled world"—with board members and high-ranking corporate officials inhabiting the former and scientists and technicians populating the latter and almost no communication passing between them. Here's where character enters: clearly, Holmes and Balwani set up the company with minimal internal transparency, which mirrored a lack of transparency vis-à-vis the outside world, and this helped keep the company's doomed schemes going.

Parenthetically, we have conducted numerous roundtable discussions with a number of board members who were focused on character issues.[16] In those contexts, there was an overwhelming belief that Leader Character matters to board governance and organizational effectiveness. That said, directors felt that Leader Character is often only brought up in boards during or after a crisis. Typically, character is not a central part of board discussions at any other time. Boards can become complacent until a significant event happens at which time character—for example, courage, temperance, justice, or drive—gets the attention it deserves. In the meantime, board members themselves may fall victim to "groupthink," in the belief that their role is to come together and reach consensus—which is true up to the point that overcollaboration begins to work against Accountability.[17]

A third lesson from the larger Theranos experience is that there were no winners, and there were many, many losers. Yes, some bilked patients got their money back, but those investors who rode the Theranos train all the way to the end of the line lost all or most of their money. This included venture capitalists, who are accustomed to unsuccessful gambles—but it also included less financially savvy board members like James Mattis, who lost the $85,000 he invested in the company.[18] Meanwhile, the main characters in the drama, including the C-suite executives, forfeited their reputations and even their careers. One might say "deservedly so"—but we should remember that all 800-plus people employed by Theranos at its 2015 peak lost their jobs. Many found themselves in professional limbo for months and even years afterward, thanks in large part to the "stain of the company" on their resumes.[19]

Beyond the walls of the company, corporate partners of Theranos, including Walgreens and Safeway, took financial and credibility hits. Doctors and their patients planned and pursued therapies based on the often-inaccurate test results provided by Theranos. Although patients in Arizona received almost $5 million in refunds from the company in a consumer-fraud settlement, there's no easy way to assess how much damage was actually done. During her time on the stand during Holmes' trial, Erika Cheung testified that she sometimes refused to run tests on patient samples because she didn't want to generate results that were likely to be wrong.[20] One patient who testified at the trial said that she learned from a Theranos blood test that she was having a miscarriage when she wasn't, which led her to start taking a new medication that could have been harmful to the fetus.[21]

For our fourth and final lesson from the Theranos saga, let's look directly at the issue of leader character, with our principal focus on Elizabeth Holmes.[22] "Elizabeth Holmes was a con artist," Arizona Attorney General Mark Brnovich bluntly told *Fortune* magazine. "In Silicon Valley, you often get folks that fake it till they make it and have a different sense of reality, and there's a certain amount of hubris and arrogance."[23] Certainly, arrogance—in a sense, the opposite of Humility—was on display in abundance in the Theranos corner offices.

At the same time, even the harshest critics among Holmes' former employees, including the whistleblowers, credit her with the ability to motivate the team. "She was a really inspiring leader," recalls Tyler Shultz. "She made every person feel like they were super important to achieving the vision of the company."[24]

Erika Cheung was similarly impressed, at least at first:

> Initially I came in starry-eyed. I admired Elizabeth Holmes. She was this female entrepreneur in biotech. What she represented to me was that you could work really hard and get to a position of running your own company.
>
> There was something very powerful about the mission she was trying to put forward: making health care accessible, affordable, allowing for price transparency when you get your blood diagnostics. It's not until you look at her as a character in retrospect that you realize the red flags and warning signs of her behavior and her personality and the kind of act that she put on to be the front face of Theranos.[25]

In Figure 3.1, we reintroduce our leader character framework, consisting of 11 dimensions and associated elements from the last chapter.

So in Holmes' story and in the testimony of her subordinates, we certainly see Drive, Courage, and—in her future orientation, her inspirational qualities, and her ability to show appreciation to team members—even a limited and corrupted kind of Transcendence. She had remarkable self-control—an element of Temperance—to the extent of rarely blinking during intimate conversations and almost always speaking in an artificially low voice.[26]

But sadly, we see serious deficits in most other areas. People with a commitment to candor and transparency (Integrity) don't deceive those around them. "We were unable to help her on the fundamental issues that she was grappling with," James Mattis later reflected, "if we only saw them in the rearview mirror."[27] People blessed with the dimensions of Collaboration and Humanity don't send private investigators to harass their subordinates. People who are Accountable don't try to blame others for their shortcomings (as Holmes ultimately tried to do with Balwani).[28] And most centrally, people with good judgment don't commit to, and then double down on, a deceptive path that is almost certain to be detected and prosecuted.[29]

What if?

What if character had been on the table from the beginning of the Theranos drama?

What if the key players in that drama had asked themselves, "What kind of character is being displayed here that shouldn't be—in ourselves and others? What kind of character are we not seeing that we wish we were?"

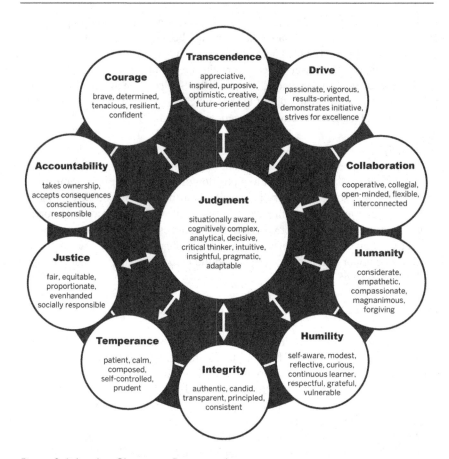

Figure 3.1 Leader Character Framework

Working from the outside in, it may seem unfair to hold Theranos' business partners up to this kind of scrutiny. In a sense, they were merely hoodwinked participants in a series of fraudulent transactions. And yet, those partners who turned a blind eye to the double-talk and exaggeration served up to them by Elizabeth Holmes actually do warrant this kind of scrutiny. "Craving growth," as the headline of a *Wall Street Journal* article put it, "Walgreens dismissed its doubts about Theranos."[30] Drive distorted judgment, Temperance, and Accountability, to a fatal extent. Walgreens' experts must have known, or at least suspected, that the claims that Holmes was making for Edison bordered on the absurd. And yet, when she refused to allow the outside verification that Walgreens had initially demanded—when they took seriously her threats to take her technology to rival drug chains like Safeway and CVS—they caved and let her have her way.

We've already touched on the character of the investors in the Theranos scheme. How could hard-nosed venture capitalists agree to be kept in the dark about the technology in which they were investing? What if they had insisted on following near-universally standard VC operating procedures, which almost always include exerting a substantial measure of control through the company's board? What if they had insisted on even a normal degree of transparency? Again, it seems, groupthink prevailed, and transparency was the victim. Even today, some of the key players involved seem reluctant to hold Holmes to account. Investor Tim Draper, for one, defends his decision to buy into Holmes' vision:

> Here's the way I look at it: She didn't lie to me. I was an investor. I lost my entire investment. And I still have the utmost respect for what she was trying to accomplish, all the work she put in, all the things she was trying to do for the world.[31]

We've also reflected on the inadequate character of the Theranos board, which seemed unable or unwilling to involve itself in the affairs of the company they were supposedly overseeing. We're reminded of the metaphor of the bad apples (Holmes and Balwani) and the bad barrel (Theranos). In this case, the metaphor can and should be extended to the barrel makers (the investors, the regulatory community, and especially the Theranos board), given that they allowed the fiasco to happen. What if there had been a system of guided conversations and discussions in place that would have helped surface the character deficiencies of Theranos' senior executives and had prevented the Courage and Drive of those executives from going unchecked? And what if, when confronted by a sordid reality—as presented, for example, by a grandson with Integrity—they had decided to be Humble and Accountable, and to demand Integrity from Holmes and Balwani?

And this brings us back our bad apples themselves: Holmes and Balwani.[32] Again, we'll focus on Holmes, and again, we preface our comments with the observation that Holmes probably didn't set out to perpetrate a fraud but made a series of bad decisions on her way down the long and slippery slope referred to earlier. But what if Holmes had combined her Courage and Drive (and her particular version of Transcendence) with some degree of Temperance and Humility? "There is no dream you can't achieve," she wrote in a 2015 tweet. "Don't let anyone tell you otherwise."[33] Well, yes, but when you allow the mindset behind that inspirational trope to solidify itself into company policy—*don't let anyone tell you that Edison doesn't and can't work*—you lose access to your judgment. Holmes' obsession with Steve Jobs is telling: although she adopted his trademark black turtleneck, filled her office with his favorite furniture, and (like her idol) never took vacations, she missed the main point of Jobs' personal quest: *getting it right*, thoroughly and seamlessly.

"He never really knew much about technology," Bill Gates once said of Jobs, "but he had an amazing instinct for what works."[34] We would substitute judgment for instinct in that sentence. Holmes lacked that judgment—increasingly over the years—and, blinded by Drive, lacked the kind of Collaborative instincts and Accountability that might have helped develop it in her. As will emerge in subsequent chapters, these kinds of *balancing* and *counterbalancing* are key to the development of strong character. Consider Figure 3.2, which summarizes the kinds of things that can happen when our eleven character dimensions are—alternatively—weak, unsupported, and balanced.[35]

The public record suggests that Holmes had little interest in introspection, or in the kind of self-awareness that might have grown out of that kind of

Character Dimension	Under-weighted (weak)	Strong character (balanced)	Over-weighted (unsupported)
Judgment	Indecision; lack of insight, rigour and understanding; resistance to change	Insightful and adaptable; situationally aware and current; solid decision making	Analysis paralysis; over-complicating decision making; no clear sense of priorities
Courage	People don't speak up; fear prevails; give up easily; little innovation	Determination and perseverance are prevalent; high resilience; "speak truth to power"	Reckless actions; stubborn; and arrogant
Drive	Lethargy and low productivity; lack of initiative	Sustained momentum around focused priorities; high productivity; passionate and vigorous	Tunnel vision; perfectionists
Collaboration	"Every person for themselves" mentality; lack of information sharing; silos	Effective teamwork enhancing productivity; diversity and inclusion evident	Conflict avoiders; people pleasing; too many people involved in decisions
Integrity	People operate from a position of self-interest and mistrust; lack of candor and transparency	Trust, transparency, and effective communication	Uncompromising, rigid and dogmatic interactions, leading to exclusionary practices
Temperance	Impatience and agitation prevalent; people are stressed and anxious	Effective risk management; thoughtful consideration; calm even under duress	Risk-averse leading to inaction; lacking urgency; often indifferent about whether something happens

Figure 3.2 The Outcomes That May Occur When the 11 Character Dimensions Are—Alternatively—Weak, Unsupported, and Balanced

Character Dimension	Under-weighted (weak)	Strong character (balanced)	Over-weighted (unsupported)
Accountability	Failure to deliver results and take responsibility; blaming culture, low ownership of issues	Ownership of problems; commitment to decisions; act in organizational interests	Difficulty delegating; obsessive and controlling; little room for learning failures
Justice	Inequities exist; favoritism and nepotism	Fairness fostering trust; clear understanding and action around systemic inequities	Recognize inequities but treat them in a rule-based rigid way that does not take into account individual differences
Humility	Arrogance and overconfidence; complacency; lack of reflection and learning	Willingness to identify and discuss mistakes; support of continuous learning	Ruminating about issues; pushover; lacking focus in learning
Humanity	Lack of empathy, compassion and consideration	Deep understanding of what is important; people felt they are seen and heard	People feel overwhelmed and suffer compassion fatigue
Transcendence	Narrow goals and objectives; failure to acknowledge and appreciate, not inspired	Commitment to excellence; clarity and focus; inspiration motivates innovation	Always thinking things will get better but no tangible sense of how to get there

Figure 3.2 (Continued)

introspection.[36] But let's play out this scenario. What if, earlier in her life, she *did* have the benefit of that impulse? To listen? To reflect? To learn? What if she had a tool that she could have used to identify her Achilles' heel and then work to offset that weakness with investments in Figure 3.2's counterbalancing dimensions and elements?

That is the tool that we have spent the better part of the past decade developing.

Finding your own Achilles' heel

The dimensions and elements of character shown in Figure 3.1 brought together our research and the research of others with practical observations from real-world practitioners. Over time, we have drawn many lessons from this diagram and the work that lies behind it, including the following:

- The dimensions of character—although manifested in markedly different ways across cultures, geographies, and eras—are remarkably consistent. It is important to your personal effectiveness as a leader to have the capacity to exercise all dimensions of character.
- The dimensions of character are interdependent and work together to determine the overall strength of our character and thus produce good outcomes.
- As explained in Chapter 2, each dimension is composed of several defining character elements. Each of these elements has an impact on the strength of the character dimension.
- Character is developed over our lifetimes, and—as Aristotle suggested—we can enhance the development of character through deliberate practice. Every situation presents a different experience and opportunity to exercise, apply, and develop character.
- *Judgment*—again, informed by the other ten dimensions—plays a central role in character, controlling when and how we choose to behave.
- That said, *all* dimensions and elements of character combine to produce good outcomes, and therefore, it's important to understand both our strengths and developmental areas.

This last point led us naturally to a central question: *how* do we achieve that kind of understanding? Diagnosing oneself is never easy, and it's particularly difficult in the often-elusive realm of character. Were there tools out there that were as rigorous as our framework, that were reliable and repeatable, and were still reasonably simple to work with? Were there tools that spoke effectively to managers—in language that they understood and embraced?

Our multiyear exploration of the character landscape convinced us that although there were relevant tools out there, they didn't meet all of our specifications. For example, we first experimented with the VIA Character Survey, developed by Christopher Peterson and Martin Seligman, whom we introduced in the previous chapter.[37] But as we also noted in that chapter, many leaders and human resource executives in the public, private, and not-for-profit sectors had difficulty fully embracing Peterson and Seligman's (2004) classification of virtues and character strengths. For one thing, the classification didn't include key virtues and character strengths that organizational leaders deemed important—for example, accountability, drive, decisiveness, and adaptability. In addition, many leaders found it difficult to figure out how some of the language used by Peterson and Seligman—including love, spirituality, humor, and zest—related to the realities of the workplace.

We are often asked why measures of personality, such as the Myers-Briggs Type Indicator, the Personality Research Form, and various self-administered tests based on the so-called Big Five personality traits,[38] don't also serve to measure character. Some virtues and character strengths may be trait-like individual differences, but character and personality traits are by no means equivalent: they have a different origin and application. For example, character is anchored in virtuous behaviors and can be developed—as opposed to personality traits, which are relatively stable and, importantly, mostly agnostic to virtue. For example, personality trait theory is about trying to explain individual differences like extroversion and introversion rather than deciding whether the trait is virtuous. We can all bring to mind extroverts or introverts who have either weak or strong character, which leads to fundamentally different expressions of this personality trait.

Character involves a set of habits of behaviors that can be learned or strengthened through deliberate practice, through the impact of context, and—sometimes—because of some intense "crucible" experience. Character addresses strengths and deficiencies, moreover, whereas personality traits just *are*. Again, we don't typically talk about a "good" or "bad" extrovert; however, we *do* emphasize strengths and deficiencies in humanity or temperance.

A second critical difference between character and personality traits centers on their operationalization. For example, the leader character framework that forms the basis for our work with executives is generally treated as a network structure that recognizes the interactions or interdependencies among the dimensions of character as well as its constitutive elements. In contrast, personality traits are typically treated as relatively independent, meaning that we don't expect that a weakness or strength in a particular trait would undermine or support other traits.

With all this as background, we were becoming increasingly interested in the interdependencies among dimensions of character: What if you have too much of X and too little of Y? At what point does a virtue turn into a vice? Thus, broadly speaking, the personality-research field and its practical spin-offs don't attempt to assert that one kind of behavior is "better" than another. Behavior just *is* and therefore invites not corrections but work-arounds. In the worst case, the focus on seemingly innate or stable elements creates an excuse for inaction: *I'm an introvert; therefore, I can't/don't need to do X, Y, or Z.* "All too frequently," as one psychologist put it, "patients insist that they are incapable of change when actually they are either unwilling or afraid to try."[39]

Although in this recounting we're still painting with a necessarily broad brush, this excuse for inaction was not acceptable to us. We felt strongly that even if personality is cast in stone—which is certainly open to question—character is not. Character research revealed that character involves a set of habits of behavior that can be learned. We were reminded of this during a conversation with an extroverted executive who had taken a number of personality-based tests. After each of those assessments, she told us, she was advised to "tone herself down"—in other words, to be less like herself. Both to her and to us, that seemed like an inadequate prescription. What that extroverted leader needed to hear about was a set of dimensions and elements that she could *work on*—not toward the goal of diminishing her Courage and Drive, but toward the goal of reinforcing her Collaboration, Humanity, Humility, and Temperance.

So how and where could she get that good guidance?

The Leader Character Insight Assessment (LCIA)

These kinds of challenges and questions eventually led us to a fruitful collaboration with a US-based consulting firm called SIGMA Assessment Systems, Inc.

Established in 1967, SIGMA has spent more than a half century developing and delivering science-based assessment products.[40] Certainly, we knew of the company through its strong reputation in the assessment field, which today extends to comprise succession planning, executive coaching, and other consulting services. We knew of SIGMA's founder, Dr. Douglas N. Jackson III, who had a long and influential career as a researcher, writer, psychologist, scientist, and innovator in the field of psychological assessment. But we also knew SIGMA firsthand: the firm had developed a leadership competence instrument that we were already using in our curriculum at Ivey, and we were increasingly coming to believe that wherever competencies reside in organizations, character could and should be considered alongside. For all these reasons, it seemed a natural fit to co-develop a character-assessment tool with SIGMA.

The result of our collaboration with SIGMA was the Leader Character Insight Assessment, or LCIA. The LCIA measures the dimensions of character and their associated elements that are shown in Figure 3.1.

Today, it is available in two versions: the self-report and the 360 report. The former is self-administered, as its name implies, and includes online scoring.[41] The individual answers a series of questions about his or her likelihood to engage in character-related behaviors—for example, "Takes advantage of any opportunity to learn from someone else" or "Steps up and takes ownership of difficult problems." What the individual receives in return is a report of approximately 50 pages, which first introduces the nature and importance of leader character—the focus of Chapters 1 and 2 in this book—and then presents the LCIA results in two forms: scores by each of the eleven dimensions and then scores in relation to each other. Throughout, the report includes practical, actionable resources (e.g., readings, podcasts, videos, etc.) designed to help the individual better understand each character dimension and its associated elements and also to assist in the process of character development.

Figure 3.3 is the overview page of a simulated report showing the individual's dimension scores in an overview format.

As you can see, our imaginary individual ranks highest on Humanity and Transcendence and lowest on Collaboration and Humility. To us, that's an interesting mix and one that's ripe with implications and opportunities. Look at the two lowest scores. Perhaps this individual (with low Humility and Collaboration) is quick

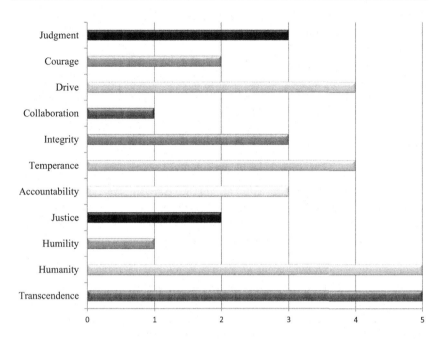

Figure 3.3 Leader Character Insight Assessment Results Overview

to tackle tough problems by himself or himself and doesn't accept offers of help easily. At the same time, he or she may be perceived as compassionate (Humanity) and inspirational (Transcendence). With this self-awareness and persistence, this person can use their Humanity and Transcendence to connect with others and share their big ideas and start to more readily accept the contributions of others—perhaps leading to more ideas being developed for the benefit of all.

We invite you to pause and ask if this profile resembles anyone you know. If so, what are the implications for what we often think about as that person's leadership style? For his or her followership style? We need to shift our frame from thinking about something as being style, personality, or attitude to taking a deeper look at who the person is with respect to their character.

The LCIA 360 report—which grew out of the earlier self-administered version—includes these same elements and also includes specific developmental comments provided by the raters whom the individual has identified. Obviously, this version of LCIA takes place in an organizational context, and the authors often work with companies to administer the LCIA 360 across some or all of their key players.[42]

Stepping back from the specifics of the report to their larger meaning, low scores on the assessment can be considered "weak character," which as the terms suggests means a lower presence of the behaviors.[43] Conversely, high scores across all dimensions can be considered "strong character," defined as a higher presence of the behaviors. "Unbalanced character" means high scores on some dimensions of character and low scores on others. As you'll recall from our earlier discussions, an unbalanced character carries with it a submerged but very real threat: virtues (high scores) may in fact turn into vices due to low scores on other offsetting dimensions. Think again about the importance of *context* as well. A context that is fueled in part by large sums of money, a fawning and uncritical press, lax regulation, and similar forces can help push a balanced character into an imbalanced one.

This brings us back to our Theranos example. As we've seen, Theranos was a corrupting context. When certain elements or dimensions of the leader's character are weak, as was the case with Holmes and Balwani, we can expect poor judgment from them. When the employees' character is weak, a powerful leader can do pretty much whatever he or she wants and reasonably expect to get away with it, at least for the time being.[44] When character is unbalanced, we can expect inconsistencies in the quality of judgment. In other words, excellence may well arise, but it probably won't be sustained. That's why character assessment is so critically important: it points and paves the way toward better judgment.

Certainly, individuals with weak character can still take action and "do the right thing"—but the barriers to doing so are strong and high. Individuals with unbalanced character may oscillate between moments of action and inaction and may lack judgment, leading to the inability to actively shape or disrupt the context.

Finally, we should underscore that these kinds of issues are generally *not* caused by evil people. Rather, they tend to be caused by good people who—by not being self-aware of their own character or by being unaware of the character of their colleagues—leave room for misjudgments. By most accounts, including Tyler Shultz's, George Shultz was an honorable person who failed to bring this kind of self-awareness to the board table at Theranos and also failed to scrutinize the characters of those around him.

Stated somewhat differently, this is not simply a moral or ethical issue; this is more completely and better understood framed as an issue of *poor judgment*: the dimension that stands at the center of Figure 3.1 and which calls heavily on the other ten dimensions.

Why it matters

It's fair to ask a question that is raised implicitly in the previous pages: Is this kind of self-assessment, or group assessment, and the conversations that should follow really worth the investment of time and money that they require? Is leader character critical, or is it simply a nice-to-have? Why does it *matter*?

Theranos is one answer to that question. leader character might have headed off a lot of miseries. But there's a far bigger picture. In a 2016 McKinsey &

Company study of more than 52,000 managers and employees, leaders rated themselves as better and more engaging than their employees did. This included 86 percent of leaders who believed they model the improvements they want employees to make while another 77 percent of leaders believed they "inspire action."

Meanwhile, a Gallup poll from the same year revealed that employees strongly disagreed. According to those employees' responses, 82 percent of managers and executives—more than four out of five—were seen as lacking in leadership skills. This deficit, Gallup estimated, costs US corporations as much as $550 billion annually.[45]

Certainly, competence enters into these assessments and calculations. But it's fair and sensible to infer, too, that a lack of leader character imposes substantial penalties on corporations—and, by extension, on those working in those contexts. It's also fair and sensible to infer that the converse is also true: the presence of character drives positive returns. So if, as we've asserted in previous chapters, character is strengthened through habit, then this argues for finding a way to adopt good habits and thereby to *exercise* character.

This is the subject of our Chapter 4.

Notes

1 See the U.S. Department of Justice's summary of *U.S. v. Elizabeth Holmes, et al.*, online at www.justice.gov/usao-ndca/us-v-elizabeth-holmes-et-al, accessed March 13, 2023, from which we derive the legal specifics of the trial and its outcomes.

2 These investors included, for example, Rupert Murdoch, Oracle founder Larry Ellison, and Tim Draper, founder of the prominent venture capital firm Draper Fisher Jurvetson. Notably, these and other investors were told that 1) the company would not reveal to them how its proprietary technologies worked and 2) Holmes was retaining total operational control over the company.

3 For a more colorful rendition of the rise and fall of Elizabeth Holmes and Theranos, see the updated January 20, 2023 edition of *Business Insider*, online at www.businessinsider.com/theranos-founder-ceo-elizabeth-holmes-life-story-bio-2018-4, accessed March 13, 2023.

4 For details on the ill-fated Theranos/Walgreens relationship, see the excerpt from John Carreyrou's book *Bad Blood*, online at https://knopfdoubleday.com/an-excerpt-from-bad-blood-by-john-carreyrou/, accessed March 13, 2023.

5 This anecdote is taken from the April 11, 2019, article in *Business Insider*, online at www.businessinsider.com/the-history-of-silicon-valley-unicorn-theranos-and-ceo-elizabeth-holmes-2018-5#lieutenant-colonel-david-shoemaker-raised-concerns-about-theranos-regulatory-strategy-to-the-fda-in-2012-after-holmes-approached-him-about-deploying-the-device-in-the-military-the-centers-for-medicare-and-medicaid-services-cms-then-did-a-surprise-inspection-in-which-balwani-told-regulators-the-device-was-still-under-development-after-battling-james-mattis-who-was-on-the-theranos-board-shoemaker-ultimately-agreed-to-a-more-limited-experiment-13, accessed March 13, 2023.

6 U.S. Department of Justice's summary of *U.S. v. Elizabeth Holmes, et al.*, online at www.justice.gov/usao-ndca/us-v-elizabeth-holmes-et-al.

7 See, for example, www.businessinsider.com/the-history-of-silicon-valley-unicorn-theranos-and-ceo-elizabeth-holmes-2018-5#in-november-2006-theranos-chief-financial-officer-henry-mosley-was-fired-after-questioning-the-reliability-of-its-technology-and-the-honesty-of-the-company-6 accessed March 13, 2023.

8 See, for example, www.businessinsider.com/the-history-of-silicon-valley-unicorn-theranos-and-ceo-elizabeth-holmes-2018-5#at-theranos-tension-was-mounting-ian-gibbons-the-chief-scientist-at-theranos-was-growing-uncomfortable-with-some-of-the-issues-the-blood-testing-technology-had-in-may-2013-holmes-scheduled-a-meeting-with-gibbons-in-which-he-expected-holmes-would-fire-him-the-night-before-he-attempted-to-take-his-own-life-he-died-a-week-later-14, accessed March 13, 2023. We cite this not as an example of character on Gibbons part but as an example of a culture that was hostile to the exercise of character.

9 The observations of and quotes by Tyler Shultz can be retrieved from the NPR article, online at www.npr.org/2022/01/05/1070474663/theranos-whistleblower-tyler-shultz-elizabeth-holmes-verdict-champagne, accessed March 13, 2023.

10 See Santa Clara University's excellent video case about Shultz, online at www.scu.edu/ethics/focus-areas/business-ethics/resources/teaching-note-interview-of-theranos-whistleblower-tyler-shultz/, accessed March 13, 2023.

11 From the Santa Clara University video.

12 See the February 15, 2022, edition of News@Ivey, which includes a write-up of Erika Cheung's role in Ivey's 2022 Leader Character & Candour Conference, online at www.ivey.uwo.ca/news/news-ivey/2022/february/stay-true-to-your-values-character-and-candour-conference/, accessed March 13, 2023.

13 From *The Guardian's* account of Theranos, online at www.theguardian.com/technology/2022/jan/03/theranos-verdict-five-key-moments-from-the-trial-that-shook-silicon-valley, accessed March 13, 2023.

14 See the aforementioned NPR article, online at www.npr.org/2022/01/05/1070474663/theranos-whistleblower-tyler-shultz-elizabeth-holmes-verdict-champagne.

15 From the Santa Clara University video. Unfortunately, weak boards are not uncommon. The collapse of Barings Bank as the result of rogue trader Nick Leeson's activities is in part attributable to minimal oversight—from the board level on down.

16 See "Leader character in board governance," by Gerard Seijts, Alyson Byrne, Mary Crossan, and Jeffrey Gandz (2019), in the *Journal of Management and Governance*, 23:227–258, online at https://doi.org/10.1007/s10997-018-9426-8 (and cited in Chapter 2).

17 Again, Seijts et al., (2019) in the *Journal of Management and Governance*.

18 Also from the story in the *Guardian*. We should note that Mattis subsequently testified against Holmes in court. See the related *New York Times* article, in which Mattis is quoted as saying he "didn't know what to believe." Online at www.nytimes.com/2021/09/22/technology/james-mattis-elizabeth-holmes-trial.html, accessed March 13, 2023.

19 See the March 14, 2019, edition of *CNN Business*, which tells the story of some of these workers, online at www.cnn.com/2019/03/14/tech/theranos-employees/index.html, accessed March 13, 2023.

20 Also from the story in the *Guardian*.

21 As it turned out, the baby was fine. See the January 4, 2022 edition of *Fortune*, online at https://fortune.com/2022/01/04/theranos-elizabeth-holmes-human-cost-fraud-faulty-blood-test-patients/, accessed March 13, 2023. We should note that the jury acquitted Holmes of the patient-related conspiracy wire-fraud count while another count of wire fraud pertaining to a Theranos patient was dismissed during the trial.

22 In July 2022, as noted, Ramesh Balwani was found guilty of 12 counts of wire fraud. We have chosen not to interpret his Leader Character here, first because his profile

appears to be very similar to Holmes and second because—as the *New York Times* observed in a November 2021 profile, online at www.nytimes.com/2021/11/23/technology/who-is-sunny-ramesh-balwani.html—"very little is known of Mr. Balwani." Much can be inferred, however, from the comments about him by Shultz and Cheung in this chapter and from Holmes's description of Balwani at her trial (*see the related note below*).

23 Again, see the January 4, 2022, edition of *Fortune*.

24 From the Santa Clara University video.

25 From an interview with Erika Cheung in the May 1, 2019, edition of *STAT*, online at www.statnews.com/2019/05/01/from-protegee-to-whistleblower-a-former-theranos-scientist-says-elizabeth-holmes-should-come-forward-and-apologize/, accessed March 13, 2023.

26 Hear both voices—her natural voice and her affected baritone—at www.youtube.com/watch?v=PjnsYz-xdOI, accessed March 13, 2023.

27 Also from the September 22, 2021, story in the *New York Times*.

28 In her closing testimony at her trial, Holmes claimed that Balwani—her former lover and second-in-command—abused her physically, emotionally, and sexually. Balwani denied all such allegations. See the December 8, 2021, edition of CNBC, online at www.cnbc.com/2021/12/08/theranos-founder-holmes-blasts-sunny-balwani-before-defense-rests.html, accessed March 13, 2023.

29 It's perhaps worth noting at this point that Holmes' father did a stint as a vice president at Enron: the scandal-plagued poster child of that previous generation and another fraud that was doomed to be detected.

30 Walgreens made the blood-testing deal without fully validating Theranos' technology, worrying that Elizabeth Holmes might balk, online at www.wsj.com/articles/craving-growth-walgreens-dismissed-its-doubts-about-theranos-1464207285, accessed March 13, 2023.

31 See the February 2, 2022, article "She didn't lie to me," online at www.businessinsider.com/theranos-elizabeth-holmes-tim-draper-respect-she-didnt-lie-2022-2, accessed March 13, 2023. Billionaire investor Tim Draper says he still respects Theranos and convicted founder Elizabeth Holmes.

32 We should emphasize that, even though we focus here on bad apples, even a bad barrel can contain plenty of good apples. Certainly, there were good apples among those 800-plus Theranos employees.

33 See, for example, www.businessinsider.com/theranos-founder-ceo-elizabeth-holmes-life-story-bio-2018-4#elizabeth-holmes-was-born-on-february-3-1984-in-washington-dc-her-mom-noel-was-a-congressional-committee-staffer-and-her-dad-christian-holmes-worked-for-enron-before-moving-to-government-agencies-like-usaid-1, accessed March 13, 2023.

34 See p. 173 of Walter Isaacson's brilliant *Steve Jobs*, published in 2011 by Simon & Schuster.

35 This figure is taken from the following book chapter: Crossan, C., & Crossan, M.M. (2023). The practice of developing leader character to elevate judgment. In T. Newstead & R. Riggio (Eds.), *Virtues and Leadership: Understanding and Practicing good Leadership*. New York, NY: Taylor and Francis Group.

36 In fact, the public record suggests precisely the opposite: her deep investment in the frauds of her life precluded this kind of self-scrutiny. For example, see her TEDMED talk at www.youtube.com/watch?v=SX7ec3uDlhs, accessed March 13, 2023.

37 Read more about the VIA Institute on Character and the VIA Survey online at www.viacharacter.org/. Christopher Peterson and Martin Seligman captured their research in the 2004 book *Character Strengths and Virtues: A Handbook and Classification* (see Chapter 2).

38 We outline the differences between character and personality traits in the article "Toward a Framework of Leader Character in Organizations," written by Mary Crossan and her colleagues. This article provides the background behind the leader character framework; see the November 2017 issue of the *Journal of Management Studies*. The Big Five personality traits are openness to experience, conscientiousness, extroversion, agreeableness, and neuroticism.

39 See Romeo Vitelli's article, "Can You Change Your Personality?", in the September 7, 2015, issue of *Psychology Today*, online at www.psychologytoday.com/us/blog/media-spotlight/201509/can-you-change-your-personality, accessed March 13, 2023.

40 See SIGMA's website at www.sigmaassessmentsystems.com/.

41 Details are available online at www.sigmaassessmentsystems.com/assessments/leadership-character-insight-assessment/#1652362352789-34d4bb04-1b2e.

42 "Key player" is defined variously by different groups. We recently worked with a professional sports franchise that included all of its athletes and coaches participating in its player-development camp.

43 We use these terms—"weak," "strong," and "unbalanced"—here for the purposes of this narrative. They, and the kind of analysis we present here, would not be included in actual LCIA results.

44 James Comey, a former director of the U.S. Federal Bureau of Investigation, commented that amoral leaders "eat your soul in small bites"—but also tend to "reveal the character of those around them." See www.usatoday.com/story/news/politics/2019/05/01/james-comey-criticizes-william-barr-says-trump-eats-your-soul/3642561002/, accessed March 13, 2023.

45 The two sets of statistics were reported in the September 9, 2019, edition of *Forbes*, online at www.forbes.com/sites/rasmushougaard/2018/09/09/the-real-crisis-in-leadership/?sh=fa5705c3ee47, accessed March 13, 2023.

Chapter 4

Exercising character

From the outside looking in, Bill Furlong should have been content.

He had a healthy and growing family and was in the midst of what seemed to be a good career. He was a senior executive of a major Canadian investment bank, for which he had successfully led several critical initiatives that had allowed him to grow both personally and professionally.[1]

Yet something was not quite right. Perhaps it was his stagnating relationship with his four children. The demands of his roles had meant sacrificing time with them—and as the oldest of his children began to reach their teenage years, he was seeing early signs of distance and mutual misunderstanding.

Perhaps it was his current role. The job he had did not seem to suit him very well—it lacked the urgency he had become accustomed to and thrived upon. He found this situation somewhat frustrating, and he was finding it harder to imagine how that might change. As an achievement-oriented person, this lack of opportunity was beginning to undermine his sense of identity. He strongly felt that he had much more to contribute.

Or perhaps it was him. He had just returned to Toronto after spending several years in London, England, setting up a new governance function focused on supporting and overseeing the dealer's rapidly growing structured and complex derivatives businesses. This had been a very challenging assignment, and he wondered if the experience had changed him somehow. In those pre-Global Financial Crisis (GFC) days, capital markets were even more hypercompetitive and hyperaggressive than usual. To properly function in this environment, he wondered if he had become a bit more guarded, more skeptical, and more cynical. Given the complexity of some of these structures and derivatives, he sometimes felt out of his depth (although, as it turned out, post-GFC, other people were as well!). As a result, he had less confidence in his own capabilities and was less willing to be vulnerable. He sometimes felt less certain about his judgment and decision-making.

In an effort to sort this all out, he did what he always did—read and think. He read all the best-selling leadership books and articles, attended various leadership courses, and even had the benefit of a bank-sponsored executive coach. But these efforts produced changes that seemed transitory—more cosmetic than fundamental. He couldn't quite put his finger on what was wrong—if anything.

DOI: 10.4324/9781003341215-5

In any event, Bill's situation seemed unsustainable to him. His current trajectory was not leading to where he wanted his career and family to end up. But what to do? Up to this point, the combination of an all-consuming career and a busy family with four young children left virtually no time for new interests or networking. Bill sensed that staying in the same job at the same bank wasn't going to solve anything. He sensed further that the real change needed to come from within himself—and that only he could do that.

"It would all be so much easier," he thought to himself, "if I only knew what direction that change was supposed to take!"

So after much internal debate, Bill decided to leave his job and find some answers. He wanted to understand what needed to change inside himself to regain an accurate, positive, and sustainable sense of self, to strengthen his relationships with his children, and to live a more balanced and truly satisfying life. And once that change was more clearly defined, he wanted to know how to make it happen. After nearly a year of reading, thinking, networking, and pursuing different ideas, Bill came across a book by two Ivey Business School professors: Gerard Seijts and Mary Crossan. Their ideas immediately resonated with him, and he decided that he would learn more about them and their research.

***

In our work with busy managers, we often start by suggesting that they pose three questions to themselves:

- *Who have I become while I've been busy doing?*
- *Who am I becoming while I'm busy doing?*
- *Who do I want to become while I'm busy doing?*[2]

Bill Furlong's situation, described previously, may strike some of our readers as somewhat extreme. Of course, not everyone shares his sense that the center of their universe, professionally and personally, is no longer growing and may even be contracting. Not everyone feels trapped in a job or work setting that feels not quite right—even one that might look reasonably attractive from the outside. And of course, not everyone carves out the time to think things through to the depth and degree that Furlong does.

But even if you don't find yourself in circumstances as vexing as Furlong's, you may share some of his concern and anxiety. Maybe you are feeling some increasing degree of disconnect between your work persona and how you think of yourself—or *want* to think of yourself. *(Who have I become?)* And maybe you see that disconnect continuing at present and on into the future. *(Who am I becoming?)* Maybe you want to steer toward something different, and you have the feeling you can contribute so much more. *(Who do I want to become?)*

Sometimes all that's needed is a change of context. Maybe your company or your job has changed in ways that you didn't anticipate and aren't happy about—in other words, an external challenge. If that's the case, you will figure out your best response to it. But sometimes, what's really needed is a change in yourself: a change in what we have referred to in previous chapters as your character. Think of the companions whom Dorothy acquires in *The Wizard of Oz*: the Tin Man, the Scarecrow, and the Cowardly Lion. They think they need a heart, a brain, and courage, respectively. In fact, as it turns out, they need to develop a character that will enable them to tap into the resources that they already have.

In this chapter, we will reinforce our premise that character can indeed be changed—both passively and proactively. Look again at our list of three questions. The first two imply passive changes: things that happened while you weren't paying much attention to character. The third question looks at character proactively: *what can I do differently going forward?*

We will provide you with an overarching framework for character exercise and development drawn directly from the work of Dr. Corey Crossan, who has been a pioneer in research on bringing an exercise-science perspective to the development of Leader Character—one that has proven itself in real-world contexts.[3] The principles and practices for exercising character described in this chapter are all embedded in an app called Virtuosity™.[4] Figure 4.1 depicts Virtuosity's home screen, which brings awareness to the habits that can be cultivated to support character development.

This app is certainly a potential asset, in part because it draws on relevant science. At the same time, there are many other ways to approach the same goals, if less directly. We encourage our readers to discover the path that works best for them—perhaps including Virtuosity.

Bill Furlong's story will recur episodically throughout this chapter to convey highlights of the character-building journey he has undertaken and is still undertaking. And while every such journey is unique, this chapter provides an overall roadmap that people who want to effect character change can trust and follow.

Bill had just finished reading Leadership on Trial, *a short book co-authored by Gerard Seijts and Mary Crossan along with two of their colleagues. It examined the reasons behind the GFC and identified as the crisis' main cause an absence of character among the leaders in the financial services sector. Although Bill's former bank had been largely unaffected by the GFC, he felt pretty certain that this analysis was correct. Bill had seen no lack of commitment and competency in the capital markets in the lead-up to the GFC—in fact, he had seen extraordinary amounts of both—but at the same time, he had observed a few instances of weak character and some truly undesirable outcomes as a result. What was really interesting for Bill was that Gerard and Mary were treating character not as a matter of ethics but rather as something at the core of who leaders are and how their decision-making occurs—their judgment.*

Their focus on character captured the essential paradoxes at the heart of leadership—"confident and humble, aggressive and patient, analytical and intuitive, principled and pragmatic, deliberate and decisive, candid and

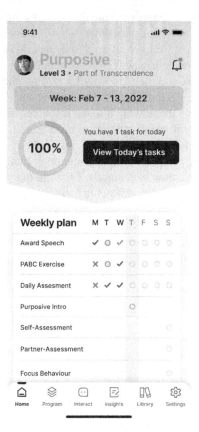

Figure 4.1 The Home Screen of the Virtuosity™ App

compassionate."[5] *The book also held out the promise that an individual's char-acter could be developed.*

Bill intuitively sensed that this novel approach to character and leadership might enable him to get to the root of what was bothering him and provide him with the avenue for the personal growth and fulfillment he had been seeking. So he reached out to Seijts, asking, "How can I get involved?"

***

Where does character come from?

Your character is the result of how you have led your life up to this point. Stated differently, character results from the accumulation of what you do all day: how you meet the particular challenges of your workplace, how you build and main-tain relationships with family and friends, which organizations and activities you participate in, how you pursue hobbies, and so forth. You make an endless series of choices, which over time accumulate and combine into a set of habits. Some of these habits are healthy and helpful to you; others are less so. The results of these habits—in terms of your emotional, mental, and physical health—may be obvious, or they may be submerged.

For many of us, these outcomes coalesce over time into a self-image, which captures and reinforces how we interact with the world. That self-image is likely to be an *intuitive* picture—one that grows out of memories and emotions rather than being determined in any systematic way. We come to think of ourselves as having a certain approach in our personal and professional relationships: "I am a nice person who supports others by including them in the decision-making process," or "I am someone who gets things done by setting stretch goals and being a straight shooter in execution," or whatever.

The problem is that these self-images are both incomplete and limiting. First, by definition, they don't include the submerged elements referred to previously. (You aren't tapping into things that have remained at the subconscious level and which you therefore can't perceive.) Second, they lock you into a self-image that is more or less fixed—*a person who gets things done*—and may well constrain your ability to thrive in a variety of new circumstances and conditions.

Now let's contrast that self-image with character. Think about it for a moment. Your character, as we've said, is the result of an unending series of choices, which over time accumulate into a set of learned behaviors or habits. Well, if that's true, then *every new day is a new opportunity to make different choices* and thereby to develop new and more effective habits. In other words, every day is a new opportunity to work on your leader character.

We've already cited Aristotle's view that the only way to be virtuous is to *act virtuously*. Your character emerges when you consciously make choices with character in mind. Becoming someone new starts with *aiming* at becoming someone new and acting on that aim.

Consider the case of Ukrainian President Volodymyr Zelenskyy, who spent almost two decades after graduating from Kyiv National Economic University—with a degree in law—as an actor, performer, producer, and executive in the Ukrainian TV and movie industries. In 2015, in the hugely successful *Servant of the People* TV series, he played the role of a high school history teacher who gets elected president. This and his previous life experiences served him well when, four years later, he was elected his country's president in real life. He was accomplished and self-confident. He had learned how to express himself in highly quotable sound bites and otherwise present himself in highly effective ways.

Then came the February 2022 invasion of his country by Russian forces. At that point, Zelenskyy almost overnight had to *be* the character-rich leader that he previously had only *played*. And while we have no reason to think that President Zelenskyy was a student of Aristotle, he subsequently embodied—to a remarkable degree—many of the character virtues that Aristotle identified many centuries ago: humanity, temperance, justice, courage, transcendence, wisdom, and prudence.[6]

Courage, for example? When the US offered to evacuate him and his family from the besieged city of Kyiv, he turned the offer down. "The fight is here," he reportedly said. "I need ammunition, not a ride."[7] Transcendence? His unshakeable optimism and conviction persuaded his countrymen—and supporters around the world—that Ukraine's cause was just, worth fighting for, and would prevail. His character-based judgment repeatedly helped Ukraine avoid catastrophic mistakes and stood in stark contrast to the stunning mistakes in judgment made by Russia's autocratic President Vladimir Putin.

How is character developed? We can point to five overlapping phases that contribute to this process, as summarized in Figure 4.2[8].

Developing a snapshot of your leader character—*discovering* character, in Figure 4.2—was the central focus of Chapter 3. What are your latent character strengths and weaknesses? Tools like the leader character Insight Assessment and the Virtuosity app help generate that snapshot, which can serve as a baseline for the larger process of character development. To reiterate two points that we've made before, first, character is not simply a nice-to-have, and second, character is always a work in progress. Character development produces well-established benefits—including sustained excellence and well-being—that contribute to a virtuous cycle that further supports character development.

This chapter focuses mainly on *activating* and *strengthening* character. It also touches on techniques for *connecting* and *sustaining* character—topics to which

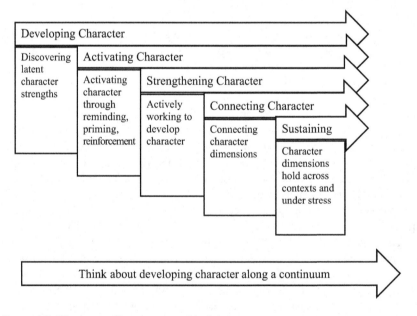

Figure 4.2 Character Development Model

we'll return in subsequent chapters. Later in this chapter, we'll present a modified version of Figure 4.1, which captures several of the key exercises introduced
in the following pages.

*Bill Furlong was reviewing the results of his leader character Insight As-
sessment. His strongest dimensions were Drive and Accountability. No surprise
there—he had built a solid reputation for getting things done under even the
most trying of circumstances. But he had scored relatively low in Humility and
Humanity. This did come as a bit of surprise to him as he had thought of himself
as a "nice guy." Bill wondered, "Maybe being nice is not the same thing as having strength in Humility and Humanity."*

*The more closely Bill scrutinized his results, the more clearly he could see
how working in the intensely competitive capital markets for more than two decades had been shaping his character. For example, on a trading floor, essentially
what is being traded is information. Trading is a zero-sum game, and if your
information is inferior to your counterpart's, then more often than not, you will
lose money. Information is therefore relentlessly acquired, constantly reevalu-
ated, and closely guarded. If your trading position is weak, then you do your
best to hide that weakness while at the same time looking to exploit weakness
and dislocation elsewhere.*

*It might all sound a bit dramatic, but in fact—as Bill found himself
thinking—it's how markets work. Vulnerability (which is a key element of humility)
is a behavior that is not prized and is not often observed. Pretty soon, a lack of
vulnerability in your professional life starts to wash over into other parts of your
life, and you become less vulnerable, less transparent, and less humble. Yet with a
renewed understanding of what humility really means, Bill understood how dam-
aging a lack of it can be because it inhibits learning and information flow.*

*Bill was beginning to see how his many years of working in capital markets
had imperceptibly yet remorselessly changed not only his character but also his
beliefs about how the working world, and maybe the whole world, works: a zero-
sum, hide-your-weaknesses game.*

***

Core beliefs: a baseline and a target in activating character

Let's begin our discussion of activating character—the first step in the larger
process of exercising character—by examining the notion of *core beliefs*. Core
beliefs are our individual narratives about ourselves, others, and the world. For
example, a person might believe on a fundamental level that he or she needs to
remain in control at all times. These core beliefs are a substantial level deeper
than the styles and self-images referred to earlier. They are our internal scripts
about how the world works. They can play either a functional or dysfunctional
role in shaping our behaviors, which in turn help shape our character.

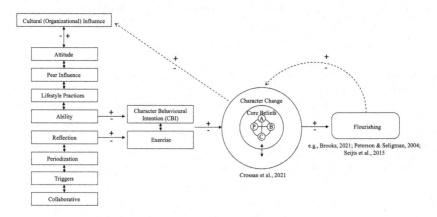

Figure 4.3 Leader Character Development Process Model

Core beliefs are something that we both *start with* and *reshape as we move forward*. You'll note that Figure 4.3—which represents Corey Crossan's most recent analysis of character development—locates them toward the center of a larger process. Note the "influence arrows" moving in opposite directions—underscoring the fact that they both *influence* and are *influenced by* other steps in that process.

You'll also note those four circles at the center of the core beliefs circle: P, A, B, and C, collectively the PABCs. These stand for *physiology, affect, behavior,* and *cognition*. The "C" (cognition) is the direct connection to core beliefs—again, our internal scripts. As for the "B" circle, think of the Nike slogan—*Just do it*—which we would restate as "Just change your behavior." But "just doing it" is easier said than done because it sidesteps the fact that when we attempt changes to cognition and behavior, both *physiology* (the functions and activities of the body) and *affect* (an expressed or observed feeling, emotion, or mood) come into play in complex ways.

For example, feeling nervous can dampen our confidence in our abilities whereas positive emotions can boost our confidence in our skills.[9] Anyone who has gone through cognitive behavior therapy, or CBT—a very common approach for people dealing with anxiety—will recognize the PABCs and confirm that you need to understand and learn how to regulate those big systems in order to make changes in core beliefs and behaviors. You can devise daily short exercises that can be done while cooking a meal, listening to music, or transforming a walking practice—exercises that start to cultivate an awareness of the PABCs.[10]

In the specific case of character development, we focus on a very select set of virtuous behaviors—a focus that helps us develop and concentrate our understanding. Maybe it would be helpful at this point to walk through an example. Let's say that your self-assessment on character (as described in Chapter 3) reveals that you are not as calm as you might like or need to be (Temperance).

Maybe you notice that you feel less calm when things don't go as you've planned. When unexpected situations arise, you can feel your heart start racing, and a blood-pressure cuff would reveal that your blood pressure is rising—your physiology at work. If the unexpected situation is threatening enough, you may experience a so-called "amygdala hijack," where you feel overwhelmed with emotional threat (affect), releasing hormones that prepare the body for flight (physiology), all of which limit the capacity to think clearly (cognition). So for many people, for many reasons, calmness is a beneficial habit of behavior to develop.

To become a calmer person, you not only need to consider how it relates to other dimensions of character but also need to learn how to regulate your PABCs that underpin all dimensions of character. For example, becoming aware that your heart is starting to race and then catching the label you attach to the emotion and why is a first step. Many people find their heart races when speaking in public and label the emotion as one of fear when a good part of it could be excitement. You need to link your understanding to the beliefs that could be triggering the emotion, such as "I'm not good at public speaking" or "I don't like being the center of attention", which could be fueled by a fear of looking inadequate or being judged, as will be revealed in Bill's story. Again, there are also exercises that move beyond better understanding to help cultivate better regulation of the PABCs. For example, breathing exercises can help with the physiological regulation of being calm.

One thing that this kind of iterative exploration tends to reveal is that as you dig deeply into a particular dimension—in this case, *calmness in the face of a loss of control*—many other dimensions of character are likely to demand attention as well. For example, you're likely to find that being more open-minded and flexible—behaviors associated with Collaboration—enables you to be more improvisational when you're addressing the unknown or unpredictable, something that gradually emerges in Bill's story. And as you develop these supporting behaviors, it's likely that your core beliefs about the need to maintain control will start to change. Ideally, you consider how the behavior you are working on relies and relates to other dimensions. You may conclude that you are putting massive stress on something like being calm because of weaknesses in other areas—such as the frustration that can arise with others, owing to a weakness in Humanity and understanding where others are coming from.

In short, the conscious activation of character relies on the regulation of the PABCs to help transform core beliefs—and thereby to help develop character. We'll return to core beliefs shortly, when we look more closely at the central role they play in activating character. For now, though, the important point to remember is that you begin the process of character activation with a set of core beliefs that affect your actions—a sort of internal baseline—but which also can be modified by your actions.

Here's an example of how this can be done. Figure 4.4 shows Virtuosity's core beliefs and PABC assessments, in addition to a series of lessons for each of them to strengthen them, including daily PABC exercises and additional ones that are stored in Virtuosity's library.

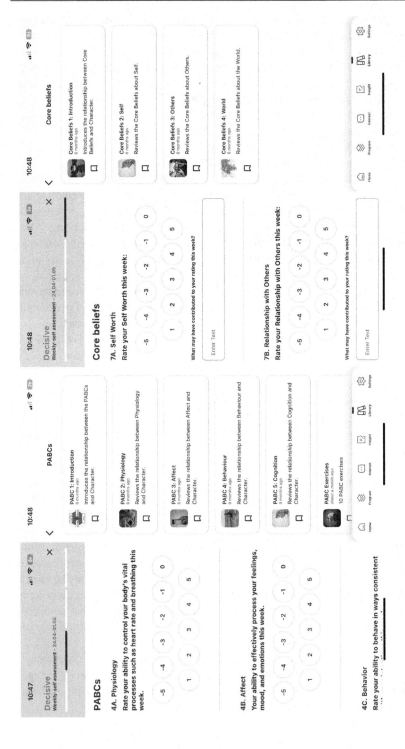

Figure 4.4 Sample of Virtuosity's Core Beliefs and PABC Assessments

Bill and Mary were getting set to take the stage to present a leader character workshop to several hundred of Ottawa's top federal bureaucrats. Bill looked over at Mary, who appeared to be perfectly calm. He could feel his own heart rate starting to elevate, his breathing getting a bit shallower, and the onset of that familiar sense of discomfort that he almost always felt before he made these kinds of presentations. Over time, he had come to expect this to be normal—simply something you (and probably everyone else other than Mary!) had to live with—even though he thought it undermined his effectiveness in presentations. "I guess that's just who I am," he had concluded.

At one point several months back, he had mentioned this to Mary, wondering aloud if maybe he needed to work on strengthening his character, perhaps the dimension of Courage. "Oh, that's not a lack of Courage you're experiencing," Mary replied. "More likely, you're experiencing a lack of Humility."

Bill was puzzled by this. He had always thought of himself as a humble person—modest, even self-effacing. But now, looking at himself through the lens of leader character, he realized that all those years in capital markets might have washed away whatever true Humility he had.

Accordingly, Bill began to realize that his weakness in Humility was the source of this discomfort. By virtue of his many years working on trading floors, he had gotten into the habit of not showing weakness—and frankly, he had to admit, that had never been his strong suit in the first place! This, again, was the result of a combination of temperament and context: rarely do weaknesses exposed in a trading environment work out well.

And now, only minutes before this presentation with Mary, Bill found himself thinking that he didn't want to make any mistakes. He cared deeply about the leader character work and didn't want to see it set back by him looking visibly uncomfortable.

No wonder he was a bit nervous.

But now, recalling this conversation with Mary about Humility and presentations, a new thought entered his mind: "I'm just here trying to share what information I have about something I think is important and meaningful. I will do the best I can. I'm not perfect, and if (and when) I make a few mistakes, it will be OK; this is a gathering of people looking to learn and share knowledge and information about leader character." Then Bill tried something a little different. Just before the presentation got underway, he began quietly repeating to himself, "Humble, humble, humble."

Immediately his heart rate slowed, his breathing settled back to normal, and he walked on stage with an authentic smile on his face—happy to greet the crowd and, with Mary, share what they knew about the importance of leader character.

***

Intention: *why* you're activating character

Now look again at Figure 4.2. To the left of the concentric circles with core beliefs at their center are two boxes: *intention* and *exercise*. Corey Crossan has determined there are two primary antecedents for character change: you have to be motivated to do it (intention), and you have to *work* at it (exercise).

To the left of those two boxes—that is, at the far left of Figure 4.2—you see a column of boxes, the top half of which are antecedents to intention and the bottom half of which are antecedents to exercise. We'll talk our way through these boxes, starting at the obvious starting point: intention. We will provide examples from the Virtuosity app following each section to help you imagine how these principles are embedded into an app. Figure 4.5 shows how Character Behavior Intention (CBI) is assessed and used for insights, with additional lessons provided to help the learner strengthen their CBI.

Crossan's research reveals that although a number of studies have established the importance of conscious attention to character development, those studies have tended to underestimate the critical role and nature of *intentionality* in that process. Intentionality can either support or inhibit character development because it influences the likelihood a behavior will be exhibited.[11] Behavioral intention represents a person's motivation in the sense of a conscious plan, decision, or self-instruction to perform a targeted behavior, and it contributes to approximately 40 to 50 percent of the likelihood of behavioral performance.[12] Why is the link between behavior and behavioral intention important? Because people tend to engage in behaviors they intend to perform, and—as we've said before—it is the repeated act of engaging in virtuous behaviors that develops character.

Back to that left-hand column in Figure 4.2: Crossan and her colleagues have developed an index that they refer to as Character Behavioral Intention, or CBI.[13] As Figure 4.2 indicates, CBI can be broken down into five antecedents: cultural (or organizational) influence, attitude, peer influence, lifestyle practices, and perceived ability. Each antecedent is influenced by the others, and therefore, strengthening one will help to strengthen another. The higher your CBI, the more likely you are to engage in character-development processes.

Each of these antecedents is deeply ingrained in us, and—depending on context—they can be difficult to change. But the lens of intentionality allows us to focus on and strengthen each of these five antecedents so that they in turn can strengthen character, more or less regardless of context.

Let's assume that you have identified a virtuous behavior that you want to target. *Cultural influence* represents the pressure you feel to perform (or not perform) that targeted behavior, based on the customary codes of behavior in your cultural context. Customary codes of behavior that embody strong character support development, whereas codes of behavior that embody weak character or unbalanced character undermine character development.

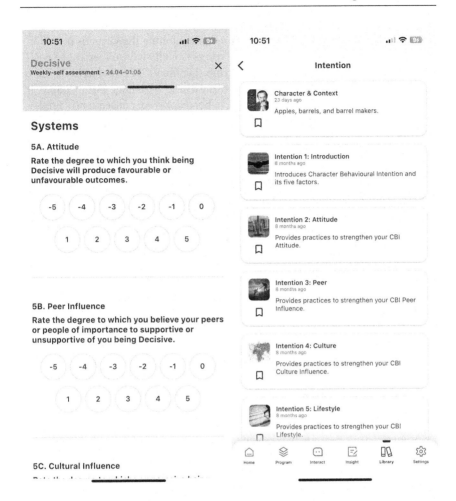

Figure 4.5 Sample of the Assessment of Character Behavior Intention

For example, organizations that overweight drive, accountability, and integrity while underweighting humility and humanity will almost certainly undermine the development of the character behaviors associated with Humility and Humanity, either consciously or unconsciously. Thinking back to the Theranos example in Chapter 3, it's clear that context is hugely important—but it's not all-determining. While cultural influence has a significant impact on the other four CBI antecedents, described later, you can limit that impact by declining to comply with normative behavior that exhibits weak character.

Attitude represents your evaluation of the targeted virtuous behavior, including the perceived consequences of the virtuous behavior and your cost-benefit analysis of those consequences. In other words, your "attitude score" is heavily rooted in what you see as the likely outcome of exhibiting the virtuous behavior, which tends to be determined by whether you personally have experienced positive or negative outcomes as a result of exhibiting the virtuous behavior or have witnessed positive or negative outcomes experienced by others. For example, if colleagues who exhibited the virtue of brave behavior were consequently fired— again, think back to the Theranos example—it makes it that much less likely that you'll be inclined to develop and exhibit bravery.

Our research, moreover, has consistently revealed that some of the virtuous behaviors are often viewed or understood only in their virtuous state, such as those associated with Drive, whereas other behaviors, such as those associated with Humility and Humanity, are often interpreted in their vice state. This underscores why it's helpful for you to understand how the dimensions and elements of character introduced in Chapter 2 interact. Understanding why, for example, vulnerability (an element of Humility) is a strength in its virtuous state can shape your attitude, and by extension, your intentionality.

Peer influence represents your perceived social pressure, from people who are important to you, to perform the targeted virtuous behavior. The peer influence score is a combination of two factors: how much your peers value a targeted virtuous behavior and how motivated you are to comply with social pressure (norms) of the peer groups surrounding the virtuous behavior. If your peers value the targeted virtuous behavior, then your focus should be on increasing your motivation to comply. If your peers don't value the targeted virtuous behavior, then your aim should be to support character development in others—a focus of later chapters.

Lifestyle represents your perceived presence of current practices that facilitate or inhibit your performance of the targeted virtuous behavior. Lifestyle can be strengthened primarily by embedding more practices that actively support your character development. For example, many people find that the goal of being calm is overwhelmed by their "to do" lists, both personal and professional. But those lists are largely within their control. Once they set realistic priorities, they set better conditions for being calm. Recognize that even priority setting is anchored in dimensions of character, whether it be strengthening Transcendence to imagine possibilities, strengthening Collaboration to help in delegating, or strengthening Humility to come to terms with a sense that only you can do something or that your self-worth is dependent on completing the tasks on the "to do" list.

Ability represents your real (or oftentimes, perceived) capability to perform the targeted virtuous behavior. Ability is strengthened when you create a development plan that is attainable, thereby minimizing the perceived difficulty of developing the virtuous behavior.

Bill knew that a single positive experience in activating Humility was not going to create the habit that he needed to ingrain in his character. He needed to be intentional and find an activity in which he would be vulnerable, would not know all the answers, and would be almost certain to make mistakes while he practiced and exercised new behaviors. But he also wanted to find a low-risk "safe space" to do this work—a supportive environment that would allow the habit of Humility to grow and strengthen. He found his answer in Bootprov, a Toronto-based improvisational acting troupe led by Kate Ashby, one of Canada's best-known improv teachers. Over the years, Bootprov (short for "Improv Bootcamp") had attracted members from all walks of life, including actors, writers, directors, IT people, consultants, executive coaches, bankers, lawyers, real estate agents, and even professional athletes.

Bill found himself welcomed into Bootprov with the proverbial open arms, and the troupe turned out to be the perfect fit. By its very nature, one can't prepare for improv because you are venturing into the unknown—sometimes in front of large crowds (Courage). Given that there is never a script, "mistakes" are bound to happen. Yet these mistakes are not only tolerated (Humanity) but celebrated and worked into the act, often to great effect (Collaboration, Humility). On those occasions when you do really mess up, you simply need to forgive yourself and move on (Humanity). You always need to support your partner and group no matter what (Collaboration, Accountability).

In other words, it turned out that Improv was a hothouse for the development of not just Humility but of many dimensions of leader character. The experience was always fun, which made committing to it very easy. And under the leadership of Ashby, who created a nurturing, no-judgment, supportive environment, it strengthened exactly the dimensions of character Bill was hoping for—and even a few more as an added bonus.

***

Exercise: *how* you're activating character

Now let's move on to discuss the tools you can use to build and reinforce your strong intention—as defined previously—to develop character.

Once again, the exercise of a virtuous behavior is the "doing," with greater frequency of that act strengthening the embodiment of a virtuous behavior. The exercise of a virtuous behavior has its own set of antecedents, presented at the bottom left of Figure 4.2.

Reflection is a virtuous behavior within the leader character framework and therefore can be strengthened through exercise. We should underscore, up front, that not all reflection is equally valuable. The *components* of reflection are important and—along with frequency—are what you can work on developing.

What's "valuable" reflection? Many people who engage in this kind of productive behavior scrutinize their mental models—their "thinking habits"—to identify and cultivate constructive ways of thinking and behaving.[14] Your goal in this kind of reflection, when you engage in it, is to *develop a daily practice*. By exercising, you'll get better at it, and this will minimize the gap between stimulus, response behavior, outcomes, and reflection. You'll be better prepared to reflect *in real time* to inform the conscious choice of virtuous behavioral responses.

There are four variables that can be embedded to strengthen the character reflective process, including a leader character framework to effectively target behaviors for development, program engagement and its relation to desired benefits, facilitators and inhibitors to character development, the use of daily assessments that capture these factors—all of which can be used to feed insights back.

In part by embedding these variables, the reflection process can help you overcome entrenched virtue-vice manifestations. It can help you discover which behaviors require attention for development and which changes you need to make to support character development. As an example of how this can work, Figure 4.6 shows some of the reflective processes embedded into Virtuosity, including leader character assessments and insights; daily and weekly self and partner assessments with insights that include program engagement tracking, desired benefits, and facilitators and inhibitors; and weekly lessons and exercises with reflective prompts that encourage the learner to reflect specifically on each behavior.

Periodization draws from a large set of exercise principles and from the literature about habits, bringing attention to the careful construction of a program to support character development.[15] Looking back to Figure 4.1 at the beginning of this chapter, you'll recall that we've depicted character development as consisting of five stages: Discovering, Activating, Strengthening, Connecting, and Sustaining. Another way of looking at this figure is to go stage by stage, left to right, and determine how often a virtuous behavior is exhibited. The first stage—discovering the virtuous behavior—implies a low frequency of embodiment. The fifth and last stage represents the sustained embodiment of a virtuous behavior.[16]

How do you move from "left to right," in Figure 4.1? Using exercise science as our foundational metaphor, we can point to five useful principles that build on one another. The first is the *Use and Disuse* principle, which is no more complex than it sounds. Using or exercising a muscle results in its strengthening whereas "disuse" (lack of exercise) results in that muscle's atrophy. The same is revealed in the habit literature: consistently exhibiting a behavior will strengthen it, and the failure to exhibit it will result in the atrophy.[17]

The second exercise-science principle we invoke is that of *Individual Differences*, which reflects the fact that individuals are unique and all have slightly different responses to exercise programs. Certainly, this holds true in the character arena, with varying contexts or stages of development calling for variations upon the exercise regime.

The third relevant exercise-science principle is *Adaptation*, which means that an individual tends to adapt to demands over time. You may already have experienced this if you've worked with a trainer or participated in workout classes:

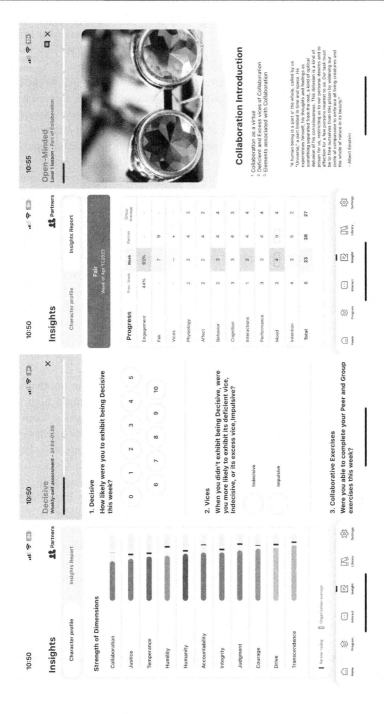

Figure 4.6 Sample of the Reflective Processes Embedded Into the Virtuosity™ App

at first you find the exercise difficult, but gradually you get better at it. The same holds true for the regimen of exhibiting a virtuous behavior. You adapt to the challenge, get better at it, and prepare yourself to act with character in a range of different contexts.

The fourth exercise-science principle is *Overload*, meaning that because a normal level of stress or load is unlikely to lead to development, a greater degree of stress is needed. In fact, character development requires *the consistent increase of load* to ensure that development continues. There's an inherent caution, here: it's difficult for character to remain static—so if it isn't developing, it is likely atrophying.

The fifth exercise-science principle that we incorporate is *Progression*, meaning there is an optimal level of overload that should be applied to achieve sustainable development. In physical exercise, a load that is excessive may result in severe injury. For example, if you haven't been a consistent runner in recent years, you shouldn't start back up again by running a marathon. Instead, a plan that begins with you running smaller increments in comfortable environments and slowly progresses to a full marathon over time is likely to yield better results. Similarly, a load applied to virtuous behavior that is over the top—meaning that, one way or another, it doesn't serve the needs of the individual—may risk trauma. If you're seeking to become more courageous in difficult circumstances, for example, you should probably begin by exercising your courage in small increments and in comfortable environments and then progress toward more demanding exercises in less comfortable environments.

The habit literature also supports this approach by describing the "motivation-threshold level." This simply means that your motivation should be high and should be supported by a relatively low or achievable threshold, which taken together will increase the likelihood that you will perform the prescribed behavior.[18] When you're just beginning to develop your character, therefore, you should begin by choosing to focus on the development of one virtue—not multiple virtues—and align your exercises with the first stage of character development. Your daily practice of reflection, described previously, will help you determine which changes you need to make, and when, as you continue to develop your character.

A *trigger* is a cue that prompts you to engage in a certain kind of behavior. Habits are generally associated with a specific stimulus, so it makes sense for you to choose a trigger to help you build your new habit.[19] Crossan has identified five different triggers that can be used depending on the focus behavior (with the acronym "SLEPT"):

1. *State:* Your mental or physical state can be used to trigger an exercise, like practicing patience when you notice your body tensing.
2. *Location:* You can create specific contextual or situational cues to trigger an exercise, like keeping a door open to encourage collaborative behavior.

3. *Event:* You can use an event or preexisting routine to trigger an exercise, like practicing "yes, and" language while watching the news.
4. *People:* You can use people who influence certain behavior to trigger an exercise, like greeting colleagues to practice optimism.
5. *Time:* You can choose a time as a stable cue that can be used to trigger an exercise, like writing a gratitude list before going to bed.

Figure 4.7, which expands upon Figure 4.1 back at the beginning of the chapter, provides an example of an exercise to develop the dimension of Collaboration, applying the Periodization and Trigger principles.

The title of the collaboration exercise is "Yes, and." It's adapted from the classic improvisation exercise, typically used to help a performer hone his or her ability to accept someone else's ideas or contributions and to build upon what has been presented. This requires the virtuous behaviors of collaboration, including being open-minded, flexible, interconnected, cooperative, and collegial.

We won't talk you through the exercise as it's depicted in Figure 4.7, except to say that the simplest form of the exercise begins with the first stage of character development—the Discovering stage—and includes an exercise trigger. As an individual adapts, the exercise progresses toward the right, aligned with each development stage and a progressively more challenging exercise.

Again, the Virtuosity app demonstrates how this works. Virtuosity has 26 levels for each of the 62 behaviors so that the exercises progressively become more challenging as the learner progresses in their levels within each behavior. Figure 4.8 shows the periodization and trigger practices embedded into Virtuosity, beginning with the option for the learner to choose their own target behaviors, followed by an exercise beginning with the discovery stage, the learner's journey overview, and finally triggers that can be selected as reminders for the prescribed exercise.

A *collaborative* approach is the last antecedent to exercise, and like the other antecedents described previously, it, too, is informed by the behavior and habit-development literature.[20] Based on that research, we can point to four techniques that can help you support the exercise of virtuous behavior. First, you should consult a trusted partner to provide consistent feedback on how they are observing character changes in you. Why? Because, first, while strengthening character will enhance your own self-awareness, it may also incline you toward an overly critical self-assessment of character, which your partner can steer you away from. And again, as noted in Chapter 3, engaging in partner or 360 assessments will minimize bias and enhance self-awareness.[21]

Second, engaging in partner feedback not only serves the individual receiving feedback. It also helps develop the assessor's character by sharpening that person's awareness of what character looks like in others (meaning, you). As we'll

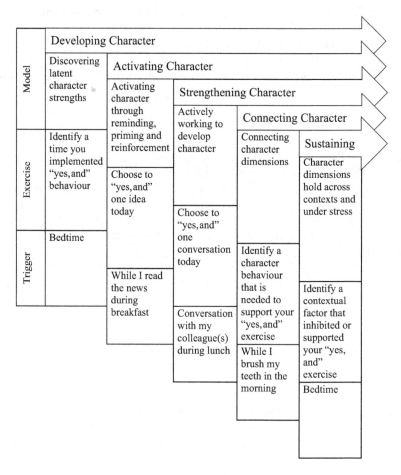

Figure 4.7 An Example of an Exercise to Develop the Dimension of Collaboration—Yes, And

stress in subsequent chapters, helping the people around you develop character is both "selfish" (in a good sense) and selfless.

Third, learning is enhanced when you engage in active dialogue. Dialogue compels you to put your thoughts into words and thereby compels you to think clearly about what you're experiencing. It also facilitates a greater depth of understanding as you exchange and engage with a range of ideas and perspectives.

And finally, engaging with others supports an accountability to character development. Focusing on this concept, Figure 4.9 shows some of the collaborative practices embedded into Virtuosity, including insights that include partner and organizational insights, choosing a partner within the app, an interact page

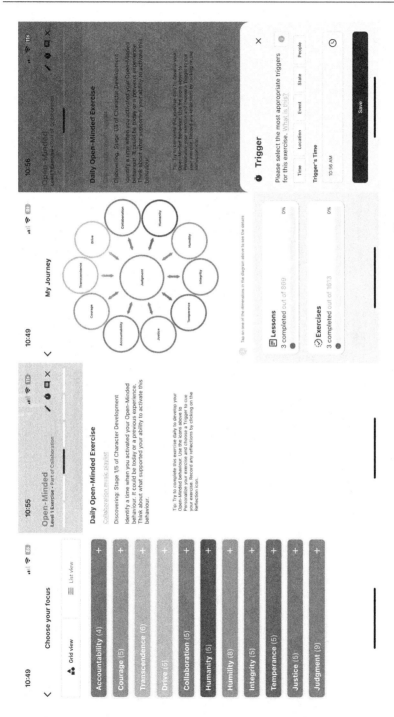

Figure 4.8 Sample of the Periodization and Trigger Practices Embedded Into Virtuosity™ App

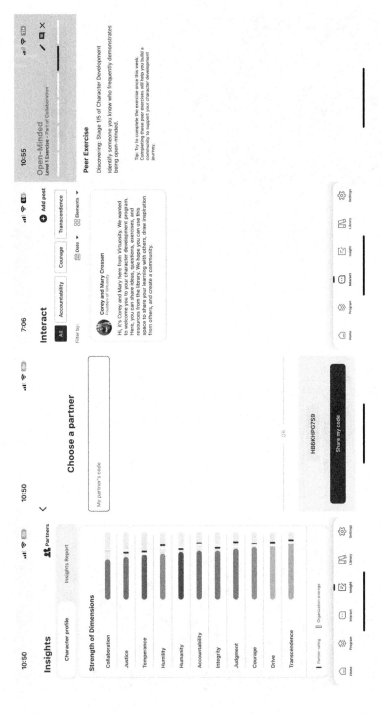

Figure 4.9 Sample of the Collaborative Practices Embedded Into Virtuosity™ App

where learners can share resources, personalized exercises, or post questions, and finally, peer and group exercises.

A parting look at core beliefs

As we noted earlier, core beliefs are scripts that we start with—and that through exercising character, we also work toward. With our run-through of character-building and our baseline core beliefs behind us, now let's look at the core beliefs that may lie ahead of us.

Core beliefs are subject to the laws of exercise science, described in the discussion of periodization previously. Core beliefs can become more functional with character development, and they can become more dysfunctional with character atrophy.

For example, let's imagine that at the outset of the kind of process described in this chapter, an individual is saddled with a core belief that the world is void of the kind of opportunity that is most important to him or her. (For our purposes here, we'll assume that it's career-related opportunity.) Well, most people would agree that this is not a very useful perspective and that it can fairly be described as dysfunctional. (Why get out of bed in the morning if there's no opportunity out there?) Now let's imagine that this same individual exercises his or her character and thereby strengthens the dimensions of Transcendence, Humility, Drive, Collaboration, Humanity, and Courage. By so doing, he or she is very likely to shift toward a new core belief—that the world is in fact *rich* with opportunity,

As researcher Carol Dweck suggests, core beliefs can be grouped into two categories: those reflecting a Fixed mindset and those reflecting a Growth mindset.[22] People with Fixed mindsets believe that they have a certain amount of ability. They also believe, however, that intelligence, talent or aptitude, ability, and other qualities are innate and relatively *unchangeable*. This perception not only inhibits their future perception of change, but it very often turns out to be self-fulfilling. (I can't grow, so I won't.) People with Growth mindsets, by contrast, believe that their abilities can continue to develop with hard work, strategies, and helpful instruction.[23]

Here's why this matters to you: you can harness your Growth mindset as a foundation to continue developing your character because you believe it can be developed with important positive outcomes. On the other hand, that colleague of yours with that Fixed mindset is unlikely to believe change is possible, which means that the all-important "intention" box in Figure 4.2 is either missing or atrophied and that colleague is unlikely to take on the hard work of exercising his or her character. Most likely, he or she will stick with being stuck and settle for becoming simply a product of context and experience. A cork floating on someone else's ocean probably doesn't worry much about the content of its character.

In short, even if your core beliefs are starting in a bad place, they certainly don't have to *end* in a bad place. Through hard work, you can make them what you want them to be.

As this book is being written, it's been more than ten years since Bill left his job at the wholesale bank. The first couple of years were challenging ones as he searched to find direction, purpose and put his finger on what he thought was holding back his full potential—what he later came to understand to be certain underdeveloped dimensions of his character.

The capital markets are very competitive, intense, and typically unforgiving. In the early days of Bill's career, this challenging environment helped to shape his character in a positive manner by strengthening his Courage, Accountability, and Drive. Over time, however, the nature and mechanics of markets can also negatively reshape one's core beliefs, turning vulnerability into a target and Humility into a perceived liability. This can easily lead to a compromised character—that is, an imbalance among character strengths and weaknesses. In Bill's case, his character may have begun to change in ways that were undermining his ability to lead, handicapping his decision-making, and hampering his relationships with his family.

Today, Bill's relationships with his children are greatly improved. He has found meaningful, purposeful, and engaging work as a capital markets regulator, board member, and executive in residence—all roles that, in varying ways, enable him to share what he is learning about leader character. Yes, his heart rate still increases before presentations—but now it represents a productive, channeled energy that Bill brings to his work and which he calls upon to convey his passion to his audiences. Most importantly, Bill has regained his sense of purpose, meaning, and contentment: a perspective that allows him to bring his best self to all that he does. Bill attributes these fundamental changes in his life not to the development of any new competencies but rather to his strengthened character.

***

Looking forward

In this chapter, we've used Bill Furlong's real-life experiences to help bring alive the processes of exercising character, with an emphasis on *activating* and *strengthening* character.

As stated earlier, Chapters 1 through 4 are mostly presented from the perspective of the individual. How does the individual understand, discover, and exercise character? Moving forward, we will retain the individual perspective to some degree, but we'll also start to increase our focus on organizational context. That shift begins with Chapter 5, which focuses on what we call *micro-moments*—the building blocks of connecting and sustaining character in the workplace.

Notes

1 Bill Furlong is one of this book's authors. His story will recur throughout this chapter. For more somewhat-disguised Furlong background, see Ivey's "Bob Franklin" case series, 9B15C038, A through D.

2 These three questions—and much of the chapter that follows—are derived from a book chapter written by Corey Crossan and Mary Crossan. The full citation is as follows: Crossan, C., & Crossan, M. M. (2023). The practice of developing leader character to elevate judgment. In T. Newstead & R. Riggio (Eds.), *Virtues and Leadership: Understanding and Practicing Good Leadership*. New York, NY: Taylor and Francis Group.

3 Corey Crossan's recent research is captured in her dissertation: Crossan, C. (2022). *Building a Model for Leader Character Development in Sport*. Electronic Thesis and Dissertation Repository, Western University.

4 See the Virtuosity website at https://virtuositycharacter.ca/.

5 Gandz, J., Crossan, M., Seijts, G. H., & Stephenson, C. (2010). *Leadership on Trial: A Manifesto for Leadership Development*. London, ON: Richard Ivey School of Business.

6 For an interesting exploration of the intersection of Zelenskyy's character with Aristotle's virtues, see the online article at https://theconversation.com/the-value-of-virtue-7-reasons-why-volodymyr-zelenskyys-crisis-leadership-has-been-so-effective-182041, accessed March 14, 2023.

7 See, for example, www.ctvnews.ca/world/zelensky-refuses-u-s-offer-to-evacuate-saying-i-need-ammunition-not-a-ride-1.5797367, accessed March 14, 2023. There is some question as to whether Zelenskyy actually said these words in this way—but there is no question about his decision to remain at the center of the fight.

8 Crossan, M., Ellis, C., & Crossan, C. (2021). Towards a model of LCD: Insights from anatomy and music therapy. *Journal of Leadership & Organizational Studies*, 28(3): 287–305.

9 This analysis draws heavily on the work of Albert Bandura, a leading scholar on developing self-efficacy or task-specific confidence. Bandura is internationally recognized as one of the world's most influential social psychologists for his groundbreaking research on the importance of learning by observing others. He died in 2021.

10 Such examples are included in the Virtuosity app, mentioned previously.

11 Conner, M., & Sparks, P. (2005). The theory of planned behavior. In M. Conner & P. Norman (Eds.), *Predicting Health Behaviour: Research and Practice with Social Cognition Models* (pp. 121–162). Buckingham: Open University Press.

12 Conner and Sparks, 2005.

13 The CBI is adapted from the theory of planned behavior, or TPB, which links beliefs to behavior. TPB posits that behavioral intention is the most important determinant of human social behavior. TPB developed out of the Theory of Reasoned Action, a theory first proposed in 1980 by Martin Fishbein and Icek Ajzen.

14 Crossan and Crossan, 2023.

15 For a detailed review, see Hoffman, J. R. (2012). *NSCA's Guide to Program Design. National Strength and Conditioning Association*. Champaign, IL: Human Kinetics.

16 Crossan, Ellis and Crossan, 2021.

17 Lally and Gardner, 2013 Lally, P., & Gardner, B. (2013). Promoting habit formation. *Health Psychology Review*, 7(supp. 1): S137–S158.

18 Lally and Gardner, 2013.

19 Brette, O., Lazaric, N., & Vieira da Silva, V. (2017). Habit, decision-making, and rationality: Comparing Thorstein Veblen and early Herbert Simon. *Journal of Economic Issues*, 51(3): 567–587.
20 Conner and Sparks, 2005; Soller A., & Lesgold A. (1999). Analyzing peer dialogue from an active learning perspective. Proceedings of the AI-ED 99 workshop: Analysing educational dialogue interaction: Towards models that support learning, LeMans, France, pp. 63–71. We use "collaborative" here to avoid confusing this principle with capital-C Collaboration: one of the 11 character dimensions.
21 Luthans, F., & Peterson, S. J. (2003). 360-degree feedback with systematic coaching: Empirical analysis suggests a winning combination. *Human Resource Management*, 42: 243–256.
22 Carol Dweck's work is summarized in her 2007 book, *Mindset: The New Psychology of Success*. New York, NY: Ballantine Books.
23 Haimovitz, K., & Dweck, C. S. (2017). The origins of children's growth and fixed mindsets: New research and a new proposal. *Child Development*, 88: 1849–1859.

Chapter 5

The power of micro-moments

Just before the jet's scheduled departure from West Palm Beach, the captain was seated in the cockpit, running through the mandatory pre-flight checklists with his copilot. As soon as all the passengers with assigned seats had boarded, the gate agent came aboard and informed the crew that he was closing the door. Obviously, the agent's main focus was to get the flight off on time.

At that point the captain spoke up. Earlier, as he was making his way aboard, he had seen a large crowd of standby passengers at the gate, and he had just been informed by his flight attendants that there were still two empty seats on the plane.

"Whoever is next on the standby list," the captain asked, "why don't you send them down?"[1]

The gate agent made it clear that he didn't appreciate the captain's interference. His job, he explained impatiently, was to get this plane pushed away from the gate *on schedule*. For this and other airlines, on-time departure was a key metric, and trying to get two more standbys on board would only slow things down. And perhaps another thought was floating through both men's minds: The flight crew would not start getting paid until the cabin door was closed and the plane's brakes were released.[2]

Nevertheless, the captain persisted. "We're here to get paying customers to their destinations. You have two paying customers out there who want to be on this plane, and there are seats available for them. So I say let's quickly get them on board." The captain outranked the gate agent, and so he prevailed. The two extra passengers were hurried aboard and seated, and the plane wound up pushing back two minutes late.

But that wasn't the end of the story. Several days later, the captain received a call on his home phone from an angry airline official, who read him the riot act for interfering with the boarding process. The irritated captain objected, saying that either the gate agent was following a flawed procedure—in which case, the procedure should be changed—or he wasn't, in which case he should be instructed to play by the rules.

Still not the end of the story: Six months later, a nearly identical scenario unfolded. Same airport, same gate, same agent. Again the captain insisted on filling

DOI: 10.4324/9781003341215-6

empty seats—six seats, this time—and again, the gate agent objected, and when he was again overruled, followed up by filing a formal complaint against the captain. This time, the airline threatened to suspend the captain for two weeks without pay. A call from the captain's union rep to management quickly put an end to that particular threat—but still, the captain was far from satisfied. He knew that other pilots had been dealing with exactly the same problem. Why didn't somebody *do* something about it?

And then, a few months later, the airline circulated a bland memo saying that standby passengers should *not* be left behind if there were seats available on a plane.

Now the captain was satisfied. "All of us have little battles we can choose to take on or to skip," he later recalled:

> Some captains feel as I do about these sorts of things, and they fight. Others acquiesce and give up. None of us likes leaving passengers at the gate, but some have decided: "I can't fight so many battles every day."
>
> I guess I haven't had what I call a "sense of caring" beaten out of me yet. I empathized with those standby passengers. But as important, leaving them behind just would have felt wrong. And so I acted.

The captain's name was Chesley B. Sullenberger III. Several years after his irritating run-ins with that particular gate agent in West Palm Beach, "Sully" Sullenberger became an overnight celebrity on a global scale. On the morning of January 15, 2009, he and his copilot, Jeff Skiles, had just taken off from New York's LaGuardia airport with 150 passengers and five crew members aboard when—about 100 seconds into the flight—their 66-ton Airbus A320 collided with a huge flock of Canada geese. Both of the jet's engines were destroyed. Sullenberger and Skiles had only seconds to decide what to do. Try to glide their way back to LaGuardia? Try to coast over to one of two nearby airports in New Jersey? Sullenberger decided that they weren't yet high enough or moving fast enough to reach any of the three airports—and that he couldn't risk crashing into a crowded neighborhood in New York City or New Jersey if the plane came down too soon.

So he decided to ditch in the Hudson River. Water landings had been tried before, usually leading to disaster. Nevertheless, daring the odds, he and Skiles pulled off a near-perfect touch-down on the river. Astonished ferry boat captains rushed to the plane from both shores as the flight attendants herded passengers out onto the plane's wings and into life rafts. Sullenberger, last off the plane, made two sweeps through the passenger cabin—now rapidly filling up with ice-cold water—to make sure there was no one still aboard.

Miraculously, no lives were lost.

"What helped me," Sullenberger later recalled, "was that I had spent years flying jet airplanes and had paid close attention to energy management. On thousands of flights, I had tried to fly the optimum flight path. I think that helped me more than anything else on Flight 1549. I was going to try to use the energy of the Airbus, without either engine, to get us safely to the ground . . . or somewhere."

Certainly, Sullenberger's tens of thousands of hours and seven million miles in the air—as a teenager taking flying lessons in his Texas hometown, at the Air Force Academy and then in the US Air Force, and finally as a commercial pilot—had rendered him immensely *competent* when it came to responding to an in-flight crisis. "For 42 years, I've been making small, regular deposits in this bank of experience," he told *60 Minutes*, "and on January 15 the balance was sufficient so that I could make a very large withdrawal."[3]

But a second, more nuanced theme emerges from the pages of his autobiography: a theme of *character*. Of his Air Force Academy training, for example, he writes:

The education we received was called "The Whole Man Concept," because our superiors weren't just teaching us about the military. They wanted us to have great strength of character, to be informed about all sorts of matters we might easily dismiss, and to find ways to make vital contributions to the world beyond the academy. We cadets often dismissed it as "The Manhole Concept," but in our hearts we knew we were held to high standards and difficult tests that would serve us well.

He writes movingly about hearing—at age 13—the famous news story about a 28-year-old woman who was raped and stabbed to death on a New York street while dozens of people in nearby apartments allegedly chose to do nothing.[4] Along with the rest of the nation, Sullenberger was shocked:

I felt this real resolve. It wasn't anything I put in writing. I was more of a commitment I made to myself, to live a certain way.

I like to think that I've done that.

I've come to believe that every encounter with another person is an opportunity for good or for ill. And so I've tried to make my interactions with people as positive and respectful as I can . . .

Everyone's reputation is made on a daily basis. There are little incremental things—worthwhile efforts, moments you were helpful to others—and after a lifetime, they can add up to something. You can feel as if you lived and it mattered.

Reflecting on his 78-year-old father's suicide in 1995, precipitated by failing health and physical pain, Sullenberger writes:

I didn't think about my father's suicide when I was in the cockpit of Flight 1549. He wasn't anywhere in my thoughts. But his death did have an effect on how I've lived, and how I view the world. It made me more committed to preserving life. I exercise more care in my professional relationships. I am willing to work very hard to protect people's lives, to be a good Samaritan, and to not be a bystander, in part because I couldn't save my father.

Strength of character. High standards. Every encounter. On a daily basis. Little incremental things. Moments you were helpful to others. More care. Not a bystander. Collectively, these phrases add up to a second Sullenberger profile: again, one of *character* as well as profound competence. No, standing up to an impatient gate agent was not a particularly dramatic moment. But it was a *formative* moment, shaped and fueled by many others that had preceded it. And while a crash landing on an icy river drew heavily on the "bank of experience," that moment also depended on the character of the man at the controls—and, again, shaped the many life moments that were to follow.

We call them *micro-moments*, and in this chapter, we investigate the power of those micro-moments.

Embracing intentionality

First, a definition: a micro-moment is that interlude between stimulus and response during which there is an opportunity to make a decision. That opportunity may or may not be perceived and—if perceived—may or may not be acted upon.

Here we focus on *perceived* opportunities. Most micro-moments are banal and mundane, with no significant consequences attached to the chosen response. *Should I stop and let that waiting bicyclist cross the street even though she's not at a crosswalk and I have the right of way?* Others, like Sullenberger's interactions with the West Palm Beach gate agent, fall somewhere on the middle of the spectrum—that is, not life or death but having the potential for a measurable impact on your own and other people's lives. And past a certain point, a micro-moment moves into a whole different realm. The bird strike on Flight 1549 led to a life-or-death micro-moment with potentially immense consequences. Sullenberger and Skiles *had* to make a decision, an incredibly complex and important decision, immediately and almost instinctively, drawing on an extremely limited toolkit. Their habits of behavior, of *character*, engrained over a lifetime, were a deciding factor.

Intentionality is a key definer of micro-moments. Recall our three questions from Chapter 4:

- *Who have I become while I've been busy doing?*
- *Who am I becoming while I'm busy doing?*
- *Who do I want to become while I'm busy doing?*

Implicit in these questions is the notion that *our character is always being forged*, for better or worse. Looking first the negative side, how do we become impatient? How do we become that person who lacks temperance? How do we become that jaded soul who's "been there and done that" and therefore lacks transcendence? How do we become that person whose ego is so large that we have difficulty accepting constructive feedback? The answer to all these questions is *by not paying conscious attention to the process of character building*—or, phrased differently, *by not embracing the intention to develop and exercise character available in our micro-moments.*

What are we, as individuals and humans, hardwired to do? Is that really hard-wiring, or is it really just an overwhelming force of habit? What would encourage us to interrupt that habit, and what would enable us to do so? How do we stop being victims of circumstance in our own lives and become agents of change?

Think about the process of developing your personal signature, in the literal sense of that word: the practiced, almost automatic scribble that you insert at the bottom of a formal letter, a personal check, or a legal document. Most likely, somewhere back in your adolescence, you came up with the very first version of that scribble. That was a moment of intentionality. Over time, that scribble evolved and "hardened" into the signature that you've been using ever since. Now it's just something that *is*. It pops up when needed and doesn't require much conscious attention from you.[5]

And that's a good thing! We don't need ongoing intentionality in our check-signing process or in the daily chores of brushing our teeth, tying our shoes, or making the morning coffee. But if we think of our character as something that is constantly evolving—something that I'm becoming while I'm busy doing—then we need to look for opportunities to inject intentionality into that process of evolution. *I've come to believe that every encounter with another person is an opportunity for good or for ill*, as Sullenberger phrased it. *I've tried to make my interactions with people as positive and respectful as I can and exercise more care in my professional relationships.* This is the potential power of micro-moments, because *it's in these moments that your character is being built.* Think of it as an ongoing, dynamic flow of potential engagements, which can be simultaneously revealing and developmental.

One caution: at the core of character, as described in previous chapters, is judgment. The behaviors associated with judgment tend to be driven more by the unconscious than the conscious. When we exercise judgment, we tend to call on the right side of our brains more than the left side—in other words, we are more intuitive than analytical.

And this is where intentionality can and should play a key role. Who do I want to become while I'm busy doing? As Sullenberger phrased it, "There are little incremental things—worthwhile efforts, moments you were helpful to others—and after a lifetime, they can add up to something."

That "something" we submit is character. And it is built in large part through intentionally deciding to take action in a certain way, in response to a stimulus either small or large.

Brick by brick, branch by branch

Again, our character is always being forged, brick by brick by brick. No, character-building is not happening every minute of every day, but it's happening far more often than we'd probably care to admit.

That's practical and sensible—but only up to a point. Our colleague Corey Crossan tells the story of a student who told her that he had resolved to stop being late for class (intentionality). "Great," she said, "how is that going to happen?" He told her that from now on, when his alarm went off—a pretty prosaic micro-moment—he would not hit the snooze button as usual; instead, he would get up immediately and start the day. "Great," she said again, "and how will you make sure *that* happens?" He thought for a minute and responded that he would have to decide every night to go to bed earlier (another micro-moment). "And what would make *that* possible," Crossan asked? "Starting dinner earlier? Not socializing after dinner?" The student took her point: that most of life's micro-moments are actually part of a *chain* of such moments. Yes, they arrive brick by brick, but they quickly assemble themselves into a wall. We either shape that wall, or the wall shapes us. In other words, if your tomorrow starts tonight, then you may need to think differently about tonight's micro-moments.

Carrying this argument to its next logical step—that is, character formation *over time*—Crossan sketched out a decision tree with micro-moments at its nodes and leadership at its end points, as shown in Figure 5.1.

You'll recall Elizabeth Holmes and Theranos, whom we considered in Chapter 3. The story begins with large doses of ambition, greed, and competitiveness.

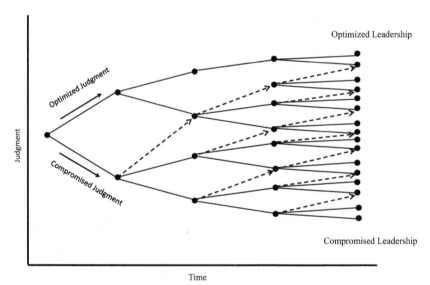

Figure 5.1 Decision Tree with Micro-moments at Its Nodes

By age 9, Holmes was telling relatives that she wanted to be a billionaire.[6] If she lost at Monopoly against her younger brother and cousin, she would storm off—once walking through a screen door in a fury. As a high school student, she intended to go into medicine but discovered that she was afraid of needles, which set her on a new path. Based on her abbreviated college education, Holmes believed that she could improve blood diagnostics enormously and eventually invented a wearable device intended to serve that purpose. But despite years of tinkering and restarts, it simply didn't work—nor did the several generations of flawed technology that followed it. Holmes ultimately raised more than $700 million in venture capital, in part by refusing to admit—to herself or to anyone else—that there was no working technology behind the company. She stacked her board with individuals who lacked a sufficient medical or technological background to challenge her. She ignored the whistleblowers who tried to warn her about Theranos' failings.

Each of these biographical snippets represents a micro-moment, or a series of micro-moments. They are the nodes in Figure 5.1, unfolding from left to right. Holmes' intentionality was all about *persisting*: again, as in Chapter 3, the "fake it until you make it" ethos of Silicon Valley. "There is no dream you can't achieve," she wrote in a 2015 tweet. "Don't let anyone tell you otherwise."[7] But persistence and tenacity can easily harden into hubris and arrogance. When they do, you are steered away from optimized leadership and toward compromised leadership. The endpoint along that path of our branching diagram is almost certain to be an unhappy one. "Elizabeth Holmes was a con artist," as Arizona Attorney General Mark Brnovich told *Fortune* magazine—a blunt definition of compromised leadership.[8]

Now think back to the stories about "Sully" Sullenberger that we used to open this chapter. As you do, imagine them as nodes along Sullenberger's own version of Figure 5.1—a journey from a young boy in rural Texas infatuated with flying to a humane leader with profound competence and character and the judgment needed to respond in the moment of crisis. The endpoint on *that* branching diagram was optimized leadership, built brick by brick and branch by branch.

Redemption through micro-moments

Sketching out biographical accounts in ways that are necessarily linear can create a false sense of inevitability. In other words, Elizabeth Holmes' long slide to con-artist status may seem foreordained—the unhappy outcome of poor decisions that, once made in their respective micro-moments, set up the succession of bad decisions that followed. It might seem as if character-building rests on a slippery slope: The failure of character at Node 4 shapes a character that is all the more likely to fail at Node 5, and so on, and so on.

But that's misleading. First of all, you can "call your own foul," in the words of Jon Hantho, president and CEO of CBI Health Group. In other words, even when you flub a micro-moment, in many cases you can go back and repair the damage. Hantho remembers an episode in which—in his own estimation—he torpedoed a multiparty Zoom conversation by addressing a colleague in unnecessarily harsh language. As soon as he got off the call, Hantho recalls, he knew he had blown it. So he called back the individual he had interacted with in that semipublic setting and apologized. He then called back each of the other participants individually and apologized to them as well, telling them, "This is unacceptable behavior on my part," and, "This is not who I am." The takeaway, for Hantho? "You just gotta nip these things in the bud. You gotta call your own fouls."

Look again at Figure 5.1, taking note of the dotted, upward-pointing arrows. These arrows are intended to make the point that, no matter where you are in your character-building, micro-moment journey, *redemption is always possible.* You can start laying bricks in new directions and following different branches— always keeping in mind character dimensions like self-awareness, courage, accountability, empathy, and so on.

To make the point, let's introduce another character: Danny Trejo. You've probably seen him in movies like *Desperado, Heat, Spy Kids*—which helped make him an international star—and *Machete*. Even if you don't know the name, you can probably conjure up the face: a huge, craggy mountainside, pitted by acne scars and the scars and broken noses growing out of decades of street fights and amateur boxing matches, festooned by a droopy mustache and often framed by long black hair. He looks, by his own laconic accounting, like the most fearsome Mexican bad guy imaginable.

"You always play the Mexican with tattoos," a reporter asked him in one of his first interviews. "Aren't you afraid of being typecast?"

"I *am* a Mexican with tattoos," Trejo responded.

But film and television were Trejo's *second* career. His first was a life of crime—some petty, some not at all petty—interrupted by frequent incarcerations in the California prison system. He was first arrested at age 10. At age 12, he blackmailed his favorite uncle into letting him try heroin. At age 14, he committed his first armed robbery and for the first time wound up in a juvenile detention facility. Both in and out of jail, he was a drug addict, drug dealer, debt collector, and enforcer, developing a fearsome reputation along the way. On the streets, each bad habit reinforced another. "I didn't know if I was pulling robberies to support my drug habit," he later wrote, "or doing drugs to support my robbery habit."

His autobiography, *Trejo*, can be read as an endless succession of micromoments, many of which involved severe consequences.[9] At almost all of those junctures, Trejo made a self-destructive choice and headed down an increasingly dangerous road. For example, at age 21, he was released from the Youth Training School in Chino—a juvenile prison informally known as "Gladiator School"—and put on an LA-bound bus with just enough cash in his pocket to get himself home. Even as he was stepping off the bus in LA, a drug dealer accosted him, and they went down a nearby alley together to shoot up. Five days later, he showed up at home with a black eye and no recollection of where he had been since getting off the bus.

In another incident, this time in a courtroom, a judge ordered the bailiff to take the handcuffs off Trejo's wrists for the judicial proceedings. The bailiff hesitated. He knew that Trejo was in a white rage at his former accomplice, Dennis—who had set Trejo up for this particular bust and who was now standing nearby in the courtroom. The judge repeated his order, the bailiff complied, and right in front of the judge, Trejo attacked Dennis in a fury. "I was sentenced to ten years," Trejo recollects.

But in some of those micro-moments, another kind of reality kept trying to interject itself and catch his attention. For example, at age 15, he and his gang of 12 decided to crash a local party, in a house off Van Nuys Boulevard. They hadn't been invited, but based on the number of cars outside, they knew it was a party worth crashing. And they came equipped: with two bottles of wine, a case of beer, a half-pint of whiskey, a .38 snub-nosed revolver, and a tire iron. They burst into the house—only to discover that they had crashed a meeting of a self-help group for recovering alcoholics. An elderly gentleman approached Trejo, smiled, and asked him his name:

"Danny." I didn't have time to think. He was so calm and friendly I was taken by surprise. I was immediately honest in a way that I'd never been with adults or the cops.

"Danny, why don't you put that stuff down outside and stay for the meeting?"

I looked around. My friends had all been surrounded by people like this man—smiling older men and women who all had coffee cups in one hand and cigarettes in the other.

"We made a mistake."

He nodded to the crate of alcohol. "You may think you made a mistake, Danny, but if you continue with that stuff, the only three destinations waiting for you are jails, institutions, or death. I'm serious."

Again, Trejo found himself in a micro-moment and, again, made a bad choice. Many more were to follow, generally with bad outcomes. But as time passed, he began to take the old man's cautions seriously—*jails, institutions, or death*—to the extent that during a stint in the Soledad state prison, he tapped into the long-submerged spiritual side of his nature and shook off his addictions. He eventually became a substance-abuse counselor himself, first inside prison and later, after completing five years of a ten-year sentence, out on the streets. Gradually, he started making better choices. One day, for example, while he was working at a body shop painting and sanding cars to support his youth-counseling avocation, his drug-dealing uncle—the one who had introduced him to heroin in the first place—arrived at the shop in a black Lincoln Continental. Dressed in fancy clothes all the way down to his $800 shoes, he looked at Danny in his greasy coveralls and gazed around the garage with disdain. "Come back and work with me," he invited his nephew. Then he put two quarter ounces of heroin and a thousand dollars in cash on the counter and walked out.

Trejo thought about it. He pocketed the cash—and left the drugs on the counter.

Not long afterward, he sweet-talked a woman at the LA Forum into allocating three dozen free Ringling Brothers circus tickets to the treatment center he had just opened. Arriving at the Forum on the night of the performance, he discovered that he had six extra tickets, each with a face value of $60. "Scalp 'em," his friend Jack advised. As Trejo considered that option—in a rather complex micro-moment—a scruffy-looking guy with five kids in tow approached him and asked if he had tickets for sale. The kids all looked different from each other, and Trejo surmised that this was a dad taking his kid and his kid's friends to the circus. It didn't look as if the dad had anything like the money he'd need to get them all in. On an impulse, Trejo gave him the tickets for free. "When I told Jack what I'd done," Trejo recalled, "he was pissed. 'Danny, you could have got three hundred and sixty bucks for those tickets.'"

"Don't worry," Trejo said. "What I did is better."

By chance, Trejo later spotted the man and his ragtag collection of kids inside the tent, having the time of their lives. He knew he had made the right call:

> I may have missed out on some cash, but getting to see that guy be a hero in front of his kid, in front of his kid's friends, seeing the expression on his face, that was priceless . . .
>
> [My co-worker and future wife] Diana witnessed this and looked at me differently. I think she fell in love with me that night. I wasn't trying to impress her or anyone else. But as I've said many times: everything good that's ever happened in my life has come as the direct result of helping someone else and not expecting anything in return. We all felt good leaving the circus.

Trejo has achieved international celebrity and financial security through his acting career over the past few decades. But it's fair to ask how his life would have been different—and perhaps better—if he had resolved his micro-moments differently and developed his character earlier. He acknowledges that his life-threatening liver cancer was almost certainly the result of years of drug abuse. He writes regretfully of his four failed marriages. "I've tried to make amends with the women [I have] been involved with simply because it was [not] their fault," he recently told an interviewer. "I was broken."[10] He recounts and regrets his unsatisfying relationships with his parents, his own kids, and other members of his family. He wonders if his film career—successful as it has been—might have been even more illustrious if he hadn't waited until his early 40s to plunge into it.

These kinds of questions can be mapped onto the nodes of our Figure 5.1. Note that our dotted-line arrows in that figure follow the rules of branching diagrams. That is, although you can change the trajectory of your character building micro-moment by micro-moment, you're unlikely to achieve total redemption—"optimized leadership," in the language of the chart. If you stumble at the start of a footrace, yes, you can regroup and cover some lost ground, but you're unlikely to catch up with those skilled competitors who *didn't* stumble out of the gate. Trejo certainly stumbled more than once. He competed ferociously once he got back up on his feet. Many people point to the difficult episodes in their life stories and say that those episodes helped make them what they are today. True enough, but a self-imposed disadvantage—like the ones described by Trejo—tends to have enduring impacts.

And while we don't like to end our lines of argument on a negative note, we need to point out a second fact that is both true and sobering. We could have included a handful of *downward*-pointing arrows in Figure 5.1 as well upward-pointing ones. (We left them out to avoid a thicket of arrows pointing in all directions.) A truly horrendous reaction in one or more micro-moments has the potential to "drop you down" significantly in terms of future possible outcomes. Cover-ups are a good example. The Volkswagen engineers and corporate officials described in Chapter 1 got caught installing "defeat devices" in their diesel cars. In that micro-moment, they *could* have come clean, grabbed an upward-pointing arrow, and perhaps even redeemed themselves to some extent. Instead, they grabbed a downward-pointing arrow: they engaged in a two-year cover-up and did themselves and their company irreparable harm. Erupting emotions can wreak the same downward-pointing havoc. Trejo's fistfight in the courtroom—the outcome of a passion-fueled micro-moment—helped earn him the stiffest possible sentence the judge could throw at him.

Making the routine nonroutine

So what are the prescriptions that we can tease out of the preceding pages? First, you need to remind yourself—practically every day until it becomes second nature—that the power to mold your character is to be found mostly in micro-moments. Thus primed, when you spot those micro-moments—where possible—you need to intentionally use those interludes to further develop your Leader Character. Your life is your laboratory. Or, to invoke a physical-fitness analogy, your life is your "character gym."

How can we break into the flow of micro-moments and thereby transform the mundane into the developmental—in other words, make the routine into the nonroutine? Think back to the 11-dimension model that we first introduced in Chapter 2 and shown in Figure 5.2.

An effective way to develop Leader Character is to pick one of these eleven dimensions that you want to work on in much the same way that you'd pick a

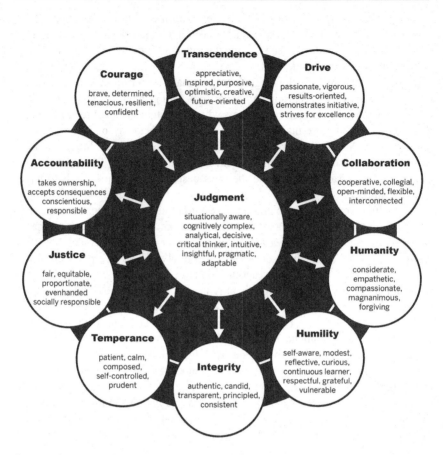

Figure 5.2 Leader Character Framework

muscle group to concentrate on in the gym. You probably have a good idea already which of these dimensions will be most fruitful for you to pursue. Keep in mind that your weakest dimension may be undermining your strongest dimension. But also keep in mind that here, we're more focused on pursuing a systematic, disciplined, and intentional approach to character-building. Once you understand and embrace that approach, you can use it to tackle multiple dimensions.

In Chapter 3, we introduced the Leader Character Insight Assessment (LCIA), a character-assessment tool that grew out of our fruitful collaboration with a US-based consulting firm called SIGMA Assessment Systems, Inc.[11] Not only is the LCIA a reliable assessment tool, but it also provides guidance and resources that you can use to strengthen your Leader Character. In the event that you do not have access to the LCIA, we provide an extract called "The Leader Character

Development Plan." This section of the LCIA presents a series of seven incomplete statements and invites you to complete those statements:

1. *The changes I want to make are . . .* Be specific. Include goals that are positive (wanting to increase, improve, do more of something), and not just negative (stop, avoid, or decrease a behavior).
2. *My main goals in making these changes are . . .* What are the likely consequences of action or inaction? Which motivations for change are most compelling? What will success look like?
3. *The steps I plan to take to make these changes are . . .* How can the desired change be accomplished? What are some specific, concrete steps (when, where, and how)?
4. *Some things that could interfere with my plan are . . .* What specific limiting core beliefs, events, or problems could undermine my plan? What could go wrong? How will I specifically address these challenges?
5. *Other people could help me in making these changes by . . .* What specific things can another person do to help me take the steps I've outlined previously? Who can provide such support (accountability buddy/clearly identified peer)? How will I arrange for such support?
6. *I will know that my plan is working when . . .* What will happen as a result of taking the steps I've outlined in this plan? What benefits can be expected? What might indicators of progress look like?
7. *As part of this development process I learned . . .* What learnings did you have as a result of focusing on the development of this dimension that could be leveraged in the development of other dimensions?

Obviously, this is an ambitious undertaking. For the purposes of this chapter, we recommend focusing (for now) on the first two questions: which changes do you want to make and why? With your chosen character dimension and your preliminary answers to these two questions in mind, start keeping what might be called your micro-moment journal. Entries should focus on things like the following:

- What micro-moments did I notice today?
- Which micro-moments did I use today to strengthen character?
- Were there micro-moments in which I didn't act with character? Why? How did affect the outcome, my relationships, and my overall well-being?
- What did today's micro-moments reveal about my character?

Over time, your journal entries should start adding up to your answer to question 7, specifically the following:

- How has my awareness changed?
- How is my character changing? What evidence do I have to support this?

- How are my decisions and outcomes being affected? What evidence do I have to support this?
- How are my relationships changing? What evidence do I have to support this?
- How is my own well-being changing? What evidence do I have to support this?

Again, this represents an ongoing—perhaps lifelong—journey. Where possible, seek input on your plan, reflections, and results from a trusted confidant. Don't expect quick or easy answers. But at the very least, look for signs that you've become more sensitive to the kinds of micro-moments that might have seemed unimportant, or even slipped by entirely, in the past.

Summing up: the three-fold power of micro-moments

Micro-moments have three distinct kinds of potential and therefore power.

The first, as we've seen, is to create and develop character. It can't be stated too strongly: Working your way through the micro-moments that arise in the course of your life—even many of the seemingly mundane moments—is the only way to develop character. Yes, the big moments are, by definition, momentous. But remember Sully Sullenberger's conviction that every encounter with another person is an opportunity for good or ill? Based on that conviction, he resolved to make all of his interactions with the people around him as positive and respectful as possible.

Danny Trejo reached much the same conclusion: "Everything good that's ever happened in my life has come as the direct result of helping someone else and not expecting anything in return." His life circumstances couldn't have been much more different from Sullenberger's—which reminds us that we have to think of each of these character-building journeys as unique—but their character-building processes are congruent. No, we can't judge Sullenberger's actions by Trejo's standards, and vice versa. Even so, along their very different paths, they wind up in startlingly similar places.

It's also worth noting in this context that dealing in micro-moments presents the opportunity for what organizational theorists refer to as "small wins": in other words, a way of redefining the scale of social problems into more manageable bites. As Cornell Professor Karl E. Weick noted, Alcoholics Anonymous is successful in part because it doesn't insist that alcoholics be totally abstinent for the rest of their lives:

Although this is the goal of the program, alcoholics are told to stay sober one day at a time, or one hour at a time if temptation is severe. The impossibility of lifetime abstinence is scaled down to the more workable task of not taking a drink for the next 24 hours, drastically reducing the size of a win necessary to maintain sobriety.[12]

Again: brick by brick, branch by branch.

The second power of micro-moments grows directly out of the first. Navigating successfully through a potential-laden micro-moment has the power to make the world a better place. Sullenberger put himself on the line repeatedly when he thought his airline wasn't doing right by its passengers. The eventual result? The airline promulgated a policy that did better by its customers. Did the standby passengers who subsequently benefited from that policy wind up treating the people around them positively and respectfully? Probably not *all* of them, but maybe some of them. Did the gate agent experience a micro-moment in which he rethought his own priorities? We don't know, but possibly.

The third power of micro-moments lies in their potential contribution to your own sense of well-being. *"After a lifetime,"* as Sullenberger reflected, "they can add up to something. You can feel as if you lived and it mattered." In fact, you don't need to wait a lifetime to derive those emotional and psychological benefits. In some cases, at least, they begin to accrue immediately and earn interest as your character develops. "Your job is to do what God wants you to do," Trejo once told an actor on a set with him who was facing a difficult personal choice in his family life.[13] "Be a provider for your family and be happy, joyous, and free. If you aren't happy, joyous, and free, you aren't doing God's work for you." This reflects the well-being benefits that accrue from living a life of character.

Our book's title builds on the metaphor of a compass: a pathfinding device. The first half of the book, which concludes with this chapter, have been about understanding how that compass works, and—at the risk of stretching the metaphor—understanding how to develop that compass within yourself and how to use it to navigate through your life's decision points, large and small.

Now we move into the second half of *The Character Compass*, in which we focus on exercising character in the context of an organization. We've already cited the example of the Theranos whistleblowers, who attempted to get their company off an established bad track and onto a better, character-rich one. Unfortunately, it's difficult to change the direction of an organization after its course is set, especially if (for example) the $700 million in venture capital that you've accepted continue to push you in that particular direction.

But what if you and your colleagues could build character into the company at every level—from the functional to the strategic, from the front line to the boardroom?

With intentionality—we argue—you can. And that effort begins with you, personally, becoming a champion of character change.

Notes

1 This story, and subsequent stories and directed quotes, are from Chesley B. Sullenberger's 2009 autobiography, originally published as *Highest Duty: My Search for What Really Matters*. New York, NY: HarperCollins Publishers and later published as *Sully*.

2   This practice didn't start changing until the summer of 2022, when U.S. airlines faced a strike threat.

3   These quotes can be retrieved online at www.historyvshollywood.com/reelfaces/sully/ accessed March 14, 2023.

4   The truth about the notorious Kitty Genovese murder—as Sullenberger points out in his book—turned out to be somewhat different, but the story as it was first reported had a strong impact on the young teenager.

5   Even so, summoning up even a long-practiced signature can present a micro-moment. On the morning of January 1, 1863, Abraham Lincoln held his traditional New Year's Day reception for a mix of military officers, diplomats, and selected members of the public—an event that required several hours' worth of handshaking. Afterwards, he went to his study to sign the Emancipation Proclamation. He noticed that his hand was trembling and decided to delay signing the document until the shaking subsided—not wanting history to think that he had doubts about his momentous action. As soon as he could, he signed in a firm hand and said, "That will do." See the article in *Smithsonian,* online at www.smithsonianmag.com/history/how-the-emancipation-proclamation-came-to-be-signed-165533991/, accessed March 14, 2023.

6   Some of these details are from the *Business Insider* biography of Holmes, online at www.businessinsider.com/theranos-founder-ceo-elizabeth-holmes-life-story-bio-2018-4#holmes-started-raising-money-for-theranos-from-prominent-investors-like-oracle-founder-larry-ellison-and-tim-draper-the-father-of-a-childhood-friend-and-the-founder-of-prominent-vc-firm-draper-fisher-jurvetson-theranos-raised-more-than-700-million-and-draper-has-continued-to-defend-holmes-14, accessed March 14, 2023.

7   These quotes or statements from Holmes are taken from the *Business Insider* article, online at www.businessinsider.com/theranos-founder-ceo-elizabeth-holmes-life-story-bio-2018-4#elizabeth-holmes-was-born-on-february-3-1984-in-washington-dc-her-mom-noel-was-a-congressional-committee-staffer-and-her-dad-christian-holmes-worked-for-enron-before-moving-to-government-agencies-like-usaid-1, accessed March 14, 2023.

8   See the January 4, 2022 edition of *Fortune,* online at https://fortune.com/2022/01/04/theranos-elizabeth-holmes-human-cost-fraud-faulty-blood-test-patients/, accessed March 13, 2023.

9   The accounts and quotes in this section are from *Trejo: My Life of Crime, Redemption, and Hollywood,* written by Danny Trejo and collaborator Donal Logue, published in 2021 by Simon & Schuster.

10 From a July 8, 2021, interview with *USA Today,* online at www.usatoday.com/story/entertainment/books/2021/07/08/danny-trejo-memoir-my-life-of-crime-redemption-hollywood/7896339002/, accessed March 14, 2023.

11 Again, SIGMA—founded in 1967—has spent more than a half-century developing and delivering science-based assessment products. See SIGMA's website at www.sigmaassessmentsystems.com/.

12 See, for example, Karl E. Weick's "Small Wins" article in the January 1984 issue of *American Psychologist*, 39: 40–49.

13 The actor was Danny Trejo's future writing collaborator, Donal Logue. The story is from Logue's "Collaborator's note" at the end of Trejo's autobiography.

Chapter 6

Becoming a champion
of character change

Let's imagine that you are the director general for leadership and learning at the Canada Revenue Agency (CRA)—the agency that runs the tax system for the Canadian federal government as well as for most of the provincial and territorial governments across Canada. It raises close to a half-trillion dollars a year in taxes and directly delivers more than $30 billion in tax refunds to Canadians, with these and other activities adding up to millions of individual interactions with taxpayers every year.

Your payroll comprises 43,000 people, including 400 senior managers. As the director general for leadership and learning, you have overall responsibility for hiring and developing and retaining those upper-level people. It's a big job.

Imagine further that one day early in 2016, you're attending a regularly scheduled meeting with CRA's Board of Management. This 15-member appointed group oversees the organization and management of the agency, the development of its Corporate Business Plan, and the management of policies related to resources, services, property, and personnel.[1] From your point of view, it's a routine meeting, and you're not expecting to play a major role—right up to the moment when one generally sympathetic board member turns to you and says, "You told us at our last meeting that thanks to demographic trends you've highlighted, we're in the middle of a major turnover wave, especially in our senior management ranks. Obviously, lots of retirements means lots of hiring. So my question is, how do we know we're hiring the right leaders?"

Do you have a good answer? What *is* a good answer? What makes for the right leaders? Certainly, capabilities and commitment count. But does character also factor into that assessment of "right"? And if it does, can you personally help steer your organization toward good outcomes—in this case, hiring the right leaders—by acting as what we call a *champion of character change*?

Initiating change at CRA

These are the questions that Sonia Côté[2] found herself pondering in the summer of 2016. She was still a fairly recent arrival at CRA, having previously spent the better part of a decade as an organizational development (OD) specialist,

DOI: 10.4324/9781003341215-7

first within the Department of National Defense (DND) and subsequently with Industry Canada, a federal agency aimed at supporting Canadian business. In both contexts, she had worked closely with senior leaders who wanted to focus on so-called "soft skills," with a specific focus on human interactions. As a result, Côté had the benefit both of working alongside supportive leaders and also of training at schools and centers in the US specializing in social justice and human rights.

But *applying* what she was learning, Côté recalls, was sometimes challenging. This was especially true of her early career at DND:

> As an OD specialist, my role was to advise leaders in the organization. And to be able to serve as that kind of advisor, I needed to assert my own leadership in that capacity.
>
> It wasn't always easy. I remember as a 25-year-old, going to advise senior officers in the organization. *[Laughs]* Sometimes it took a lot of time for me to get to that level of credibility, because within DND at that time it was thought that life experiences were overwhelmingly important, and so what would a 25-year-old be able to teach a senior civilian or military leader? As a result, I put a lot of focus on self-discovery—on finding my own sort of power, and figuring out how to use it.

So by the time Côté arrived at CRA, she was well versed in the literature of organizational development, and she also had learned how to assert herself and her ideas within a sometimes-skeptical bureaucracy. Both skill sets would come in handy as she attempted to answer the question put to her by the Board of Managers: *how do we know we're hiring the right leaders?*

Looking back, Côté stresses that she didn't interpret the question as being critical of her work to date, but rather as good guidance and an implicit green light from her board:

> No, I never see this kind of question as aggressive—you know, "Why didn't you do that?" Instead, I see it as an opportunity to reflect on what we're currently doing, and to look at other possibilities. In effect, that question was just what I needed to be able to go back to my team and say, "Look at our state of affairs. Look at the demographics. We know we're going to have high turnover in the next years. So what's the opportunity here?
>
> As opposed to look at it negatively and saying, "Oh, the sky is falling on us! We're losing all of our leaders! How will we get by without all that knowledge that's leaving?"
>
> So yes—"it's something that we need to look at, but we need to see it as an opportunity to define what's important to us, and to signal to the organization the types of leaders that we want to have within the Agency."

During her stint at Industry Canada, Côté and her team had worked with senior faculty leaders at the Ivey Business School on the general challenge of developing business acumen in their leaders. Those discussions had centered on leadership challenges—and had become increasingly focused on the three Cs described in our introduction: *competencies, commitment,* and *character.* At CRA, Côté reflected further on this model, thinking it might help answer her board members' "right leaders" question. She read and reread articles on the subject of character, which was then a topic of increasing interest both in business and business schools. At the same time, she initiated a series of discussions about the three Cs model with her then deputy commissioner, John Ossowski.[3] "Yes, we have a clearly delineated list of key leadership competencies (KLCs) that we use in our recruitment processes," she would say in those discussions, "which is the competencies side. But I don't see the equivalent on the character side."

In fact, CRA—like other Canadian federal government departments and agencies—did have the benefit of well-defined KLCs to help guide candidate selection, learning and development, and performance and talent management. Côté increasingly saw these metrics as tools that were important but at the same time insufficient. And she knew that other leaders within CRA shared that view:

Along the way, it became more and more clear that it was important to elevate character alongside competence in order to hire and develop leaders. The main reason why I was so interested in thinking about looking at character, and supplementing the competency piece, is because I'd been working for ten years with senior leaders in government—the deputy ministers, who were hiring the Assistant Deputy Ministers (ADMs) for the organization. And every time we sat around the table, they told me that the existing processes were insufficient—that these processes weren't giving them the opportunity to get to know the leader sitting in front of them, and determining if they were making the right hiring decision.

So that really was the trigger.[4]

As she related this and similar stories to Ossowski, Côté shared an emerging conviction: by themselves, she believed, KLCs focused solely on competence (and interviews tightly structured around those KLCs) wouldn't necessarily lead to CRA hiring the right leaders.[5]

Côté remembers Ossowski responding positively. "Assuming you're right," he said, in so many words, "why don't you get in touch with your contacts at Ivey and put that challenge on the table?"

In July 2016, Côté got back in touch with faculty members at Ivey, hoping to find someone who would be willing to address a CRA Executive Forum then being scheduled for mid-October: the first in an anticipated annual series. Mary Crossan—one of the authors of this book—fielded the inquiry. She agreed to attend the October session and facilitate a workshop on character-based leadership.

That meeting, held in Ottawa, brought together some 400 CRA executives, collectively dubbed within the organization the "EX Group."[6] They were told in advance that, among other topics, the meeting would address the future leadership needs of CRA's EX community and would generate self-awareness and reflection on leadership style and growth. Côté and Ossowski opened the meeting and kicked off the morning panel discussions. After lunch and a speech by the Clerk of the Privy Council—the senior civil servant in the Canadian government and head of the country's public service—Crossan took the floor. She introduced the leader character concept, explaining its eleven dimensions, the complex ways that those dimensions come to bear on each other in real-world settings, and the implications for leaders (at all levels) in those organizations.

Crossan recalls that her sense, going back to the beginning of the morning session, was that the EX Group attendees were genuinely happy to be there and pleased to be sharing perspectives and (in many cases) meeting face-to-face for the first time. This sense of excitement carried through her session, with participants expressing excitement about embracing leader character in their particular corner of CRA.

So how would that be done? How would Côté and her colleagues meet the expectations that they had raised?

Pushing the change: part one

The comments that Côté heard at the EX Group forum only reinforced her sense that hiring was the place to start—a conviction that in part grew out of the unsatisfactory recruitment processes then in place at CRA. "Recruitment was one of the biggest pain points in HR," she recalls. "So it was an opportunity to change things around so that people could see the potential, and experiment with it, and then become advocates and champions of character in different ways."

But the existing staffing practices and guidelines did not encourage experimentation or innovation. Like all federal agencies, CRA followed an executive qualification standard that applied to all potential hires. It stipulated that, at the entry level, candidates' KLCs had to be assessed through a structured interview, a third-party validation of those KLCs, and structured reference checks. The prescribed KLCs (last revised in 2015) were as follows:

- Create vision and strategy
- Mobilize people
- Uphold integrity and respect
- Collaborate with partners and stakeholders
- Promote innovation and guide change
- Achieve results

Experience was assessed at the screening phase, and knowledge was usually evaluated as part of a written test or included in the structured interview. The system was designed to promote fairness, to ensure a level playing field in the hiring process, but in fact lent itself to clever manipulation: a challenge faced by most organizations using structured interviews. Many candidates who applied to EX positions were familiar with the KLCs and were often trained by professional coaches and mentors to make sure they understood the KLCs and—in the interview setting—were able to provide examples of behaviors demonstrating each competency. This often created a rehearsed, one-sided delivery, mostly consisting of candidates listing accomplishments and examples of KLCs they had shown in the past.

All in all, as Côté recalls, it was an unsatisfactory process:

> We in the federal public service were renowned for taking notes, not making eye contact with the candidate, and not engaging in a meaningful dialogue. Candidates were being asked the same questions, again with limited eye contact from board members. They often left without having shared much about their leadership. Structured interviews have their advantages, but we wanted to explore an option that provided more opportunity to get to know the individual being interviewed.

The interviews were conducted by ad hoc boards of interviewers who typically included senior executives. But because there was very little interaction between the participating board members and the candidates, they were often left wanting to know more about who these candidates actually were and how their individual approach to leadership might have evolved over time.

Côté realized that she would need help breaking through these kinds of logjams. It was also becoming clear, based on inquiries from several colleagues, that the EX Group forum had stimulated interest across the extensive CRA network. That interest needed to be managed—in other words, served by a single coordinated initiative rather than a collection of freestanding initiatives. In the spring of 2017, therefore, Côté and her team sent out a request for proposals, seeking outside experts who could do the following:

- Provide strategic advice on how to integrate character-based leadership successfully in the CRA organizational culture.
- Review existing EX assessment tools used at CRA for recruitment purposes and identify opportunities to integrate character-based leadership in addition to the assessment of KLCs and enhance these assessment tools to allow CRA to assess character-based leadership and KLCs in the recruitment of leaders at the executive level.

Crossan, the facilitator at the Ottawa workshop, submitted a proposal on behalf of Ivey. When that proposal was accepted by CRA in July of 2017, she began working through a system for enhancing leadership selection at the agency by—as an emerging catch phrase distilled it—"elevating character alongside

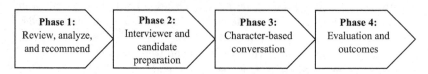

Figure 6.1 Leader Character Strategic Roadmap

competence." This phrasing was purposeful: competence was *not* being down-graded in the selection criteria; character was being upgraded.

The project that emerged from Crossan's work unfolded in four phases, as depicted in Figure 6.1.

Phase 1 involved identifying all aspects of the selection process that invoked the concept of "competence," in one guise or another, and suggesting ways that character could be embedded alongside that competence reference. This was a large universe of component parts, ranging from job postings to interview questions to reference checks. For example, job postings would henceforth include the following statement: "Canada Revenue Agency seeks to attract candidates who demonstrate leadership character. Dimensions of character include courage, drive, accountability, transcendence, humanity, humility, collaboration, temperance, integrity, justice, and judgment."

Phase 2 focused on interviewer and candidate preparation and comprised of two related activities. The first was running optional information sessions for inter-viewers to get them comfortable with a character-based interviewing process—in other words, one that was less the sort of staged, set-piece conversation described previously and more of a "human to human" conversation. Second, candidates were invited to a voluntary workshop to introduce them to character leadership and to help them understand that the selection process would be different from the kinds of competence-based interviews the candidates might have experienced in the past. For example, the character-based assessment was designed as a conversation around a coffee table with comfortable chairs and couches. No papers or writing instruments would be in evidence during the conversation; notes would be made directly after the candidate left the room.

Phase 3 involved shaping—but not scripting—the conversation described previ-ously. Again, the focus was on an *authentic* conversation, not one that is so programmed that the candidate is merely telling the interviewer what they think is expected. Why? The more the interviewers probed, the more likely they would be to get to levels of detail and insight that revealed whether the story was real or something that was tailored or fabricated. Programmed stories, Crossan explained, don't have a richness to them because they are not *lived* and tend to break down when probed. It was also important to note that the conversation was not about testing whether someone was telling the truth; rather, the conversation was meant to provide an authentic opportunity to learn about the candidate's character.

Yes, questions could be provided to launch and support the process, but those questions would rarely dominate the conversations, which would tend to be more organic in nature. For one of the staffing processes at CRA, for example, all candidates would be required to write a letter or submit a video explaining why they wanted to work for CRA, then—in many cases—something from that letter or video would serve as the launch point for the conversation.

Phase 4, focused on evaluation and outcomes, will be described in the next section.

Crossan presented this four-phase proposal informally to CRA in September of 2017, and it was presented again and approved in October at the second annual EX Group forum. The next two months were spent developing a pilot program to test the plan, and its first three phases were implemented on a trial basis, beginning in December when the first revised job postings—greatly reduced in length and explicitly focused on character dimensions as well as KLCs—were distributed. Board member training began in January of 2018, with Crossan sitting in as an advisor, and the revised interview process was launched in February, with the help of volunteers from two key branches and one region.

In all, this trial run in the spring of 2018 comprised 65 interviews involving three separate CRA business lines. Of the 65 applicants interviewed, 30—that is, fewer than half—were assessed as having well-developed character. While that might sound surprisingly high, it is actually in line with experience elsewhere. Why? Because, simply stated, leader character has been a blind spot in many organizations. In situations where—for example—dimensions such as Drive, Integrity, or Accountability are operating as vices without support from Humility and Temperance, there's a good chance that leaders will not have had the opportunity to develop their character.

One innovation in the process involved a successful effort to move the evaluation of the relevant KCLs to the written tests that *preceded* the in-person interview, thereby allowing that interview to be more character-focused.

Interest continued to grow across the CRA and—increasingly—across the broader federal civil service. All of this interest kept the phones ringing. "The team and I have been busy answering calls and messages from other government departments," Côté wrote in an email to Crossan in June of 2018, "and I've been reflecting on potentially creating an interdepartmental senior management committee to discuss character-based leadership and its implementation in HR programs across the Federal Public Service." Meanwhile, a second and third pilot now needed to be readied for launch. Preparations were underway for a June workshop in Ottawa, and a national videoconference, scheduled for the fall, was looming. And all the while, of course, Côté also had to attend to the ongoing duties of her job as director general.

Not surprisingly, she realized that she was reaching the limits of her capacity and that she needed help. It was, she recalls, an important turning point:

> One of the pivotal moments was putting on the table the funding request for building the team. And on that point, I was very clear. I said, "If the branch doesn't get the funding for this, we will have to scale back. The pace and the additional work on the team need to be recognized and funded appropriately." I was asking the organization to support me in the way that was required to continue on the path of infusing character within the Agency.

CRA leadership reviewed Côté's business case and—in a clear validation of her character-related efforts up to that point—approved her request for up to a dozen new team members.

Pushing the change: part two

One of those new team members was Steve Virgin,[7] hired into the newly created position of director of character-based leadership beginning in July 2018. Appropriately, Virgin was selected in part based on his demonstrated competence and relevant experience and in part based on his character interview. As Côté recalls:

> We interviewed about ten individuals, and Steve really did stand out. He didn't have a traditional HR background, but he had all of the life experiences that were required to start elevating the character leadership approach to another level. And, of course, we were looking for balanced character dimensions, and he demonstrated them all the way.

Although new to CRA, Virgin was far from a novice in the field of leadership. After spending three decades in the Canadian Armed Forces, including numerous tours of duty as a submarine captain, Virgin moved into the ranks of management. He served for three years as Deputy Commander of Canadian Special Forces—an executive position—and then two more years as a business manager in the federal government. Beginning fairly early in his career, he was engaged in selecting military officers and continued to focus on talent management, succession planning, and the selection of future executives in his subsequent government posts. As he recalls:

> I had seen plenty of bad leadership in my career, and also plenty of good. And although I didn't know much about Ivey's and Sonia's work in the character area, I got a pretty good understanding from the job advert. And I just thought, "This is a chance to make a *difference*. This is what lights me up—influencing leadership development."

The truth is, I've never lobbied for a job in my life. I had some interesting jobs in the military, and I never lobbied for any of them. Each time, they just called me up and asked me if I would do it, and I kept saying yes. But in this case, when I came out of that interview, I found myself saying, "Oh, I hope I get this job!"

He got the job and got to work. Right out of the gate, to Virgin's surprise and satisfaction, his boss made a point of giving him significant latitude. Côté was heading off to Portugal on a long-overdue vacation and basically turned over the keys to Virgin. "She welcomed me," recalls Virgin, "and said, in so many words, 'Work out our strategy for implementing character across CRA and I'll see you in a month.' And that big-picture style of leadership continued after she got back. I would check in with her on something and say, 'I think we should go this way on this, Sonia. Do you think I'm crazy?' And maybe she'd give me a little course correction, but otherwise, it was carte blanche."

Like any good manager coming into a complex organization without existing networks, Virgin started touching base with colleagues across the agency, whose employees at the time numbered 43,000. But he didn't give himself the luxury of the typical "100-day listening tour," or even the 30-day version. He told Côté that he'd listen hard on day one and keep listening—especially toward the end of making himself an expert at spotting and developing character—but that he also intended to start making changes on day two.

One of Virgin's early innovations was the development of an intensive training session for all board members who would be called upon to assess character in candidates, lasting a day and a half. Lessons had already been learned from the pilots that had been run before Virgin's arrival; now the organization had to build on those lessons, learn new ones, and leverage that understanding across a much broader base. "That's going well," says Virgin, "but we're learning all the time."[8]

Another significant innovation led by Virgin and his team was creating an opportunity for the candidate to have a post-interview feedback session, most often with the chair of the screening board. That opportunity was offered to all candidates, whether they were successful or not. This debrief in some ways resembled the interview—that is, a candid conversation intended to respect and be helpful to the candidate. Both strengths and weaknesses associated with the dimensions of character were discussed, and more specifically, the elements and behaviors that support the dimensions were discussed. For example, it was common for the debrief to provide encouragement to candidates to strengthen their authenticity—an element of Integrity—because candidates often struggle with displaying their authentic selves when they are preoccupied with what others think of them. Obviously, this challenge can be particularly acute in an interview setting.

"While it's only a few moments in time," says Virgin, "the debrief from the character interview can be some of the most meaningful feedback that one ever gets in a professional career. That's what we're getting fed back to us, by and large."

Certainly, not all candidates take advantage of the opportunity to debrief, and of those who do, not all are uniformly satisfied with the process and its outcome. But many clearly are. As one candidate who was not successful put it:

> That feedback session really was a conversation. The interview board was able to use information from earlier steps in the process to formulate meaningful questions that were specific to me, as a candidate. I had the opportunity to be myself, and the final feedback was very useful—focusing on both my strengths and areas that I should consider for my leadership development. So I'd say that the character interview is a positive departure from the normal hiring approach, and I look forward to the next competition, when I intend to apply again, and pursue my goal of becoming an executive leader in CRA.[9]

While Virgin was listening, learning, and innovating—from day two onward—he was also putting together his allocated ten-person team. On that front, however, he moved more slowly. "I didn't hire the tenth person until about 18 months in," he recalls. "It was a very deliberate pace, slow burn, aimed at bringing in the right people." And that deliberate pace, he adds, was part of a bigger vision:

> Sonia and I were determined to build something that would stick. All too often, organizations fall into the trap of what I call "episodic strategy." I'm not an expert in strategy, but I knew from my previous employment that all too often, organizations embrace a series of short-vision, short-term strategies. Sonia and I had great discussions about that. "This has got to be *enduring*," we'd wind up agreeing. "This has got to be something that's going to be there for the Agency for the long-term."

Toward that end, they adopted a conscious strategy of *plan, do, measure, adjust, experiment, and explore*. "You can substitute whichever change-management terms you want to use," says Virgin. "But we agreed back in 2018 that the foundation of our strategy had to be to deliberate, deliberate, deliberate. Yes, we took measured steps, in implementing everything that we've done. But we had to deliver the goods, and they had to stick."

As of this writing, Côté and Virgin's team has conducted more than 900 character-based interviews, working their way up level by level through the CRA executive ranks, so that today, *all* executive interviews include a character component. They have also offered character-related developmental opportunities to many thousands of CRA employees in the agency's middle and lower ranks. This was an important balancing step, says Virgin. "We didn't want the interview to become the be all and end-all—the test that you did or didn't pass.

Actually, as we see it, the development side is the profound part. We have to keep finding ways to develop our new and ongoing leaders over time."[10]

The growth in demand for that kind of development, says Virgin, "exceeds our wildest dreams." One example: the Agency's surveys of subordinates regarding their managers' leadership skills used to be based solely on competence; today, they are also based on character. To date, 32,000 people have submitted these "blended" evaluations of 5,000 managers—"a phenomenal resource for future development," Virgin suggests.

Virgin is also proud of his team—none of whom are in the executive ranks but all of whom put in long hours to make their shared initiative a success. For her part, Côté also applauds the dedication of the team, which she says has inevitably embarked on its own character journey—an almost inevitable side benefit of engaging in character-related work as she sees it. And like Virgin, she, too, points to the widespread impact of the program, vertically as well as horizontally:

There's not a week that goes by that I don't have someone—a colleague, or someone from another department, or someone internally—who says, "Hey, I was at this session, and it made a difference for me. And keep on doing the work that you're doing, because it makes a difference."

And the other point of pride is being able to engage with the very senior levels of the organization and find ownership of the initiative. For example, I sit in on the Commissioner's management committee meetings every week. Very often, as we're having a strategic conversation about one of the Agency's programs, someone will raise a hand and make the link with character leadership. We might be discussing our strategic planning framework, and one of my colleagues might ask, "Have we thought about how that links up with character, and what we need to do to demonstrate that?" And for me, that's a proud moment, because as a collective, we are seeing the benefit of leader character and its integration into key approaches, programs, and services. This is how true change happens.

Côté and Virgin have also been involved in more than four dozen engagements with some three dozen other government agencies and departments, interactions with more than a dozen private-sector companies, and a number of conferences. Many of the organizations they're interacting with are now learning lessons that CRA learned a half-decade ago—but of course, these newcomers have the benefit of precedent and guidance from the CRA team. "I'm proud of the fact that this initiative is so far-reaching, and has such impact," says Virgin. "It's affecting people in a much deeper way than I think many people realize."

Obviously, becoming a champion of character change—the focus of this chapter and of our deep dive into CRA's recent history—is neither a simple nor a short-term challenge. Sonia Côté, later joined by Steve Virgin and other team members, worked long and hard to elevate character alongside competence, as they set out to hire and develop leaders within a complex agency. That work continues today. We've presented their story in some detail, in part because that degree of granularity helps make the point that championing character change depends a great deal on *context*—on your ability to tailor the concepts of leader character to the needs of your particular organization.

We'll underscore that point by looking briefly at a second example of championing character change, this time in a very different setting. Then we'll review the kinds of lessons that emerge from, and in some cases cut across, these two examples.

A private-sector parallel

Our focus in this case study is Porter Airlines, a Canadian regional airline that began operations in 2006 and has enjoyed steady growth since then. Traditionally, it has served Canadian and US cities mostly within easy striking distance of Toronto, relying on between two and three dozen Dash turboprop planes. The COVID-related global collapse in air travel in 2020 hit all airlines—including Porter—hard. Porter suspended all service from March of that year until September 2021: almost 18 months. Most of the airline's 1,500 employees were furloughed for the duration.

But even in the depths of the COVID-related recession—when most airlines were reeling, scaling back, and fighting off bankruptcy—Porter was laying the groundwork for a significant expansion of its operations. In July 2021, it announced that it would be purchasing up to 80 new Embraer jet aircraft and in 2022 would start flying to more distant cities in the US, Mexico, and the Caribbean—an expansion that would require a major expansion of Porter's payroll. Almost 1,000 new hires joined that payroll in 2022 alone.[11]

This kind of dramatic growth obscures another kind of quiet success that Porter has enjoyed in recent months: Despite the so-called "Great Resignation" in the wake of COVID, close to 75 percent of the airline's pre-pandemic workforce has returned to work at Porter. Why this high level of loyalty? One answer lies in the fact that Porter extended fully paid health-care benefits to all of its employees throughout the 18-month suspension of service and otherwise kept in regular touch with its furloughed employees during the course of the pandemic. But that was only part of a bigger picture: Porter has a long-standing culture of listening to its employees, which has led to its enjoying higher than average employee-engagement rankings than its peers. In 2019, just before COVID, the airline not only turned in its best financial performance ever; it also recorded its highest-ever levels of employee engagement.

Lawrence Hughes is Porter's executive vice president and chief people officer. Before joining Porter in 2015, Lawrence operated a human resources consulting firm and also held operational and human resources leadership roles for

West 49 Inc., Rogers Communications Inc., Roots Canada Limited, Dylex Limited, and Hudson's Bay Company—all places where he learned lessons he is applying today.

Hughes draws a direct-line connection between employee engagement and skilled managers:

> Here at Porter, the place where we found the biggest ROI, in terms of driving engagement, was in developing our leaders. We can do all we want at the corporate level, in terms of policies and programs, but if a team member has a leader who they don't respect, and who isn't strong in those core leadership skills, then engagement will suffer. So that's been our big focus, in the last several years—really developing leaders, and ensuring that our leaders are leading in ways that are productive, transparent, and in keeping with the culture of the organization.[12]

Hughes attended a two-day HR Management Institute Canada event in Ottawa in early November 2021. There he heard a presentation—"Sustained Excellence through Leading with Character"—by Gerard Seijts, a faculty member at the Ivey Business School and also one of the authors of this book. Hughes saw parallels between Porter's ongoing efforts to develop leaders and the Ivey team's work and asked Seijts to present his framework as part of a larger Porter leadership retreat in Toronto the following April. About 125 senior leaders from the airline attended the event, and again, Seijts' presentation was well received.

The collaboration between Porter and Seijts was gaining momentum. In September, the April group reconvened—now joined by an additional 125 Porter managers—to attend a daylong session on leader character. The agenda included a deeper dive into the application of leader character to diversity, equity, and inclusion initiatives, live polls and film clips, a case discussion, and the administration of the Leader Character Insight Assessment (see Chapter 3) to all attendees. Seijts then led a debrief of the LCIA to help the participants begin a process of reflection and development based on their individual results.

The following month, Hughes asked Seijts to return to Porter to make a brief presentation to his eleven-person HR group. The participants had recently taken the LCIA, and Seijts worked with the team on a debrief and interpretation of their scores.

In a recent conversation, Hughes summarized the foundations, evolution, and current state of the Porter/Ivey collaboration:

> I'm so fortunate in my role as an HR leader to have a board, and the rest of the executive team, who understand the value and the importance of developing leaders, and are fully committed to making that investment. Everyone gets the correlation between strong leaders—people who are leading with

character—and their ROI as it relates to business results and team member engagement.

The concept of Leader Character really resonated with the values and principles that we place on leader development at Porter. When we looked at the principles and values of our own Accountable Manager program and then married it up to Leader Character, it was inspiring and compelling.

So we're going to continue to develop leader character. What's next? I'm not an expert in curriculum development, so I can't say for certain. But we're going to continue to work with Ivey and find out how we can keep this alive, and make it stick, and support our leaders in developing leader character.[13]

Porter had a number of key advantages already in place before Seijts began working with Hughes and his team. First, of course, there are the distinctive characteristics of the realm within which Porter competes: a low-margin, highly competitive industry where the level of customer service can be the key differentiator. Front-line employees help make customers happy, and great managers help keep front-line employees engaged. This dynamic summarized in Figure 6.2.

This implies Porter's second advantage: the airline's management was committed to leadership development—perhaps the main reason they hired Hughes in the first place. Third, in Hughes, they had a strong and experienced champion of leadership development, who was able to leverage the strong corporate culture that was already in place by focusing on a set of core values. Fourth, they had in place a formal short-term incentive plan for leaders, which included accountability for engagement within their teams: a strong and compelling link to leader character. Again, people are more engaged when they respect their leaders, and leaders with character are more likely to command that respect.[14] And finally, they had a cohort of middle and senior managers who already had demonstrated strong commitment and key competencies and were open to hearing about new ways to develop their leadership potential.

In these two relatively brief case studies, we've tried to show what's distinctive about the evolution of leader character at CRA and Porter. CRA is a much larger organization and is itself part of a vastly larger organization: the government of Canada. CRA is a half-decade into its embrace of the leader character framework—that is relatively far along—and is now serving as a resource for

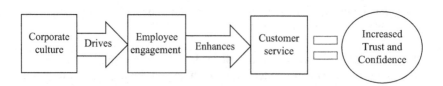

Figure 6.2 People, Engagement, and Culture Matter

other groups in both the public and private sectors. Porter is only in the early stages of engaging with leader character, but they started with a strong foundation of values, which they realized was necessary but not sufficient. With the added organizational complexities associated with doubling their workforce and tripling their fleet of aircraft, they are scrambling to preserve and strengthen their positive culture.

So again: different contexts. But let's look at some of the lessons that cut across these and other contexts in which the leader character framework is now being explored and applied.

Lessons for character champions

We present these lessons in the order that you may encounter certain challenges. They include both general prescriptions and suggestions that are more specific to the content presented in this chapter and—where relevant—also include parenthetical references to related character dimensions:

- *Start with yourself.* First and most importantly, being a champion of character—and mastering the kinds of character-based selection described in this chapter—starts with understanding and developing your own character. The preceding chapters focus on this challenge and how to master it. But remember that it's a challenge that never ends. "It takes a lifetime to master and perfect," says CRA's Côté. "It's much like being an athlete who is training to compete at the highest levels. That training doesn't stop."[15] (Humility, Accountability)
- *Keep a close eye on context.* What are the unexpected outside factors—the black swans, the bolts from the blue—that can come to bear on your change process? The COVID-19 pandemic certainly challenged virtually all organizations and their ongoing change processes. But chaos intruding from the outside isn't necessarily a bad thing. Porter used its 18-month suspension of operations to strengthen ties with its furloughed workforce. More than 7,000 CRA employees who were *not* call-center agents volunteered to answer the phones to help their fellow Canadians deal with unexpected tax and benefit issues during the pandemic. *Character* came to the fore—and was there to be channeled and managed. (Transcendence, judgment)
- *Look for allies.* You almost certainly can't be a successful champion of character on your own, so you'll need to find allies within the organization. Look up and down the ladder. Look sideways. Consider an internal stakeholder analysis, an approach that Côté and her CRA colleagues used. "What I realized, during these years of exploration," says Côté, "was that there were a number of what I'd call 'disruptors'—people at all levels of the organization who felt like me, and who believed that when it came to recruiting and developing great leaders, it wasn't enough to focus on technical abilities alone."

She found allies in what at first seemed like unlikely places—for example, within the agency's IT group, which included individuals who started out as self-proclaimed skeptics ("Hey, we're *technically* oriented") but wound up embracing the initiative. Her colleague Steve Virgin underscores the point: "We knew that this couldn't just be 'by HR, for HR.' We had to build coalitions, we had to get people on our side, and we had to *influence*. We had to get them in the tent." (Collaboration)

- *Bring people together.* In the same spirit, find ways to co-create. Share the fun as well as the burdens. In particular, don't overlook existing colleagues with overlapping mandates. "You have an organization that's accustomed to operating a certain way," observes Côté. "Changing that system requires more than one voice. So we needed to work with our existing HR professionals, who were used to working within the guidelines that had been in place for years and years. I often referred to them as our engineers. They're the people who will actually change the policies and practices. If we don't involve them from the get-go, then we run the risk of not being able to implement effectively." CRA's original pilot programs, for example, were set up by a working group that included the relevant director generals and their teams. This is also good advice when working upward in the hierarchy. "You've got to tread carefully," says Virgin, "so you don't create the perception that you're doing this as an indictment of the current leadership." (Humanity, Collaboration, Humility)

- *Don't overengineer it.* Yes, invoke the theory, but find ways to let it resonate with people naturally. In that kind of effort—as our Ivey colleague Jeffrey Gandz advises—*be open-minded but not empty-minded.* (Humility, judgment)

- *Start with pilots.* As is true for most entrepreneurial and intrapreneurial ventures, it's best to invent, experiment, and learn in small bites. Create a critical path of risk-taking and follow that path, changing it as you go. Register some successes, and then seek resources to expand the initiative. (Temperance)

- *Go as fast as possible, but not too fast.* In the same spirit, avoid the bridge too far. "We're definitely going more slowly than the system sometimes demands of us," says Côté. "But one of our roles is to put a foot on the brake when necessary. We have to ensure that it's a very deliberate and credible approach. We have to ensure, for example, that we're training our board members effectively, and that our candidates are fully aware of what's expected of them, in this new way of being. Why? Because if we *didn't* put in that effort, it could put the whole approach at risk." (Drive, Courage, Temperance)

- *Pick a point of intervention that has significant potential for leverage.* Most likely, your initiative will have to compete with others for corporate resources and brain space. "Right now," says Porter's Hughes, "there's a tremendous amount of pressure on the organization as we gear up to launch the new E2 jet fleet, at all levels—from our leaders right down to our front-line people."[16] That means that Hughes has to find the right levers to pull and the right language (leadership driving engagement driving customer satisfaction) to describe those levers. Fortunately, leader character initiatives have a way of making their own friends because they effect change on multiple levels, professionally and personally. "In retrospect," says Côté, "I'm glad we started with staffing, because what happens when people serve on boards and participate in the interviews, something lights up, and they start realizing that this new process is unique, and productive, and it's enabling us to really see the person in front of us. And it has an impact on both sides of the table. When you're the candidate, this new process helps activate the character dimensions that are important for leaders, which eventually starts changing the behaviors and the cultures within the organization." (Transcendence, judgment)

- *When you interview, interview wisely.* If your change process involves interviews, be creative—but at the same time, guard against the kinds of mistakes that can happen when you get away from structured interviews. Structured interviews were invented for a reason: to avoid bias. That's why Steve Virgin's team at CRA invested heavily in designing training sessions for the board members who would be involved in candidate interviews, with a focus on unconscious bias. What does it look like? What does it feel like? How can it be surfaced and weeded out of the screening process? And how can leader character development be used to mitigate unconscious bias? CRA also adopted a policy where at least two of the board members who are involved in interviews for executive positions have to be members of "employment equity groups," as defined by the Employment Equity Act.[17] (Justice, Humanity, Accountability)

- *Stay humble.* As Steve Virgin phrases it, "When we built the team, we probably lacked a bit of humility. We became the *specialist* team, and maybe got a little bit full of ourselves. I was using metaphors like the Avengers—trying to fire the team up, and make them feel like they were doing something special. Because they *were* doing something special. But maybe we disenfranchised some other players, especially in the early days." (Humility)

- *Expect opposition.* Not everybody will embrace your ideas on day one. Maybe it's just a matter of time and persuasion on your part. "It's fascinating to see a senior person approaching an interview process, and pooh-poohing it," says Virgin. "And then they do it, and they become converts." Or maybe they're not converts and never will be. Then what? "This is a topic that people tend to shy away from," says Hughes. "If you have a leader who is not aligned, and is in the background undermining what you're trying to do, then ultimately that person needs to exit the organization, because one or two detractors can really do a lot of damage. Research tells us that it takes five 'cheerleaders' on your team to negate the impact that one tuned-out person can have." (Courage, Integrity)

- *Be patient and persistent.* Elevating Leader Character alongside competence takes *time.* Yes, it's important to embed the language of Leader Character into corporate practices and documents—such as CRA's Corporate Business Plan and its Agency Workforce Plan—but those kinds of relatively quick, top-down fixes are rarely enough. The most powerful way to elevate character alongside competence is to *activate and encourage the development of character of the individuals within your organization*—and that takes time. Over time, individuals who are developing character will begin to identify and change practices that are not character-aligned. In other words, organizational culture is a reflection of the character of the individuals involved, and their character leadership will be the driving force behind organizational transformation. The good news is that for most individuals and organizations, elevating character alongside competence comes as a welcome change. There's no need to force implementation; rather, the transformation can be allowed to emerge through the conversations and actions that arise from a variety of interventions, including workshops, seminars, management briefings, and experiential sessions like improv or meditation. But again, this takes *time*. Be patient. This is equally important in the assessment end of the process. CRA, for example, says it's still too early in the change process to assess whether the candidates they hired have grown. Côté, Virgin, and their colleagues say that they see reason to be optimistic but, at the same time, argue that a longer time horizon is needed to track results (although recall that some of the research we presented in Chapter 2 is providing very positive evidence). Says Côté. "You have to wait for that transformation to happen." (Temperance)

- *Keep the bigger picture in mind.* Is this initiative that you've launched bigger than your department or your functional area? Virgin recalls that he and Côté had many conversations about whether the leader character effort should be seen as a strategic opportunity for CRA: "I remember some people asserting that it wasn't our job to export character to the entire public service. As in, "Hey, this is for *CRA*, not everybody else." And Sonia and I discussed it, and we decided, 'This is a strategic opportunity for CRA. We're not just in the tax business; we're a major federal department, and we believe in leadership, and this could influence government." Looked at from the other direction: what parts of your organization *don't* need to learn what you're learning about leader character? (Transcendence)
- *Be brave, and be a champion.* You need *character* to be a champion of character change. Right? It takes courage to see something differently than anybody else sees it and to act on that vision. And it also requires a strategic mindset: given our limited resources, where do we need to put our focus? At times, that's very tiring—but champions persevere. "It's about continuing to push for something that I strongly believe in," says Côté. "It's about having enough faith to jump in without knowing exactly what the outcome will be, and continuing to have that faith all along the way. And finally, it's about admitting that from a character perspective, you constantly have new things to learn. And in a way, that's a relief. I don't have to feel like that as a leader,

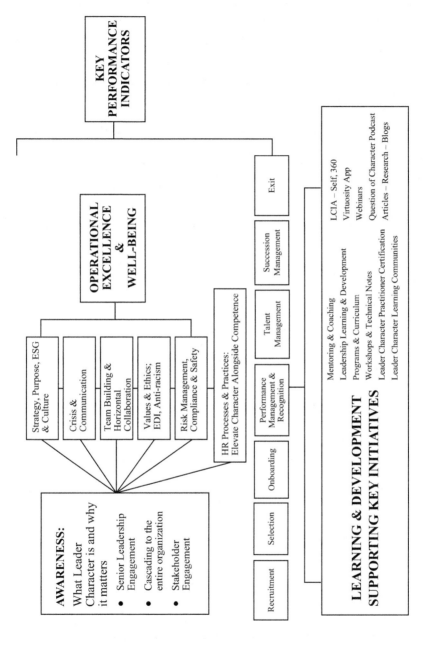

Figure 6.3 Leader Character Strategic Roadmap

I need to know it all, but I can show up, show vulnerability, trust the team, and trust that it will work out." (Courage, Transcendence, Drive, Humility)

Those of our readers who are familiar with the field of change management will certainly recognize many of these prescriptions. That should come as no surprise: when you become a champion of character change, you are advocating, embodying, and facilitating organizational transformation. You become, literally, a change agent.

In this chapter, we've focused on developing people and teams through leader character, which often involves change agents at work in the Human Resource area. But as our Strategic Roadmap—which we introduced back in the introduction and which we include again as Figure 6.3—indicates, HR is only one of many corporate activities in which leader character can be embraced, leading to enhanced operational excellence and individual well-being.

In our subsequent chapters, we'll look at how change agents can make a difference—and leader character can be embraced—in several of those other areas.

Notes

1 This administrative/structural information is from CRA's website, online at www.canada.ca/en/revenue-agency/corporate/about-canada-revenue-agency-cra/canada-revenue-agency-structure-operational-framework.html.
2 The views expressed by Sonia Cote are her own.
3 We first introduced John Ossowski in Chapter 2, in the context of his next job after CRA: president of the Canada Border Services Agency (CBSA).
4 Unless otherwise noted, the direct quotes in this chapter are from our interview with Sonia Côté and Steve Virgin on November 1, 2022.
5 Much of this discussion draws upon the 2021 article "Elevating leader character alongside competence in selection: A case study of Canada Revenue Agency" by Mary Crossan, Sonia Côté, and Stephen Virgin, published in *Organizational Dynamics*, 50: 1–14.
6 Details of the forum are from the agenda circulated in advance of the meeting.
7 The views expressed by Steve Virgin are his own.
8 These quotes are from episode 6 of the podcast by Bill Furlong and Mary Crossan, "How is Canada Revenue Agency Embedding Leader Character?" online at www.youtube.com/watch?v=oYi0hXeo1Pk, accessed March 14, 2023.
9 Also from the article "Elevating leader character alongside competence in selection: A case study of Canada Revenue Agency."
10 Also from the podcast.
11 This information was obtained from www.travelweek.ca/news/an-incredible-year-of-opportunity-porter-airlines-has-big-plans-on-the-horizon/, accessed March 14, 2023. See the expanded routes at Porter's website: www.flyporter.com/en-ca/about-porter/who-we-are/porter-and-embraer accessed, March 14, 2023.
12 From the Oven Ready podcast "Flying High—How HR Took the Initiative with Employee Engagement," online at https://ovenreadyhr.com/flying-high-how-hr-took-the-initiative-with-employee-engagement/, accessed March 14, 2023.
13 Unless otherwise noted, the quotes in this chapter are from our interview with Lawrence Hughes on November 17, 2022.

14 Studies have revealed that virtues and the use of character strengths are associated
    with job satisfaction, motivation, work engagement, well-being, and work perfor-
    mance. Representative research includes the following: Miglianico, M., Dubreuil, P.,
    Miquelon, P., Bakker, A. B., & Martin-Krumm, C. (2020). Strength use in the work-
    place: A literature review. *Journal of Happiness Studies*, 21: 737–764. Park, N., &
    Peterson, C. (2009). Character strengths: Research and practice. *Journal of College
    and Character*, 10(4). https://doi.org/10.2202/1940-1639.1042. Monzani, L., Seijts,
    G. H., & Crossan, M. M. (2021). Character matters: The network structure of leader
    character and its relation to follower positive outcomes. *PLOS One*, 16(9): e0255940.
15 Unless otherwise noted, the Côté quotes in this section are from the podcast "How is
    Canada Revenue Agency Embedding Leader Character?"
16 Unless otherwise noted, the Hughes quotes in this section are from our interview with
    him on November 17, 2022.
17 For details, see the federal government's write-up of the Employment Equity Act
    and Workplace Equity Program, online at www.canada.ca/en/employment-social-
    development/corporate/portfolio/labour/programs/employment-equity.html.

Chapter 7

A culture of character

Looking back, it's easy to see where Boeing's troubles started.

In late December of 1996, the world's largest manufacturer of commercial aircraft—and Washington state's biggest employer until 2021—announced that it was acquiring its archrival, St. Louis-based McDonnell Douglas Corporation, for $13.3 billion.[1]

The move seemed to make sense from a competitive standpoint. Boeing had a huge backlog of orders, and McDonnell Douglas had idle factory capacity. The combined company would be better positioned to compete with Lockheed Martin for military contracts and with Airbus Industrie—the European leader—in the commercial aviation field. On paper, at least, it appeared that the acquiring company would dominate the continuing business: Boeing CEO Philip Condit would continue in that role, and McDonnell-Douglas' CEO Harry Stonecipher would become the president of the combined entity, which (over the objections of the McDonnell-Douglas camp) would be called Boeing. Two-thirds of the new company's directors would be members of Boeing's existing board. This reflected not only the dominant flows of money involved in the transaction but also the recent history of the two companies. Boeing was riding high whereas McDonnell Douglas had experienced a number of recent setbacks, including an unsuccessful bid for a critical Pentagon contract. In short, Boeing was a proud and successful company with a sterling reputation, and McDonnell Douglas was—by many measures—failing.

At the time, few observers raised questions about the implications of bringing these two corporate cultures together. But the truth was that they were significantly different, and those differences had inherent perils.[2] McDonnell-Douglas was less focused on engineering prowess and more on financial maneuvers—including corporate stock buybacks—designed to jack up its share price and make Wall Street happy.[3] The company patterned itself on Jack Welch's General Electric, where Stonecipher had cut his managerial eyeteeth, and this translated into a relentless focus on a particular financial metric: return on net assets (RONA). But RONA was and is a manipulable measure: a company that can keep its income stream reasonably stable while cutting its asset base can improve

DOI: 10.4324/9781003341215-8

its RONA, at least temporarily. For a manufacturing company, however, choosing not to invest in the plant and equipment—or even selling off entire factories and outsourcing production—is likely to lead to competitive disadvantage in the long term. By the time of the merger, McDonnell-Douglas' manufacturing capacity was woefully out of date, and its competitive posture was slipping.

Boeing, by contrast, was an almost pure engineering culture, focused on designing and building the best commercial jets in the world. Its employees considered themselves to be part of an extended family—one which effectively dominated its still relatively small and relatively isolated Seattle hometown. The company had a long tradition of making whatever investments were needed to make its fleet safe and providing the materials and training required by the pilots who flew those planes.

Those foundations began to crumble shortly after the merger. One telltale sign came in early in 2000, when the previously sleepy union representing Boeing's engineers called a strike to protest benefit cuts proposed by the company. What followed was the largest white-collar strike in US history up to that point, comprising 23,000 people in six states—a strike that many observers concluded was unnecessary in light of the relatively small amounts of money that were at stake. One federal mediator involved in the difficult negotiations aimed at settling the strike confessed that he thought the marriage between McDonnell-Douglas and Boeing was doomed to fail. Why? Because, he said, the former McDonnell-Douglas executives were "hunter killer assassins," whereas the Boeing execs—in other words, those who were supposedly running the merged company—were "Boy Scouts."

Another telling episode came in May 2001, when CEO Condit decided to move the company's headquarters to Chicago.[4] Why? "When the headquarters is located in proximity to a principal business," he explained, "as ours was in Seattle, the corporate center is inevitably drawn into day-to-day business operations." But one could argue—and some *did* argue—that having corporate immersed in the reality of designing and building aircraft was one of Boeing's longtime strengths rather than a weakness. In this move, we can see once again the pervading influence of Jack Welch's General Electric, which in the mid-'70s had moved to a 60-acre campus in Fairfield, Connecticut, to bring together under one roof those corporate executives responsible for "long-range planning, resource allocations, and overall direction of the company."[5] Not incidentally, Fairfield provided a safe remove from the kinds of factories that had made GE a leading US manufacturer in previous decades.

Harry Stonecipher accumulated power and largely overshadowed his new boss at Boeing in the five years leading up to his mandatory retirement—at age 65—in June 2002.[6] But he remained on Boeing's board, along with John McConnell, and his influence continued to be felt. Then came an unexpected twist: Condit was forced to retire the following year after Boeing became ensnared in an Air Force procurement scandal, and Stonecipher came out of retirement to succeed him. He picked up where he had left off with his relentless cost-cutting: outsourcing key manufacturing processes and then squeezing those subcontractors. And in a 2004 interview with the *Chicago Tribune*, he was straightforward and unapologetic about his intentions for Boeing:

> When people say I changed the culture of Boeing, that was the intent, so that it's run like a business rather than a great engineering firm. It is a great engineering firm, but people invest in a company because they want to make money.[7]

Many people saw Stonecipher's return as the final chapter in McDonnell-Douglas' "reverse takeover" of Boeing. Meanwhile, there were more chapters to come in what might be called GE's concurrent cultural takeover of the company. Early in 2005, Stonecipher was caught in an affair with a female Boeing lobbyist based in Washington.[8] He was fired in March—only to be succeeded by Jim McNerney, a fellow Boeing board member who was then CEO of the Minnesota-based 3M Company.

McNerney, a longtime GE executive, had been one of the three finalists to succeed the retiring Jack Welch; when that job when to Jeff Immelt in late 2000, McNerney went to 3M. There he embarked on a RONA crusade of his own, cutting the payroll by 8,000 jobs—about 11 percent, including many older workers—and slashing investments in plants, equipment, and R&D. Yes, during his four-year tenure, 3M's profits doubled and its stock price rose 30 percent—but the effect on morale was devastating. Employees watched as their proud and innovative company was whittled down and hollowed out, actively disinvesting from its future.

One employee, chemical engineer Art Fry, had achieved almost mythic status for his co-invention of the Post-it note in the late 1970s. Responding years later to the strictures of the McNerney regime, he said bluntly that he wouldn't have been able to pursue his invention if he had been constrained by McNerney's brand of relentless cost-cutting in his day. "What's remarkable," he declared, "is how fast a culture can be torn apart."[9] And beginning in 2005, the same CEO responsible for tearing apart 3M—Jim McNerney—was entrusted with the already collapsing culture at Boeing.

A 2006 interview with *FlightGlobal* provides some veiled insight into how McNerney perceived that cultural challenge, a year into his tenure:

> Someone asked me once: "Aren't you impressed at the massive differences between GE and 3M and Boeing?" And there are huge differences. There are big differences in terms of products and services provided. But there are also a lot of similarities. And I happened to be at the center of all three companies in one form or another wrestling with the issue of a proud-culture, high-performing company that had gotten a little inward. But 3M and Boeing,

they're great people. There's a couple of generations of the best chemical engineers in the United States went to 3M. And the same thing on the aeronautical side here at Boeing. So it was more a matter of re-engaging, facing the company outward again, whether it's customers or ethics and compliance or all the things that the outside is asking of us that we should be doing anyway. I think GE 20 years ago went through a similar thing, and I probably learned from that.

I think the Boeing folks never lost faith in themselves and pride in their products. I think they were very disappointed in some of the things that went on and wanted to address the issues. I found them willing to address the issue. I sat down in town hall meetings and raised the issues that we had, talked about ways forward, about attributes and values. And I found them very responsive. I probably would be kidding myself if I said that everybody in Boeing was totally rejuvenated after I've been here for a year, because that's not true. But I think there's a broad acceptance of the change agenda. We're all working it. It's early days. These things take many, many years. But it's more re-tapping into a fundamentally ethical culture that had lost its way in a couple of areas than it is having to recreate a new culture out of the ashes.[10]

A company that had grown inward. A culture that had lost its way. We will return to the Boeing saga in our next chapter, when—in the context of risk management—we explore the tragic story of Boeing's 737 MAX 8. For now, suffice it to say that one clear lesson from Boeing is that culture is in large part determined by the folks at ground level—in Boeing's case, generations of employees (mostly engineers) who were committed to making the best and safest planes possible. But it is also determined by the handful of individuals who occupy the highest ranks of the corporate structure. They are uniquely positioned to create and strengthen that culture as they did over Boeing's first half century; they are also uniquely positioned to tear it apart.

A different approach to culture building

For something of an antidote to our unfolding Boeing story, let's now turn to St. Louis–based Barry-Wehmiller Companies, Inc., whose longtime leader Bob Chapman received the 2022 CEO of the Year award from the Society for Human Resource Management Foundation.[11] The award is given annually to corporate leaders who "demonstrate innovative and impactful business practices leading to better workplaces and a better world by serving as visionaries, innovators and change agents."

A press release from the SHRM Foundation elaborates:

The Committee selected Bob unanimously for the CEO of the Year Award after considering some of the largest multinational companies on the globe because there was specific, tangible proof that the culture Bob envisioned and nurtured resulted in that rare business that has done well financially while also providing an amazing work experience for its employees. BW is an exemplar employer because of Bob's unwavering commitment.

At first glance, Barry-Wehmiller (BW)—a manufacturer of industrial equipment and provider of engineering consulting services, with a recent history of focused acquisitions—might not seem to be an obvious place for business visionaries to be steering toward a better world.[12] Founded in St. Louis, Missouri, in 1885, BW for several decades sold bottle-pasteurization and bottle-refilling machinery to local brewers like Anheuser-Busch. The family-owned company limped its way through the Depression, reviving somewhat after Prohibition was repealed in the US. Significant change started to come to BW in the early 1950s when the company hired its first non-family CEO—Bill Chapman—who bought out the Wehmiller family in 1963. In 1969, Chapman asked his son Bob to join the company. The younger Chapman spent the next half decade rotating through various roles in the business: a training that served him well when his father died unexpectedly in 1975 and—at age 30—he was forced to take over as the company's CEO.

It was a rocky start, made much rockier by the fact that BW's bankers—rattled by the sudden succession—called in the company's loans. The banks had reason to be nervous. BW was losing about a half-million dollars a year on $18 million in annual revenues, and having its $3 million line of credit taken away looked like it might be a fatal blow. Not seeing other alternatives, Chapman cut costs dramatically, including deep cuts to the payroll. "The human cost of this," he later recalled in his memoir, "was something I just didn't think much about."

The bitter medicine worked—along with external trends like an ecology-driven trend toward reusable bottles. Within a half decade, revenues had almost quadrupled, and the company began taking baby steps into new realms, including overseas licensing arrangements. But just as quickly, the outside world turned hostile, and—once again—the banks quailed and suspended BW's credit lines. It was a vicious merry-go-round, and one that Chapman was determined to get off. After once again going through the painful process of widespread layoffs, Chapman came up with a novel idea: diversify the company through selective acquisitions to avoid being unduly hurt by future downturns in BW's existing market segments.

The main problem with that strategy was that even after this most recent recovery from a near-death experience, BW had limited resources with which to acquire anybody. Chapman's team addressed this challenge through the sale of its UK operations, which created an unexpectedly large pool of capital. But still, BW had to be disciplined. That meant acquiring businesses that no one else wanted—and even in that pool, being extremely selective. It also meant focusing on acquisitions that were asset-intensive and which manufactured products that had robust aftermarkets for those products. This would make capital investments more predictable, over the long run, and perhaps create more reliable income streams.

This approach was part of an ambitious larger growth strategy, with the stated goal of increasing revenues significantly—and for much of that decade, it worked.[13] Meanwhile, another important story line was unfolding. CEO Chapman had a series of three revelations that changed the way he thought about the culture of his company. The first came when he visited a new acquisition in South Carolina in the early months of 1997. Getting to the plant before it opened one morning, he saw early-arriving employees enjoying each other's company as they argued good-naturedly about the ongoing "March Madness" basketball tournament—an annual focus in many US workplaces. But when the workday started, Chapman noted, it seemed as if the fun stopped abruptly. Why shouldn't *work* be fun, he wondered? He subsequently experimented at that facility with some team-based competitive incentives—including modest financial rewards for the winning teams—and sales went up 20 percent the following quarter.

Chapman's next epiphany came in church. One Sunday, he was struck by the fact that his minister, who had the congregation's attention only an hour a week, nevertheless exerted a profound impact on his flock. At least in theory, he himself had his employees' attention for a full 40 hours a week. Couldn't he somehow use that time to add more meaning to their lives?

That same question next arose in a different guise at the wedding of one of his friend's daughters. Watching the proud father give the bride away, Chapman asked himself, *Wasn't everyone somebody's daughter?* And didn't that increase the responsibility of an employer to help people lead more satisfying lives?

To be sure, these revelations arrived separately and gradually over the course of a half decade. But they came to a head in 2002, when a member of BW's marketing department asked Chapman to make a video focused on key financial metrics as the measure of the company's recent successes. Chapman declined and instead—with his three revelations in mind—convened a group of BW's senior leaders at an off-site to come up with an aspirational statement about leadership at the company. The result was a document called the "Guiding Principles of Leadership (GPL)," which centered on two core ideas:

- *We measure success by the way we touch the lives of people.*
- *We are committed to our employees' personal growth.*[14]

Leadership, according to the GPL, would be based on trust. It would bring out and celebrate the best in each individual. It would allow for teams and individuals to have a meaningful role, inspire a sense of pride, and challenge individuals and teams. And finally, it would "liberate everyone to realize true success."

Through the GPL, the company committed itself to effective communication, identifying and tracking metrics that allowed "individuals and teams to relate their contribution to the realization of the vision" and to developing leaders who were "visionaries, coaches, mentors, teachers, and students."

The GPL was an explicitly *cultural* statement. "The document we created," said one of the managers who was present at the off-site, "exemplified how we wanted everyone to treat each other. We had described a 'perfect culture' that we would all like to aspire to achieve."[15]

Friendly skeptics from within the company soon stepped forward. How was this different, they asked pointedly, from similar statements by a host of other companies—Enron, for instance—whose cultures soon proved corrupt? Chapman took the question seriously, devoting something like a quarter of his time to listening sessions across the company. He also took concrete steps to institutionalize the tenets of the GPL. These included, for example, setting up an internal training program, Barry-Wehmiller University, in 2008 to offer leadership training to all employees who wanted it. The curriculum, focusing intensively on communication and listening skills, was well received, and the program was soon fielding three applications for every available seat.

But the true test of the GPL-defined culture came in the Great Recession of 2007–2009, when BW experienced a 35 percent drop in new orders. Would the company revert to the slash-and-burn measures it had used in previous downturns? Chapman was determined that it would not. Instead, his team came up with a package of cuts that amounted to corporate-wide shared sacrifices. With agreement from the company's unions, all employees were asked to take a four-week unpaid furlough, with each employee choosing when to temporarily go off the payroll. Individuals electing to retire early received generous buyouts. Executive bonuses and corporate matches to 401(k)'s were halted, and Chapman cut his own pay from $875,000 to $10,500.

It worked—and quickly—thanks not only to these and other economies but also to a rebounding economy. The following year, BW turned in its best financial performance ever. Some of those profits were used to make employees' retirement plans whole retroactively. In effect, BW had turned a potential disaster into a resounding success. "Because of the way we chose to respond," Chapman later wrote, "the financial crisis actually ended up being a blessing in disguise for us."

In Chapter 6, we focused on individuals who serve their organizations as what we called "champions of character change." Those individuals can play a unique and critical role in challenging circumstances—for example, when an organization faces a major generational turnover, as did the Canada Revenue Agency in 2016, and when a company (such as Porter Airlines) contemplates a dramatic, rapid upgrade in the scale and scope of its operations. In this chapter, we look at how the influence of those champions can be leveraged for significant change in specific areas, adding up to thoroughgoing organizational shifts.

Of course, *context* is critical. The Boeing and Barry-Wehmiller stories related previously remind us that for significant character-oriented change to occur, the leadership table has to be set correctly. Leaders (at all levels) have to work actively in support of a corporate culture that sustains character. The kinds of heavy-handed cuts that Boeing engaged in (for example) actually contribute to the *atrophying* of character. And yes, organizations can also get culture wrong by (for example) overweighting on Collaboration and Humanity and underweighting on Drive and Transcendence, leading to what some apprehensive leaders might describe as a "soft" culture. A strong, character-infused culture supports individual well-being and, in the aggregate, sustains excellence.

That character-infused culture can't be left to its own devices. It has to be nourished in good times and defended in bad times. It has to be used as a sounding board when a far-reaching strategic move—such as an acquisition—is contemplated. But it also has to be consulted when a corporate leader succumbs to the "flavor of the moment" and proposes to push off in a new and alien direction. Boeing's embrace of the GE culture, in the same timeframe that it was being overwhelmed by the McDonnell-Douglas ethos, is a case in point.[16]

The Boeing and Barry-Wehmiller stories also remind us that culture changes not only from the top down but also from the bottom up. Without strong rank-and-file support, in other words, cultural change is unlikely to take root.

One way to develop that kind of character-infused culture—as we argue in the following pages—is for the organization to embrace the leader character framework. That organizational embrace builds on the kind of individual commitment to leader character that we've discussed in previous chapters.

Toward a culture of character

In management literature, culture is usually looked at through one of five lenses: values, stories, frames, toolkits, and categories. Throughout this chapter, we draw on all five.

Also in this chapter, we continue our overall shift in emphasis from the individual to the organization—but we still will make the case that individual character can be, and *should* be, a foundation of culture. As professor emeritus of psychology at the University of Maryland Benjamin Schneider argues, an organization's culture does not exist as something separate or distinct from the people who work there. "The attributes of people," he writes, "not the nature of the external environment, or organizational technology, or organizational structure, are the fundamental determinants of organizational behavior."[17] All too often, leaders try to initiate change in their organizations by changing their processes, systems, and structures, when in fact it's the *people*—leaders, managers, and employees—that need changing first, or at least in parallel to structural change, in order to achieve the set goals.

Our emphasis on the people in a human system underscores our conviction that the system being transformed is *not* just the sum of its parts. In fact, it's the interplay among these actors that creates transformation. In theory, then, *all* of those actors should participate in the transformation. In real life, as Jenn Bitz[18] of the Canada Border Services Agency (CBSA) points out, "Culture change isn't about changing every single person's mind. It's about creating movement. It's about creating a context for transformative change. And once your movement reaches a critical mass, that kind of change gets much, much easier."[19]

Bitz, whose voice will appear frequently in the following pages, works with John Ossowski, whom we introduced in Chapter 2 and who retired in 2021 as the president of CBSA.[20] In that chapter, we briefly described how Ossowski's team at CBSA—the second-largest law enforcement agency in Canada—attempted to address workplace-based cultural challenges that had begun to emerge among the agency's 15,000 employees. In this chapter, we dig deeper into how that transformation unfolded, including a related exploration of equity, diversity, and inclusion (EDI) issues.

Culture, declares Ossowski, is key:

Wherever I've been, I've focused on the culture of the organization. Maybe I've paid too much attention to Drucker: "Culture eats strategy for breakfast." But I really do think it's important. We started on a major transformation process when I arrived here [at CBSA], because the organization found itself in a tough spot financially. We were at the end of a pretty tight restraint period. Volumes were growing. We needed to move forward, but we were somewhat adrift. There was a good vision of what needed to happen, but there wasn't really a strategy in place. The first questions I asked were, "Do we actually have the culture, and the commitment, to go down this road together? And what's it going to take? And why hasn't it happened yet?"

Again, the thing that I keep focusing on is the culture, and the impact that leadership has on the culture of the organization. There's an intentionality here that's so important, around the language and the understanding of yourself as a leader. I'm from the West Coast, right? This is one of those West Coast terms: *Energy follows intention.* What you bring as a leader is that energy. Well, what are your intentions? Where do they come from?

In a 2019 document, CBSA outlined a three-phase strategy for inclusive cultural change—diagnosis, articulation of the vision, and implementation—only the first of which the agency so far has committed to paper.[21] But as we'll see, CBSA is well along into the implementation of their phases 2 and 3. Through much of the following discussion, we'll adopt the broad-brush outline presented in that paper. We'll also provide fine-grained practical approaches to all three phases, both at the CBSA and other organizations.

The starting point: diagnosing the existing culture

You can't change a culture without understanding your starting point. Unfortunately, simply applying a cookie-cutter approach—that is, using something that's worked elsewhere—just won't work. You have to dig deep to figure out what *your* organization needs before you can start deciding how to get there. As Jenn Bitz puts it:

> The diagnostic phase is critical. We spent more than a year on it. During that phase, we gathered as much feedback as we could from employees. We drew on survey data that already existed, but we also worked with employees to make *sense* out of those numbers. If you stay at the symptom level, you're going to come up with the proverbial band-aid. The more you discover the underlying patterns, the better your interventions are likely to be.

One obvious starting point is the *external environment*. What's going on out there in the world that may be determining your current culture and may help or hinder your efforts to change that culture? Consider the example of Silicon Valley, with its famously normative sectoral culture. Are there comparable regional or industry norms—*the way business is done around here*—that come to bear on your company? Are you regularly subjected to regulatory interventions or media scrutiny—and if so, how has that shaped your culture?

Moving inside the organization, you need to consider your history and the kinds of *legacies and momentum* it may have created for you. What events do you look back to with pride (or dismay)? What's your current footprint: small/big, centralized/dispersed, and so on? Has your company been through a reorganization, merger, or divestiture, and if so, was a new culture deliberately created to heal and unite the workforce? Are you dealing with the aftermath of previous failed transformations? (If so, skeptics may abound.) To whom are you currently accountable, and what metrics are included in that accountability? The answer may not be as obvious as it sounds, as John Ossowski sees it:

> It's partly about how you've been incentivized to lead. In my case, I won't get any extra promotion or performance pay for doing CBL [character-based leadership] in CBSA. It's more about, did I keep my minister in a good spot, and did I deliver on government priorities? That's the bottom line. Well, people have to unpack that, and ask themselves, 'Well, how do I actually *achieve* that result?', right? And then take the time to think that through.

In a related vein, you'll probably want to identify the *positive themes* in your current culture. Having good, pride-inducing stories to point to is useful in and of itself. At the same time, stories and storytelling are also useful in conveying lived experience—in other words, in helping us understand who we are and why. Stories serve as connective tissue that can be critically important if and when the organization comes under stress. And finally, stories are what we *actually remember*, so they are one of the most powerful tools in your tool kit.

While that positive reporting is underway, it's also helpful to begin to identify *what's missing* in the current culture. Who's privileged by circumstance? On the flip side of that coin, who's *not* flourishing and why? Is trust present? Is it possible for people in your organization to have tough conversations? In many situations, people lack the language they need to have those kinds of conversations.

Again: look for holes in your shared *language*. What's missing? A pure "business case" or "game plan" tends to omit the kind of connective tissue that—as explained previously—can be provided by storytelling. You and your colleagues need to get beyond bullet points and sound bites to what's *real*. Is there vestigial language which was adopted with good intentions, way back when, that now makes (at least) some people less effective?

This is not necessarily about *supplanting* existing language—e.g., "maximizing shareholder value"—but *putting that language within a new context of character*. And without getting ahead of ourselves, we should point out that an effective infusion of character in the company may make that company *far better* at generating strong returns for shareholders, among other things.

As you can guess, none of this happens easily or quickly. According to John Ossowski:

> We had to examine the language that we used in the past and translate that to the CBL (Character-Based Leadership) language. We had to think through how to begin to embed it as a real foundational part of the organization, and who we want to be, and how we want to lead our folks. Well, all of that took *time*—but it was part of the cultural shift that we wanted to effect in the organization.

The exploration of language is likely to uncover *disparities of perspectives* among key groups. Which current experiences and visions are shared, and which aren't? Sometimes perspectives shake out along obvious fault lines (for example, managers vs. the managed), but sometimes, other fault lines predominate: national, regional, cash cows vs. rising stars, and so on. Which disparities seem to run deepest, and why?

All of the work described previously prepares you to conduct an effective *root-cause analysis*. Certainly, your company has challenges. (All do!) Can you explain where they come from? Are there systems, processes, and practices that are driving them? What are the predominant mindsets of your workforce? What are the stories we're telling ourselves? Sometimes, as Ossowski explains, they are driven in part by new or inexperienced leaders:

> This is especially important for new executives, new leaders. One thing I always say to them is, "Remember that you've likely gotten to where you

are because you were the star analyst, the star performer *yourself.* And now you're achieving results through others. So you're really responsible now for the messages that you send, and the tone that you set, in every single conversation—because you're now the *leader.* You need to understand the culture of your organization, and take responsibility for that culture, through your leadership."

Other times, as explained in previous chapters, it's the result of over-rewarding competence at the expense of character or overrewarding certain dimensions of character and underrewarding others. Sometimes the culture permits, or even promotes, unconscious biases and passive bystanders, suggesting a lack of shared identity. In Jenn Bitz's view, this was a real issue at CBSA:

When we conducted our culture diagnostic, we uncovered some root causes for some of the underlying tensions and divisions within the organization. And one of them was a lack of shared and meaningful identity. So we recognized early on that we were not going to achieve the desired culture transformation, or the needed strategic renewal and modernization of the organization, unless we tackled that issue. We needed to build a shared and meaningful identity— and more recently, a shared sense of *purpose.*

Many organizations discover, to their dismay, that their cultures are impaired by the lack of opportunity for *reflection.* There is a growing body of research that shows "good" people can get involved in character-deficient behavior if organizational processes, systems, and structures don't allow them to stop and consider the consequences of their actions. For example, a plethora of studies have revealed that a broad range of organizational attributes—such as an egoistic ethical climate, performance expectations, skewed reward systems, competitive behavior, arrogant executive behavior, status differences, and peer pressure—can fuel bad decisions. This challenge exacerbates and is exacerbated by a lack of organizational purpose. Resolving these issues is not simply a matter of structural changes to compensation, values, or purpose. As mentioned earlier, the changes need to be in the human connective tissue of relationships, which is both the essence and reflection of organizational culture.

The kind of diagnosis sketched out in the preceding pages is likely to be more difficult and time-consuming than you might expect at the outset. (As noted, CBSA took more than a year to conduct theirs.) To be useful, a compelling diagnosis requires input from many, many people—and this, in turn, implies a necessary action at the end of the diagnostic phase. "If you're going to gather all this feedback from employees," says Jenn Bitz, "you're going to have to reflect it back to them. That takes courage, but that's what's needed. So that's what we did."

We'll focus on communicators and effective communication in subsequent sections. But even at this stage—before any visions are defined or concrete actions proposed—letting your colleagues know that you've heard them is not just a courtesy but a practical obligation. You need to bring them into your diagnosis, which tees up the prescription that is to follow.

Next: articulating the aspirational culture

The second phase in character-based cultural transformation is to articulate the culture to which the organization aspires—in other words, to *say where you want to go*. This phase is all about *ends*, as opposed to the means that the organization will use to get to those ends. ("Means" is Phase 3.) If the goal is to elevate character alongside competence, for example, this is when that important statement gets made.

Any such effort picks up the "positives" discovered in the diagnostic. It may also explicitly state challenges that you intend to address as a group—the things that you are determined to change—but it's worth keeping in mind that aspirational statements generally tilt toward the positive.

Some sort of overarching vision statement is a key building block. CBSA's vision statement reads, "At CBSA we are One Team founded on Trust. We have shared sense of purpose, we value and care for each other, and our workplace is psychologically safe."

Note the positive emphasis on a shared and meaningful *identity*, migrating toward *purpose*—again, deficits that were identified through the CBSA diagnostic. Note, too, the emphasis on a *human* system, as opposed to a cut-and-dried system of inputs and outputs. This process is all about understanding human behaviors and, based on that understanding, saying how you're going to *shift* selected behaviors. It's about making the implicit explicit. Going forward, *who will we be* as we're making our small and big decisions each micro-moment? And it's about the power of bringing your whole self to work, which leads not only to more individual fulfillment but also to better organizational performance.

The process of cultural definition should "go deep," providing as much specificity as possible without driving off potential readers/listeners. Which language, root causes, mindsets, and incentives does your organization seek to change? "We articulated what our desired culture was," recalls Jenn Bitz, "and we defined a whole set of outcomes in pursuit of that desired culture." At the same time, the leaders of the initiative looked for ways to communicate those specifics in a way that would resonate with the whole organization. "Just sharing a logic model won't cut it," Bitz continues. "You need to bring it alive."

Toward that end, the language of leader character proved particularly helpful. As Bitz explains:

In this phase, we relied heavily on the Leader Character model. If you look at our logic model, you'll see character woven all through it—the concepts, the dimensions of character, and so on. In particular, the table that's part of the model—defining the behaviors that you'd see in an organization if this dimension were present or absent—was extremely helpful for us. It gave us a language to use to describe the behaviors that we were seeing or not seeing, and also the behaviors we were looking for in our desired culture.[22]

John Ossowski underscores the importance of a shared and powerful language in this definitional phase:

> It's in part because the [Leader Character] language is so accessible, and it's also in part because it's so practical. . . . What's interesting is that, when they're exposed to these ideas, everyone is excited right away—as opposed to these assessment tools, with their colors and letters and so on. It's about real language, that people can understand and instantly relate to.
>
> For me, it's like that Apollo 13 scene when they dump a bunch of random stuff on the counter and someone says, "O.K., how do they use this stuff to get back home?" This, for me, is another thing that I have that I can bring to the table to achieve the result. I've been through a bunch of other tools—such as Myers-Briggs, or other things—and you come out of those with a color, or a few scrambled letters, and that's it. And there's no conversation to be had, except to say, "Well, I'm this, and you're that." Maybe there's a bit deeper unpacking about how you relate to each other, but generally, that's it. Character-based leadership goes well beyond that.

Let's take this opportunity to revisit the eleven dimensions in the leader character model, with a focus on how those dimensions are manifested in organizational culture—and how they might be called upon to *improve* that culture.

Humility is a key engine for *learning*, especially around self-awareness and, vulnerability. Without humility, we're not going to be open to the possibilities that are presented to us. People who reveal humility acknowledge their strengths and limitations, understand the importance of thoughtfully examining their own opinions and ideas, and embrace opportunities for personal growth and development. They are intensely self-aware, and they do not consider themselves more important or special than others, including if they possess great talents or have a record of great achievements. Humble individuals respect, understand, and appreciate the strengths and contributions of others. Their willingness to be vulnerable allows them to participate in uncomfortable conversations about each other's behavior.

Integrity is about authenticity and candor. We're often ill-equipped for the conversations that we need to have, and our organizations are disadvantaged when people don't feel comfortable presenting an authentic self in the workplace. People with integrity demonstrate a high moral standard and ensure their decisions and actions align with their personal beliefs and values. They are committed to doing the right thing, whether anyone is looking or not.

They value openness and honesty and are therefore candid in their communications, especially during challenging conversations. We should be careful not to conflate Integrity and Character—in other words, Integrity is a *dimension* of character, not a substitute for the word "character."

Temperance helps us deal with difficult subjects by giving us the patience, calm, and self-regulation we need to be able to work through them. People with temperance remain levelheaded when discussions in the workplace become heated or volatile. And yes: while the redress of injustice demands swift action, those actions are likely to be far more effective, and enduring, if people remain self-controlled, composed, and calm during their design and implementation.

Justice: Most cultural changes eventually come to grips with the organization's inherent degree of fairness and equity. People with a deep sense of justice strive to ensure that individuals are treated fairly while remaining objective themselves and keeping personal biases to a minimum. They provide others with the opportunity to voice their opinions on processes and procedures and to seek redress for wrongdoings inside and outside the organization.

Accountability: You can put all of these pieces in place, but if you don't have a sense of who you're accountable to and how you will act on that accountability, it may not matter. What will you *do* with this new knowledge, and how will you do it? People who demonstrate accountability willingly accept responsibility for their words, decisions, and actions. They are willing to step up and take ownership of challenging issues and can be counted on in tough situations. They are also conscientious and will admit when they are wrong or have caused harm. Those who possess strong accountability take ownership of their flawed decisions or misguided behaviors and engage in continuous learning and personal development to root out their own biases.

Courage often grows out of Accountability. People with courage do the *right thing* even though that action may be unpopular, may be actively discouraged, or may result in a negative outcome for themselves. They show an unrelenting determination, confidence, and perseverance in confronting difficult situations. They step into unfamiliar territory, handle uncomfortable conversations, openly address problems, and push for the necessary changes.

Transcendence: Think back to the Nelson Mandela story that we recounted in Chapter 1. People with the gift of transcendence see possibility where others do not. Mandela somehow understood that the game of rugby could be put to work in the vanguard of reconciliation and even help facilitate South Africa's eventual return to the international community. Transcendence is not about a particular policy objective. It's about purpose: *what is the higher ground to which we aspire?*

Drive is a critical component of sustained organizational excellence. So what does "excellence" mean in this organization? What's our "results orientation," and how can we move that agenda faster than we have in the past—moderated, of course, by attributes like dignity and civility? People with drive strive for excellence, have a strong desire to succeed, tackle problems with a sense of urgency, and approach challenges with energy and passion. They make it possible for the organization to create transformative, sustainable change.

Collaboration: People who value collaboration actively support the development and maintenance of positive relationships. They encourage open dialogue and don't react defensively when challenged. They can connect with others on a fundamental level and in a way that fosters the productive sharing of ideas. Collaboration is both the process toward a character-infused culture and one hoped-for endpoint: *how do we get together on this?* We need to be interconnected to get this done. We need to cooperate, so we need to be collegial and open-minded. The *team* is key, and collaboration underpins the effective team.

Humanity: People who engage in behaviors that reflect humanity demonstrate a genuine concern and care for others. They appreciate and identify with others' values, feelings, and beliefs. They understand that people are fallible and offer opportunities for individuals not only to make mistakes but also to learn from them. Humanity helps us see past the visible differences among people to their true individuality and inherent worth.

You'll recall that *judgment* sits in the very middle of the leader character framework, modifying and being modified by the other ten dimensions. When it comes to ambitious cultural change—which involves issues like hierarchies, resource allocations, stakeholder balancing, and so on—a very practical kind wisdom is needed, which we call judgment. Character-infused judgment draws on insight and intuition as much as it relies on intellect and critical thinking. A leader of culture change is always situationally aware, deciding "what is needed now" by having the pulse of their organization and a clear "north star" that guides them.

Note that we present these eleven dimensions in fairly general organizational terms—at the 50,000-foot level. This is appropriate for Phase 2: the aspirational/definitional phase. Again, the goal of this phase is to define desired outcomes, without necessarily defining specific paths toward those outcomes. For example, the organization might declare that it aspires to *transform passive bystanders into active bystanders*—in other words, into the kinds of people who won't tolerate "small" misbehaviors like aggressive joking. In this phase, though, the initiative's leaders might decide to leave the *means* to that end (e.g., "implement bystander intervention training for employees to develop the behaviors and confidence needed to recognize and respond to bullying, intimidation or incidents of racist behavior") to Phase 3, as described later. Remember: *bringing it alive* is an overriding principle, which usually argues for staying out of the weeds.

In short, the audiences of this aspirational statement need to come away both *informed* and *energized.* They need to hold some shared core ideas in their minds, and perhaps their hearts, as the organization heads into its third and final phase of character-based cultural change. Toward that end, Jenn Bitz says, "We put a heavy emphasis on becoming *one team*, founded on trust."

It was a goal, she emphasizes, that drew heavily on all the dimensions of leader character.

The payoff: designing and delivering the desired culture

Let's assume that you've prepared and presented a powerful and persuasive summary of the character-infused culture to which your company aspires. How do you design and deliver upon that hoped-for future? What are the concrete steps you should take, in which order?

"At this stage," says Jenn Bitz, "everything we're doing is working toward that desired culture. We are working to shift behaviors in a whole range of different ways. We monitor the impact of each intervention, and adapt as we go." And character-based leadership, she adds, is central to that effort. Returning to the language of Chapter 6, here is where champions of character-based change need to step forward.

First, *be optimistic.* Be the person who every day says, "I *know* we can get there!" In fact, the kind of purposeful character-based intervention you're attempting is still pretty rare, and you may have to work against that sense of novelty and discomfort. "Be confident," advises Bitz, "that you can bring to the organization what it needs to transform its culture. I've ignored many people who have told me what I'm doing is impossible."

Meanwhile, *watch out for changes in the larger context* that may call for some recalibrations in your plans. John Ossowski realized that COVID-19 created a whole new overlay of obligations and concerns for his culture-changing initiative:

> Today, what with remote work and Zoom calls and so on, it takes that extra bit of effort that it didn't used to, because you don't have those casual interactions that we're accustomed to. Everything's structured in a new way, at least temporarily. And I'll be honest: I'm a little bit fearful for the hybrid workforce of the future, in terms of how leaders will lead as effectively in that space. I think that's really hard. I worry for those workers of the future who just want to stay home locked in their bedrooms and staring at their screens, because that's really going to have an impact on their character development.

Based on your diagnostic work and your description of your aspirational leader character-infused culture, you now need to *develop an implementation strategy* for achieving that culture. This requires thinking on two levels: individual and organizational. The individual level is important because, as we've stressed in previous chapters, leader character takes root at that level. But it's also important because the individuals in your organization have to feel that they're getting something out of this effort personally—especially if they perceive any risk in your initiative. They have to understand that the initiative is about creating ways that they can *bring their whole selves to work*: an outcome that most people enthusiastically endorse once they understand it. You're proposing to *create new opportunities*, with them and for them. The fact is, people respond to the (true) assertion that leaders can be found *anywhere in the organization* and that your proposed change initiative is designed to make that possible.

This inevitably introduces the organization level, which needs to be explored concurrently. What are the systemic and structural barriers that prevent individuals from being and doing their best? How can we work together to break down those barriers? For organizations as well as individuals, character development is all about taking the unconscious and making it conscious—and then fixing what's outmoded, ineffective, or unjust.

Of course, every implementation plan is different. But there are some touchstones that most organizations wind up considering in one way or another. For example, do you need to change the organization's recruitment and selection systems? Do you need to change the definition of "cultural fit" away from "cloning what we already have"—that is, hiring people in your own likeness—to "how well this candidate's values align with those of the organization"? Do you need to address succession planning, which is one of the most powerful ways to link opportunity to aspiration and transcendence? Do you need to change leadership development programs? How about informal mechanisms aimed at mentoring and coaching? How about the whole world of incentives, ranging from compensation to recognition?

As your planning starts getting more and more specific, *look for allies*. We discussed this same challenge in the previous chapter, from the point of view of a champion of character change. Certainly, look up the ladder. Your senior leaders need to enable, endorse, and *trust* you—and they will need to be able to draw upon attributes of leader character (for example, Courage, Humility, and judgment) to do so. Says Bitz:

> Partners within the organization are so important. Back at my former employer, Public Safety Canada, I was fortunate enough to have had two senior executives who were extremely supportive and who served as visible and active sponsors. Having those champions at senior levels is key. And the good news is that in a lot of cases, those leaders can see the value in this, and are happy to step forward.

This last point suggests an important parallel effort: making investments to *develop the leaders you need*. Senior organizational leaders can contribute to the character development of both individuals and of the organization itself by modeling the behaviors associated with the character dimensions they want to see throughout the organization. They can also coach and mentor employees so that they can succeed in the cultures leaders want to create, hiring and promoting those who demonstrate the appropriate behaviors and providing the resources and personal engagement in character-based formal leadership development processes and programs. As you review the leadership team that you need to work with, do you see ways to reinforce individual executives in the principles of leader character? Do you see ways to build and reinforce bonds across that team?

Of course, managing your bosses requires tact and skill. But if you step carefully, you may be rewarded with positive responses from unexpected directions. Bitz recalls once such response:

> I've been working with our senior exec team, to help them build trust and lead by example. One of the members of that team recently said to me, "You know, Jenn, what I appreciate about what we've achieved with this team is that we inspire each other not to be jerks." Well, isn't *that* an important observation? Haven't we all been in teams where that wasn't the case?

Concurrently, you need to *develop lateral allies*. Some of this work has already begun as you've worked with colleagues to diagnose the company and to articulate a desired future. For example, you've probably begun working with partners on the human resources team, as suggested in Chapter 6. These are critical potential allies, especially those who work in the leadership-development area. It's worth noting that as a rule, cultural transformation has *not* been located within the HR branch, so you may find that these professionals are happy to be welcomed in as key players in your implementation phase.

Another key lateral resource, mentioned previously, is the communications team. Assuming that they have responsibility for internal as well as external communications, they know how to speak in terms that employees will respond to—and they have communications channels waiting to be deployed in support of cultural change. Again, *stories* are key, and good communicators know how to use them. As Bitz points out:

> We've invited employees to tell their own stories, which we share on our internal website. And they're not necessarily the typical kinds of stories that celebrate hard work and getting the job done at all costs. They're about *human* actions. Humanity, humility, collaboration, temperance. Interacting with the public, which is what more than half of our people do all day, at the border. About people helping each other out, about the joy and heartbreak of our jobs. And this underscores, "This is what we want. This is what we're looking for." It's about the *how*, and the *who*, as much as the what.

A third group of potential lateral allies includes your organization's strategists, planners, and risk managers (and even IT managers, which is where CRA started, as noted in Chapter 6). These are functions that traditionally stay out of "who we are" initiatives in favor of "what we do" strategies. But you can and should make the argument to these colleagues that your effort is aimed at enhancing the performance of the whole organization. "When you introduce leader character," argues Bitz, "you are actually fostering efficiency and productivity." In bringing these kinds of quantitatively-oriented colleagues on board, you need to persuade them that the "serious work" of the organization is not elsewhere but actually begins *here*, in your initiative, with their help. As soon as you have data to support this assertion, provide it to those colleagues.

So yes, allies up the ladder and sideways are important. But once again, it's important to always remember that these kinds of formal partnerships can only take you so far. Ultimately, it's about grassroots engagement. Once again, you need to *motivate and recruit each individual employee*. As Bitz puts it, "You need people within the organization to step up and say, '*I'll* take the lead on this!' And that's what will make the changes possible."

A related prescription that grows out of this kind of motivation: *strive for character contagion*. Maybe you'll start your implementation with a focus on leaders, traditionally defined. (Especially where resources are limited, you have to start somewhere.) But at the same time, you should be sniffing out every opportunity to infuse a leader character–based culture throughout the organization: a fast-moving change process in which each convert brings along the next.

Perhaps it goes without saying, but you should *be prepared for surprises*. Despite all of your due diligence in the diagnostic culture-articulation phases, unexpected legacy issues (good and bad) are very likely to pop up. For example, you may start encountering what might be called "identity issues," meaning that certain people or groups of people conclude that their professional identities are being challenged by the process you're leading. Well, is there some truth in that? If so, is some sort of recalibration of the implementation needed? Keep in mind, too, that these kinds of objections—even hotly presented—may be indicators of success. How so? People are feeling engaged enough to call the organization out on this particular issue. In other words, as Bitz argues, someone shining a spotlight on what seem to be emerging paradoxes and contradictions may be a momentum indicator:

> These may mean that you're on the right track. If you're hearing, "Hey—you said X, but what's actually happening is Y," that means that you're starting to create healthy feedback loops, that employees are starting to believe that things *are* changing, and that they want you to know where they're *not* changing. It means that they're starting to have that sense of agency, and to believe that speaking up matters. They're demonstrating what I call a fine-tuned Hypocrisy Meter.

These are circumstances that will require more good judgment to work through. Most likely, a superficial response probably won't be enough. Can your critics be persuaded to help you come up with a nuanced, effective one?

From day one of the implementation phase, but especially as time passes and new cultural foundations are put in place, *establish ways to measure progress.* These may include both informal and formal measures. In the former category, keep an ear out for new kinds of conversations that are occurring, an increasing number of "Aha!" moments, and new testimonies about how people are feeling in this new environment. Do people report an enhanced sense of personal dignity, or acceptance, or psychological safety (even if they don't use these exact words)? Conversely, is bad behavior becoming less frequent and therefore more visible? Don't be surprised if there is a profusion of these kinds of informal measures. Says Bitz, "It's like watering a desert."

Combine your findings in this realm with more formal, trackable metrics—for example, survey-derived data. Natacha Prudent, director general, Management Cadre Programs, CBSA, provides one example:

> Based on our year-over-year tracking, I can say with confidence that the agency's efforts to incorporate Leader Character into our practices has contributed to a 9 percent improvement in CBSA's public service employee survey results—basically, in the trust and confidence measures vis a vis senior management, and in the area of leading by example. This is huge, and a great outcome for the agency.

Specific innovations may generate new kinds of data—for example, changing the organization's weighting in recruitment and selection criteria—which may in turn suggest future iterations in this realm. This is a path to both reinforcing what's already been done and improving upon it.

And finally, *be patient and persistent.* "Culture change takes years," says Bitz, who points out that as of this writing, CBSA is well into its third year of character-based cultural change. "Temperance is absolutely needed!" Referring to the total number of people in the CBSA workforce, she adds, "We're not at 15,000 yet. But we'll get there."

When you run into roadblocks and frustrations—which you will!—remember that experience at CBSA and elsewhere suggests that cultural change gets easier as time goes on. Bitz says that at some point, the effort reaches a tipping point:

> It's like an avalanche. Once that last little change in temperature happens, or that last little shift in the wind comes along, it sets off that avalanche. Then you can step back and let it do its thing.

One last suggestion as you work toward that avalanche: invite your colleagues to "write the story that has yet to be written"—in other words, a prediction of something that the organization is about to do of which they'll be incredibly proud. When you've gathered enough submissions, bring them together in a collective document, and invite your colleagues to explore this document in search of common themes.

If you've done your job well—and if the avalanche is close at hand—those common themes will be there to be found.

EDI: a focused intervention

Now let's look sideways at an important topic that often arises when organizations attempt large-scale, character-focused change: equity, diversity, and inclusion, or EDI. Why are these topics often interrelated? In part, it's because strengthening character makes it easier for individuals and organizations to address the EDI agenda. In fact, we argue that the two are inseparable: *to succeed at EDI, you need to draw on character*. Character leadership supercharges EDI, by bringing the full individuality of the person—their best self—to the table. As co-author Seijts recently wrote:

> If we really want to address systemic racism in organizations, we must first attend to the people who work there. This is because their individual and collective character, revealed through behavior, drives and determines organizational processes, systems, structures, and culture. . . . Character equips people with consciousness and the conduct to embrace and cultivate equity, diversity, and inclusion in their organizations and in their lives.[23]

"If your organization is considering or is in the midst of an EDI initiative," confirms Natacha Prudent, "Leader Character can be an indispensable ally in making that initiative successful."

First, some EDI background: the goal of EDI is to increase the representation and degree of inclusion of identified communities—often but not always ethnic/racial minorities and women—and to reduce the career-success gaps between privileged and nonprivileged communities.

Many people, especially privileged people, underestimate the need for EDI. They don't comprehend the emotional cost that minorities incur through the process of "armoring up" to try and achieve organizational inclusion. The truth is that adopting a particular style—that is, dressing, talking, and presenting oneself in certain prescribed ways—can be psychologically taxing. And the higher up the corporate ladder one goes, the more costly that process of "strapping on the armor" can be. If presenting an "executive presence," as traditionally defined, means projecting a certain look, or sound, or body language, that may pose a high and unfair hurdle. This is especially true if, as is the case for many minorities, good coaching and mentorship toward that end has not been readily available.

What happens if those hurdles are too simply high? Here we arrive in the realm of self-fulfilling prophecies: the people who are wearing these kinds of psychological hobbles probably *won't* succeed, and the organization will therefore lose access to their particular kind of talent and potential. In many cases, that's a significant loss. Here's one way of looking at it: people who've been marginalized by society and who have *still* had initial success within an indifferent (or hostile) organization most likely have developed a well-honed sense of Justice and judgment, among other qualities. If those people leave, some measure of Justice and judgment goes with them.

But what if a different standard were applied? For example, what if "executive presence" were defined as *strength of character*—derived from lived experience and combined with demonstrated competence and commitment?

EDI is not a new addition to the corporate agenda. But the very durability of the EDI challenge underscores the point that organizations have struggled with it for a long time and continue to struggle with it today. Why? Because EDI *tests* and *challenges* character—and because until recently, organizations haven't really had a working definition of "character," because they haven't had the toolkit of leader character to draw upon; they've been stuck.

Stated positively, if we can couple EDI with the language of leader character, we can begin to crack this difficult and durable nut—as in, "What does EDI require in terms of humility? What does it require in terms of humanity? What parts of accountability have I not fully developed, which are needed to move this important agenda item forward?"

As John Ossowski puts it:

> Looking at EDI from the Leader Character perspective: again, the language transcends the different cultural backgrounds you might have. These are universal attributes. It doesn't matter what your heritage is, or what culture you might have come from. These are universal attributes. The neutrality of the language that everyone can buy into.

This may sound straightforward or even easy, but in most cases, it's not. When EDI is brought into an organization, as noted, it tests the character of the individuals involved. At the same time, though, leader character—tested and strengthened—*supports* EDI. This dynamic is summarized in Figure 7.1.

In other words, a balanced, well-developed character equips individuals with the coping skills to withstand or outright oppose negative situational

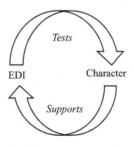

Figure 7.1 The Dynamic Relationship Between Equity, Diversity, Inclusion, and Character

pressures. This places them in a strong position to address the numerous work-place challenges—often built directly into organizational processes, systems, and structures—associated with implementing initiatives that support EDI. Meanwhile, character helps individuals thrive because they reap the rewards stemming from consistent good judgement and hence contribute to sustained excellence of individuals, organizations, and communities. Character there-fore acts as both a personal resource and as a coping mechanism for initiating and sustaining positive change in organizations.

We've already presented a version of Table 7.2, summarizing the organiza-tional consequences of an excess or deficiency of our eleven character dimen-sions (see Figure 3.2). In Figure 7.2,[24] we tailor that table to focus on EDI.

Dimension	If Present	If Absent
Accountability	Ownership for decisions, behaviors, and outcomes; recognition of how individuals contributed to or upheld unjust practices	Denial of injustices embedded in organizational practices and policies; failure to deliver on EDI metrics; culture of blame; and hence individuals' potential is limited
Courage	Openly address problems and opportunities; challenging decisions are made; calling out of racist behaviors and micro-aggressions; EDI initiatives thrive	Lack of conversations; satisficing rather than maximizing is the norm; moral muteness prevails; resistance to EDI initiatives is unaddressed
Collaboration	Inclusion thrives; benefits of diversity are realized through forging deep, personal relationships; sharing of a common goal	No trust and information sharing; deep sense of individualism; individuals remain focused on self (feelings, outcomes, positions)
Drive	Proactive in addressing injustices and racist behaviors; sustained momentum around EDI-focused priorities	Lethargy towards solving EDI challenges; racial inequalities persevere; no improvement in engagement or EDI metrics
Humanity	Deep understanding of what is important to all stakeholders; and a culture of respect, caring	Failure to acknowledge the importance of critical social interactions and issues; lack of genuine interest to improve the lives of all

Figure 7.2 Impact on Building Cultures of Equity, Diversity, and Inclusion (EDI) When Character Dimensions Are Present and Absent

Dimension	If Present	If Absent
Humility	Willingness to identify and discuss personal mistakes and biases; support of continuous learning and personal development as it pertains to EDI	Arrogance and blind-spots; no listening; lack of perspective-taking; and individuals are unaware of the impact of their behavior on others
Integrity	Transparency and candor for effective communication and problem-solving; a principled approach to tackling obstacles to EDI initiatives	People operate from a position of self-interest; gaslighting or manipulative response to causes of inequity and injustice; and mistrust remains or develops
Judgment	Awareness of own biases; recognizes biases in others; acknowledges the need for healing; responds in a thoughtful manner to EDI challenges; able to understand the complexity of dismantling systemic racism	Absence of reflection and learning; lack of what shaped deeply-held personal beliefs and beliefs in others; and challenges in reasoning effectively (and respectfully) in uncertain and ambiguous situations
Justice	Biases are kept to a minimum; wrongdoings are addressed; trust and respect deepens among individuals; an atmosphere of psychological safety develops to address the challenges with EDI initiatives	Inequities in treatment (continue to) exist; no resources and opportunities are made available to systemically marginalized individuals; and tensions rise
Temperance	Thoughtful consideration to EDI; remains calm, composed during difficult conversations; resists compulsive behaviors	Unable to control emotions in difficult, tense situations; and conflict ensues
Transcendence	Acknowledges the opportunities and possibilities of creating a more just organization; hope for and confidence in a better future	Failure to acknowledge and appreciate the opportunities associated with EDI initiatives; a win—lose perspective toward EDI; deep cynicism

Figure 7.2 (Continued)

Just like the larger cultural-change agenda discussed previously, every or-ganization's approach to EDI is necessarily different. Based on your diagnosis and vision statement, you can and should design an implementation plan that's most relevant to your circumstances. That said, here's a possible sequencing of key activities based on one company's recent experience:

1. First, *activate accountability and temperance*. This is a first step toward get-ting people comfortable with new ways of thinking—and keeping that pro-cess civil.
2. Second, *connect with others from diverse backgrounds*, and show a genuine interest in them. This will inform your change agenda and, at the same time, activate Humanity and Cooperation.
3. Third, *diagnose and root out biases*. Be prepared to hear things like, "My success is all self-created," meaning that everyone should be able to pull themselves up by their own bootstraps. This is overwhelmingly untrue: many successful people are also privileged people. But how will you make that point and still recruit that person as an ally?
4. Fourth, in your initiative's implementation phase, *embed changes in policy* to ensure sustainability. Your company's leadership will eventually change; your EDI focus doesn't have to leave with the departing CEO.

As with cultural change, described previously, look for ways to *create an ava-lanche*. Again, story-telling can play a key role. Character contagion is a natural phenomenon that can be pushed toward the good. Studies have shown that people are motivated to engage in positive, virtuous behaviors and to perform good deeds when they see someone else perform positive, helpful acts. People generally tend to mirror others' kindness and generosity across different types of helping behav-iors and different types of people in need of help. Thus, the spread of behaviors, attitudes, and affects from one individual to another can be a powerful contributor to initiating and sustaining change in the area of EDI. Meanwhile, leaders have to communicate their intolerance of intolerance and act in ways that reinforce EDI-related initiatives—not least by allocating resources to those efforts.

What not to be

As we've seen, corporate culture is inextricable from character and is defined both from the top down and from the bottom up. We've also seen, in the examples of Boeing and Barry-Wehmiller, that corporate culture is ever-changing—always susceptible to improvement or corruption. It's worth noting that BW today is not the same company that it was during the crisis of the Great Recession, and what-ever comes next for BW in terms of culture will certainly be different from the BW culture of today. Comments on the Glassdoor website from a recently retired St. Louis-based network engineer make the point:

> If you like a challenge, then BW is a place for you. IT (specifically operations) is run very lean. This can be a good and bad thing—good in that you get a hand on everything you want to, bad in that you can never really finish anything you started. You have to be self-directed, especially if remote. But don't worry— you'll find that there is plenty to do, and boy, will there be lots of fires . . .
>
> Leadership is a mixed bag. In my time, I found pockets and some great leaders. People who work here for the most part are great, but very over- worked, and most of them do not even know it . . .
>
> Culture was very strong when I started. They really did push the "every- body matters" culture, and for the most part, it was well received. That was back in 2015. In 2022, the company was pretty much like any other in corpo- rate America. The culture is still there in pockets, but nothing like what it was. Please: if you are looking to work at BW, don't do it for the culture, [because] as of [this] writing you will be disappointed . . .
>
> Bob is trying to leave a legacy. His son Kyle recently took the reins, and has a much more business mind set. This has certainly been reflected in the culture . . .
>
> Advice to management: You need to seriously look at the leadership struc- ture, and bring back some of the culture. Remember what got you to where you are today.[25]

Remember what got you to where you are today: sound advice both for compa- nies that are riding high and those that are heading for the rocks. But how do you "bring back" culture? (Presumably there are many at Boeing who would like to hear the answer to this question.) Or even more challenging: how do you create a "from-scratch" culture, infused with leader character, where that kind of culture hasn't existed before? How do you mix an EDI initiative, which is likely to be challenging enough in its own right, into that kind of culture reformation?

We are convinced that leader character speaks to both challenges, in part be- cause for most people, building character in their professional lives concurrently builds character in their personal lives. Again quoting Jenn Bitz:

> People very quickly relate this to their personal lives, and in a very positive way. You'll hear people say, "This is really going to help me in a conflict that I'm having with someone right now." In other words, people discover that it contributes to their own well-being. And don't we all want more of that? Of course we do. In this complex fast-moving, 24/7 world, something that helps us care for ourselves and feel better is always going to be welcome.

We'll conclude with a four-word cultural prescription offered to Jenn Bitz by a senior executive at CBSA, perhaps partially in jest: *don't be a jerk*. Yes, it sounds simplistic, and even a little silly. But turn it over in your mind: if no one in our work group or in our personal lives acted like a jerk, wouldn't that be a desirable culture? Wouldn't our teams be *great*? If we rewarded people for having integrity, being candid and transparent, and for exercising great judgment, all in balance, wouldn't that be the culture we all wanted to live in?

Notes

1 Much of this story comes from a merger-related article in the *New York Times*, online at www.nytimes.com/1996/12/16/news/boeing-to-buy-mcdonnell-douglas.html, accessed March 14, 2023. According to the *Seattle Times,* Boeing was displaced by Amazon in 2021 as the state's largest employer. See www.seattletimes.com/business/amazon/amazon-surpasses-boeing-as-washington-states-biggest-employer/, accessed March 14, 2023.

2 This section draws substantially on *Flying Blind: The 737 MAX Tragedy and the Fall of Boeing,* Peter Robison's compelling account of the merger and its tragic aftermath, published in 2021 by Doubleday.

3 See, for example, "McDonnell dividend to jump 71%," by John Holusha, in the October 29, 1994 edition of the *New York Times*. According to the article, the stock buyback—and associated three-for-one stock split and dividend increase—was Harry Stonecipher's first major action as CEO, Online at www.nytimes.com/1994/10/29/business/mcdonnell-dividend-to-jump-71.html, accessed March 14, 2023.

4 See "The long-forgotten flight that sent Boeing off course," *Atlantic*, November 2019, online at www.theatlantic.com/ideas/archive/2019/11/how-boeing-lost-its-bearings/602188/, accessed March 14, 2023. The article's title refers to the stunt that Philip Condit performed to reveal which city had won the bidding for Boeing's headquarters: Chicago, Denver, or Dallas. On the day of the announcement, Condit's plane filed a flight plan to each city. Only after the 737 was airborne was its destination revealed: Chicago.

5 See the article "G.E. plans move to Connecticut," published in the July 3, 1971, edition of the *New York Times*; see www.nytimes.com/1971/07/03/archives/ge-plans-move-to-connecticut-shift-of-headquarters-here-to.html, accessed April 10, 2023.

6 Harry Stonecipher was actually more highly compensated than Philip Condit during his first year at Boeing. He claimed to be keeping a list of promises that Condit had made to him as part of the price of the merger and extracted a series of concessions from Condit that seemed to substantiate the claim; see *Flying Blind,* pp. 59–63. Also, Stonecipher "made a forceful, threatening first impression," according to a generally positive article in the *Seattle Times,* online at www.seattletimes.com/business/stoneciphers-blueprint-built-a-stronger-boeing/, accessed March 14, 2023.

7 See *Flying Blind,* p. 88

8 This revelation was made more awkward by the fact that Harry Stonecipher was one of the architects of the company's recently promulgated ethics policy. See the March 14, 2005, edition of the *New York Times,* online at www.nytimes.com/2005/03/14/business/wife-of-ousted-boeing-chief-seeks-divorce-after-50-years.html, accessed March 14, 2023.

9 From *Flying Blind,* p. 102; and also from the *New York Times* obituary for 3M's research chemist Spencer Silver, who first developed the not-too-sticky adhesive that was put to use by Fry. See the May 13, 2021, edition of the *Times*, online at www.nytimes.com/2021/05/13/business/spencer-silver-dead.html, accessed March 14, 2023.

10 From the June 26, 2006 *FlightGlobal* interview with Jim McNerney, online at www.flightglobal.com/the-flight-interview-james-mcnerney-boeing-chief-executive-transcript/68115.article, accessed March 14, 2023.

11 A write-up of the award is online at www.packworld.com/supplier-news/news/22499239/barrywehmiller-companies-inc-barrywehmiller-ceo-bob-chapman-named-tharse-ceo-of-the-year-by-society-for-human-resource-management, accessed March 14, 2023.

12 The Barry-Wehmiller and Bob Chapman stories related here are drawn largely from Harvard Business School Case 9–717–420—"Truly Human Leadership at Barry-Wehmiller"—and from *Everybody Matters: The Extraordinary Power of Caring for Your People Like Family,* a 2015 book written by Bob Chapman and Raj Sisodia.

13 In fact, according to the cited Harvard Business School Case, between 1989 and 2013 the company's revenues grew from $20 million to $1.6 billion.

14 The GPL is online at www.barrywehmiller.com/story/history, accessed March 14, 2023.

15 This comment by Maureen Schloskey is also online at www.barrywehmiller.com/story/history, accessed March 14, 2023. The authors of the document signed it at the bottom of the original document—"one of the proudest moments of my life," Schloskey later said.

16 Peter Robison, in *Flying Blind* (page 74), also recounts the story of Boeing CEO Philip Condit becoming enamored of Harvard Business School Professor Clayton Christensen's 2001 argument that great companies were able to couple and decouple their mundane and high-skill businesses in ways that allowed them to minimize the negative impacts of business cycles. "We've got to do this," Condit said—a personal embrace that soon rippled out across the organization. Ironically, by 2014, Christensen himself was backing away from the idea (page 114).

17 Schneider, B. (1987). The people make the place. *Personnel Psychology*, 40: 437–453.

18 The views expressed by Jenn Bitz are her own.

19 This chapter draws heavily on three podcasts produced by two of this book's authors: Mary Crossan and Bill Furlong. It includes numerous quotes from the subjects of those podcasts: Jennifer Bitz, Director General, Culture, at the Canada Border Services Agency, or CBSA (unpublished podcast): Natacha Prudent, Director General, Management Cadre Programs, CBSA, podcast at www.questionofcharacter.com/episodes/episode-01-leader-character-101a-r9rxc-3r552-3y9df-baf3j-4zexg-j8bst; and John Ossowski, whom we have introduced in earlier chapters, and who as of this writing is president of CBSA, podcast at www.youtube.com/watch?v=_Ics2GCCs1I.

20 Ossowski also made a brief appearance in Chapter 6, as a result of his stint as the leader of the Canada Revenue Agency.

21 See "CBSA Culture Diagnostic," December 2019. The diagnostic can be found here: https://www.ivey.uwo.ca/leadership/research-resources/reports/cbsa-culture-diagnostic/

22 We include a modified version of the table to which Bitz refers in our discussion of EDI-specific initiatives that follows.

23 Seijts, G. H., & Milani, K. Y. (2022). The application of leader character to building cultures of equity, diversity, and inclusion. *Business Horizons*, 65(5): 573–590; online at www.sciencedirect.com/science/article/abs/pii/S0007681321001300?via%3Dihub, accessed March 14, 2023.

24 This Figure is taken from the Seijts and Milani (2022) article.

25 On the Glassdoor website at www.glassdoor.com/Reviews/Barry-Wehmiller-Reviews-E17686.htm, accessed March 14, 2023.

Chapter 8

Character's role in risk management

The first crash of a Boeing 737 MAX 8 occurred on October 29, 2018, just outside Jakarta's Soekarno-Hatta International Airport.[1]

A sensor on the left side of the Lion Air jet, outside and below the pilot's window, had a small but lethal misalignment. This "angle-of-attack" (AoA) sensor was designed to help keep the plane from stalling, and mechanics inspecting the plane had failed to spot the misalignment. Now, just after takeoff, the Lion Air's jet's nose started bucking and plunging violently, resisting the pilots' increasingly desperate efforts to pull it up and gain altitude. The onboard Quick Reference Handbook—provided by Boeing and now frantically consulted by the pilot—gave no answers. The pilot and co-pilot fought with the plane, but to no avail. It crashed into the sea, nose down in a nearly vertical position, at 500 miles per hour. All 189 people aboard perished.

Over the following month, Boeing publicly insisted that the plane was safe and that the crash was the result of pilot error and bad management on the part of Lion Air. But slowly, an alternative story began to emerge: that Boeing had installed software on the plane that could effectively take over control of the plane's horizontal stabilizer and had chosen not to tell anybody about it. When that software program got bad data from the faulty AoA sensor, it effectively wrested control of the plane from the crew—and forced it down.

These two conflicting stories co-existed for several months, until March 10, 2019, when a second MAX 8 crashed shortly after takeoff from the Addis Ababa airport in Ethiopia. This crash killed all 157 people aboard. Finally, the real story came clear: a string of computer code, misinformed by errant data from the errant AoA sensor, was overriding pilots and crashing airplanes.

The 737 was originally conceived in the late 1960s as a no-frills, low-end plane, for use by smaller airlines in secondary markets low-end airports. It reused a lot of components from the earlier 727 but did away with some of that predecessor craft's more expensive components. Nevertheless, in that era, the 737 was subjected to rigorous testing. When problems came up, they were fixed. If pilots testing the plane made suggestions, they were listened to. If safety was in question, senior management allowed the project to go over budget and fix the problem.

DOI: 10.4324/9781003341215-9

The plane first flew commercially in January 1967. Early sales were dismal, but then fate intervened. A DC-10—McDonnell Douglas' response to the 747—crashed outside of Paris in 1974. When a second DC-10 crashed near Chicago in 1979, a federal judge grounded the entire DC-10 fleet: a draconian intervention that hadn't happened in more than 30 years. Sales of the DC-10 plummeted, and the 737 now had a market opening.

Boeing kept up the heat on its archrival by designing and introducing two more new models—the 757 and 767—both of which had far more sophisticated cockpit controls than the 737. But the humble 737 held its own in a changing marketplace. Prompted in part by deregulation, the three leading US airlines adopted a hub-and-spoke strategy, which required a fleet of smaller jets to shuttle passengers to and from a "hub" airport en route to their ultimate destinations. The 737 fit into that strategy perfectly.

That was the good news. The bad news was that Airbus in 1984 introduced its 150-seat A320. Not only was it wider than the 737—providing more comfortable seating to its passengers—but it had more sophisticated cockpit controls. First overseas and then in the domestic US market, airlines started buying the plane, which prompted Boeing to introduce new and bigger versions of the 737. But this kind of iterative tinkering led to new problems. Two 737 crashes in the early 1990s led investigators to speculate that the aging aircraft was starting to reach its limits. "We believe the airplane is trying to tell us something," commented the head of the National Transportation Safety Board at the time.[2]

Airbus scooped up more and more of Boeing's former customers. In 2003, the European upstart officially became the world's largest manufacturer of commercial airliners, delivering 305 planes to Boeing's 281.[3] Even so, the 737 hung in there, selling some 7,000 units in the 1990s, serving as a much-needed cash cow that accounted for something like a third of Boeing's profits. But in an effort to protect those margins, Boeing took the plane down market—for example, requiring customers to pay extra for items formerly included as standard equipment. One of those extras was a second AoA indicator, this one mounted in the cockpit—an "extra," by the way, that neither Lion Air nor Ethiopian Airlines chose to purchase.

Airbus kept up its innovating ways. In 2010, it began taking orders for what it called the "A320neo," with "neo" standing for "new engine option"—in other words, more powerful. By the following July, Boeing—faced with the potential desertion of stalwart customer American Airlines, among others—announced plans for a new, far more powerful 737: soon to be dubbed the "737 MAX."

The plan made Wall Street happy because the redesigned 737 would cost only $2.5 billion, as opposed to the $20 billion that an entirely new plane would cost. On the other hand, the 737 was already almost a half-century old—in fact, the 13th generation of the plane. Boeing was now playing catch-up—if that. At a board presentation in 2012, the 737 MAX was described as "stingy with a purpose." The informal slogan proposed for the design team was "more for less."

Outside-world trends also were converging in worrisome ways. A continuing federal push for deregulation led to, among other things, a gradual ceding of authority from the Federal Aviation Administration to the manufacturers that it supposedly regulated.[4] At the same time, bare-bones customers like Southwest were demanding no increases in pilot training and built large financial penalties into their orders if changes to the 737 required any such extra training. And this was no small threat: by 2019, Southwest had ordered 246 of the planes.[5]

Against that backdrop, Boeing made the fateful decision to leave the cockpit of the 737 more or less unchanged. This meant that unlike its 30-year-old siblings, the 757s and 767s, the revised 737 still wouldn't have an electronic checklist to help pilots respond to various kinds of alerts. This was in an era when a generation of older pilots was retiring; in their places increasingly were younger pilots who were accustomed to—and reliant upon—more modern flight decks.

It wasn't that Boeing made no changes to the 737. For example, it introduced a new MCAS (Maneuvering Characteristics Augmentation System) software program to help control the pitch of the plane to prevent stalls.[6] But these changes were downplayed by Boeing as unimportant—and therefore not subject to review by the FAA. Again, such a review was a real outside-world threat: In the worst scenario, the FAA could require recertification of the entire aircraft, which in terms of schedule and budget would have represented a disaster for Boeing. And even short of that, the agency could ask for more pilot training in simulators:

> Though software was convenient, a concern was that the FAA would treat it as a new feature that would jeopardize what employees began referring to as a "program directive": no simulator training. Keith Leverkuhn, the MAX program manager, tracked the training issue as one of a half dozen "risks" that he updated superiors about regularly.[7]

The FAA, increasingly compliant in the face of Boeing's demands, agreed to minimal certification standards. But some Boeing engineers weren't satisfied with leaving the plane's alert system in a half-modernized state: old hardware with new (and submerged) software. As journalist and Boeing chronicler Peter Robison recounts:

> One of the most vocal was Curtis Ewbank, a graduate of Embry-Riddle Aeronautical University then in his late twenties . . .
> In 2014, Ewbank was among a group of flight controls experts who started raising questions about how erroneous information from the plane's sensors might compromise the MAX's safety. Sensors like the angle-of-attack vanes or the pitot tubes, which measure airspeed, sit outside the plane. They're vulnerable to bird strikes, damage from jetway equipment, or other obstructions . . . Ewbank and the others urged implementation of a backup system

called "synthetic airspeed" already in use on the [787] Dreamliner—essentially a computer program to compare values of all the sensors. If an illogical reading came from any of them—such as the AoA vanes linked to the new MCAS software—it would be deactivated.

In rejecting the safety enhancement, managers twice cited concerns about the "cost and potential (pilot) training impact."

"People will have to die before Boeing will change things," Ewbank was told by his manager.

When Ewbank and the others raised the idea a third time in a meeting with the MAX's chief engineer, Michael Teal, he cited the same [objections] as he killed the proposal. Keith Leverkuhn, Teal's boss and the MAX program manager, later said he never even heard of the idea.[8]

Ewbank left Boeing in 2015, frustrated by his company's skewed priorities. "I was willing to stand up for safety and quality," he wrote in an internal complaint later forwarded by Boeing to the Justice Department, "but was unable to actually have an effect in those areas."[9]

The following year, a top Boeing pilot name Mark Forkner "flew" in the 737 MAX simulator and reported several hours later—in a late-night email exchange with a colleague—that the plane was "running rampant." He blamed the problem squarely on MCAS. He then reflected that in his conversations with regulators, he had lied, "unknowingly," about the circumstances under which MCAS would kick in and the fact that the program was designed to reactivate itself repeatedly.

"It wasn't a lie," the colleague wrote back immediately. "No one told us that was the case."

"I'm levelling off at like 4000 feet, 230 knots," Forkner went on, further reflecting upon his experience in the simulator, "and the plane is trimming itself like crazy. I'm like, WHAT? . . . Granted, I suck at flying, but even this was egregious."[10]

Chief engineer Michael Teal claimed in testimony before Congress in the wake of the 737 MAX crashes that he didn't know that MCAS could activate itself repeatedly—an attribute that could greatly increase a pilot's difficulty in controlling the airplane.[11] He also testified that he didn't know that the 737 MAX had only one AoA indicator—arguably something that the plane's chief engineer should have known.[12] For his part, Teal's boss, Keith Leverkuhn, told the House Transportation and Infrastructure Committee that he didn't consider the 737 MAX program a failure and that a larger "industry standard" was actually to blame:

I think based on our understanding and our assumptions of flight crew actions, that [using a single AoA sensor] was a mistake. Clearly what was in error was our assumptions regarding the human machine interaction. Because the process relied on the industry standard of pilot reaction to a particular failure. And what was clear post accidents was that assumption was incorrect.[13]

A footnote, and perhaps a grim foreshadowing: the 737 MAX's first test flight came in January 2016, just under three years before the Jakarta disaster, with several thousand people gathered outside a suburban Seattle factory and many more employees watching online. The two very experienced pilots in the cockpit fired up the jet's massive engines—and to their surprise, the aircraft responded by rolling forward several feet. It turned out that no one had set the parking brake. And the pilots, as good as they were, had overlooked that item in the preflight checklist.

Not for the first or last time, the "human machine interaction" had generated a surprise.

Risk and risk management

How much risk did the 737 MAX pose to Boeing? To its employees? To its customers? To its shareholders?

Perhaps the worst way to answer these questions is after the fact. By that backward measure, of course, the 737 MAX posed enormous risks—many of which, tragically, came to be realized. Hundreds of people lost their lives, and thousands of loved ones, friends, and colleagues suffered those losses. The company's formerly sterling reputation took a major hit. The 737 MAX fleet was grounded for two years, leading to massive legal snarls and lost sales. All told, Boeing lost an estimated $20 billion. Last and least, Boeing CEO Dennis Muilenburg—who at first blamed everyone except his own company for the disasters—lost his job, although his hard landing was softened by a $62.2 million golden parachute.[14]

Of course, a far better way to conduct a risk assessment question is prospectively—that is, looking into the future, spotting liabilities that are lurking out there and figuring out ways to try to manage those liabilities. Most often, this is accomplished through an Enterprise Risk Management (ERM) program.

"Risk management" is one of those business terms—like portfolio diversification, planned obsolescence, cost/benefit analysis, and so on—that sound clear and concrete to the ear and *don't* sound like a ground for ambiguity or debate. But as it turns out, that's not even close to true. A check-in with Google, for example, turns up references to the *four types of risk management*, the *five essential steps of a risk management process*, the *seven principles of risk management*, and so on—a confusing welter of concepts and processes.

As you dig deeper, it becomes clear that risk management—and by extension, a corporate ERM—is more or less what a company chooses to make of it. In some contexts, the ERM is both a framework and process, which can comprise things like risk taxonomies, risk registers, risk three lines of defense, risk dashboards, risk mitigation plans, and risk heat maps. The analyses generated through the use of these kinds of tools may wind up being presented to executives, the risk committee of the board and/or the entire board, and/or outside parties, sometimes including borrowers, investors, rating agencies, and regulators. But because every context is different, every ERM is unique as well.

Are there also commonalities? IBM has produced a template that describes a "typical" risk-management process as follows:

> At the broadest level, risk management is a system of people, processes and technology that enables an organization to establish objectives in line with values and risks.
>
> A successful risk assessment program must meet legal, contractual, internal, social and ethical goals, as well as monitor new technology-related regulations. By focusing attention on risk and committing the necessary resources to control and mitigate risk, a business will protect itself from uncertainty, reduce costs and increase the likelihood of business continuity and success. Three important steps of the risk management process are risk identification, risk analysis and assessment, and risk mitigation and monitoring.[15]

Risk management, continues IBM, "is a nonstop process that adapts and changes over time. Repeating and continually monitoring the processes can help assure maximum coverage of known and unknown risks."

We should underscore four things, at this point. Note that the first word in IBM's list of ERM components is "people." People exercising good judgment—up and down the corporate ladder—make risk management possible. This is the central focus of this chapter. There's no "judgement-free zone" when it comes to risk management because there's no people-free zone. Even credit-card scoring algorithms—seemingly rational, remote and bloodless—rely on human-made judgment rules and on people making those judgments.

Second, as the IBM template points out, risk management is an ongoing, mutable process that requires constant attention and tweaking. It can't be tied up with a bow and put on the shelf as a finished product. Again, an effective ERM calls for well-timed interventions by people exercising good judgment.

Third, a comprehensive ERM considers both external and internal risks as well as risks that sit squarely on the interface between the corporation and its outside-world constituencies. In the case of Boeing, this last category would include, for example, the training of the pilots for its client airlines. It's worth stressing that we're *not* focusing here on threats to a chosen corporate strategy—although of course, those kinds of threats are part of a bigger picture. As noted, MAX program manager Keith Leverkuhn tracked the pilot-training issue as one of a half dozen "risks" about which he updated superiors regularly—but Leverkuhn's concept of the word "risk" appears to have been focused narrowly on risks to the corporate strategy rather than the larger universe of risks.

And finally, an effective ERM addresses both the "hard" and "soft" aspects of business. It's usually easier to focus on the hard and quantifiable, but doing so tends to create an incomplete picture. The FAA's 2020 summary of its review of the 737 MAX disasters, for example, focused exclusively on design, training, and maintenance issues—and stayed well away from the kinds of cultural and character issues that we explored in Chapter 7 and which contributed so power-fully and tragically to the 737 MAX story.[16]

The management consulting firm Arthur D. Little (ADL) also conducted a postmortem risk analysis on the 737 MAX, and that analysis didn't shy away from pointing to flaws in Boeing's corporate culture.[17] According to ADL, Boeing was guilty of a host of organizational, cultural, and technical failures and was notably negligent in its management of risk. The ADL report pointed to four "key risk indicators" (KRIs) that should have provided early warning signs and enabled Boeing to avoid disaster:

- Staff complaints
- Staff under pressure (according to ADL, 39 percent of Boeing employees felt they were under undue pressure)
- Simulator testing results (including the incident, included previously, of the MCAS system "running rampant")
- Errors by engineers (including an unforgiving calendar that resulted in blue-prints being produced at twice the normal rate, which often arrived at the factory full of errors)

As we look for the common thread in these KRIs, we once again arrive at the intersection of *people* and *judgment*. Who was complaining about what, and why? Who was putting whom under pressure, and was it "undue" pressure? Who decided to downplay or ignore the results from the simulator, and why? Why didn't someone fix the bad-blueprint problem? Who decided that those kinds of mistakes weren't a *real* problem, in need of an immediate solution? And if these decisions were put through the filter of micro-moments, as discussed in Chapter 5, what would be revealed?

These are *judgment* calls, not technical calls. And as we have said before, wherever great competency resides—as it did, and does, at Boeing—great character must reside too. Competency with weak or unbalanced character is simply an accident waiting to happen. And it's not difficult to make the case that in many of the most egregious operational failures in recent years—including Enron, the global financial crises, VW, Theranos, the *Challenger* and *Columbia* space shuttle disasters, FTX, Silicon Valley Bank, and so many others—the real root problem was *poor risk management that stemmed from poor character-infused judgment.*

Judgment, risk, and character

To dig deeper into these kinds of questions, we need to borrow a framework—the 4I model—from the field of organizational learning.[18] That model helps to illuminate the processes associated with moving from individual insight to the kinds of collective and organization decisions associated with judgment and learning. The framework rests on the idea that effective learning takes place when four interrelated "i" processes (*intuiting, interpreting, integrating,* and *institutionalizing*) take place. These can be summarized as follows:

- *Intuiting* is predominantly about preverbal pattern recognition, characterized by individuals sensing a threat or possibility and "talking at the edge of their thinking," often using metaphors and analogies to convey something that they struggle to articulate. Notice that being intuitive is a character behavior associated with *judgment,* which as we've seen is all too often undermined in organizations. For example, in most organizations, it's frowned upon to speak before you can clearly articulate an idea—preferably with data to back it up and a solution that at least appears to grow out of that data. Otherwise, the speaker can be ridiculed and their reputation tarnished, bringing forward a seemingly half-baked idea. In such a context, it takes a lot of Courage, Accountability, and Humility for people to risk engaging—but short-circuiting this process can mean missing key insights. Stated positively, organizations that create psychological safety can reap great benefits from turning these intuitions into innovations and ideas.
- *Interpreting* is both an individual and collective process as individuals try to make sense of their experiences. Rarely can one person go from intuiting to interpreting without the help of others to draw out their thinking. As with all of these processes, all dimensions of character are heavily implicated. But the behaviors associated with judgment—such as being situationally aware, analytical, cognitively complex, and a critical thinker—can be centrally important in shaping what people see and how they make sense of it.
- *Integrating* is the challenging process of creating some kind of shared reality. It can be fraught with many challenges, as we discussed in our earlier examination of diversity, equity, and inclusion. Being open-minded, flexible, and interconnected (a few of the behaviors associated with Collaboration) and exhibiting Humanity and Humility are critical to generating a coherent and robust perspective. But this is the ideal. All too often, we see major disconnects between one group and another, with senior leaders dismissing insights and advice from either or both.
- *Institutionalizing* involves embedding new actions and interpretations into the routines, rules, information, systems, strategy, and structure of the organization. This is where decisions to institutionalize—or *not* institutionalize—can have far-reaching consequences, such as we saw in the Boeing case.

Although these processes are presented here from the individual to the organizational level, they are actually interdependent, meaning—for example—that what gets institutionalized impacts all of the other processes. This explains the challenges associated with *culture,* where processes like selection, promotion, and reward influence what the individual pays attention to (intuiting and interpreting), whereas *structure* tends to dictate who talks to whom (integrating), and systems like quarterly report and budgeting having a heavy influence on investments (institutionalizing).

Our research—and real-world experiences like that of the Boeing 737 MAX—argue strongly that *character is an essential underpinning to organizational learning and both are essential to all organizational practices.* Think back to the earlier chapters of this book, which focused on the dimensions and elements of character development at the individual level. What kinds of individuals do we want doing our intuiting and interpreting? Clearly, we want individuals whose character is well developed—which means, among other things, that they bring excellent judgment to the table. The same holds true at the organizational level, where interpreting continues and integrating and institutionalizing also come to the fore. What kinds of teams should dominate these processes? Again, we want teams with strong collective character and sound judgment that is supported by the other ten dimensions.

Another way of looking at these same challenges and opportunities is to think about the impact of character at three distinct levels:

- **Character activation at the individual level**

"Character activation" refers to the awareness and intentionality needed to exercise character (despite situational pressures) and how the different character configurations (that is, weak, strong, or unbalanced) influence learning. Character activation requires not only the awareness of the dimensions of character but also the intention to practice character. While character can be activated, it can also be deactivated—when, for example, leaders don't listen to the advice being given, which can hurt accountability among employees who (rightly) wonder why they even bother.

- **Character contagion at the group level**

By "character contagion," we mean that character activation in one person can lead to character activation in others (for better or worse). Group character also impacts group learning through role modeling, where one individual can act as a role model for acceptable behavior. Character contagion can involve not only the spread of one character dimension in a group but also the activation of other dimensions.

As noted, character contagion is not always positive and can be dysfunctional when someone with unbalanced or weak character undermines the character of others. One of the notable instances of this negative character contagion is someone with strong integrity, accountability, and drive—and at the same time, with low humility, humanity, and collaboration—operating in a self-righteous manner that comes across as bullying within the organization.

If the bully has a position of power or influence, this can easily undermine the courage of others.

• Character embeddedness at the organization level

"Character embedding" means that character can be institutionalized in organizational processes and practices, such as hiring and promotion. In addition, leaders can legitimize character dimensions in organizations, which could then become a permanent attribute of the organization's culture, impacting all of its members.

As in previous chapters, we need to underscore that while character may operate in its virtuous form—leading to positive influences on the organization—it can also operate in its vice state, with important implications for practitioners about how some dimensions of character tend to be overweighted and others underweighted in organizations. To cite an example from an entirely different realm, climbers die on Mount Everest not only because scaling that peak is inherently dangerous but also because something like half of the climbers tackling the mountain are inexperienced.[19] Yes, Drive is key—but a measure of Humility can save your life.

The Boeing saga provides multiple appalling illustrations of middle- and senior-level managers failing to intuit, interpret, integrate, and institutionalize learning effectively—or even at all, in some cases. The pilot who struggled with MCAS in the 737 MAX simulator worried that he had misled regulators about the circumstances under which the rogue software program would kick in. "It wasn't a lie," his colleague responded. "No one told us that was the case." The project's chief engineer didn't know, or understand, key things about the MCAS system and related hardware. That chief engineer's boss, in turn—a Boeing VP—never heard anything about these debates and wound up relying on "industry standard" estimates of how humans (pilots) would interact with machines (jets) under certain conditions: the "human machine interaction."

In other words, at least as that VP saw it, Boeing's mistake lay in relying on standards derived from past industry-wide experience—true enough as far as that went. But all along, the *actual* answers and the truly relevant standards had been trying to percolate their way up through the Boeing system and had been thwarted—in large part through deficits in dimensions of character that eventually led to poor judgment in identifying, assessing, and adjudicating risk.

How unusual is the Boeing story? How often do large corporations, unwittingly or even intentionally, take on risks that may be large enough to be existential—risks that might have been managed through individual and organizational character? The answer is, *probably more often than we'd like to think.*

In January 2023, *Science* magazine published an assessment of a number of studies conducted by two in-house scientists at Exxon (now ExxonMobil) in the mid 1980s.[20] The model that those two researchers produced back in the 1980s was only one of many then being generated inside the multinational energy giant, some of which made their way into print in relatively obscure journals toward the end of the 20th century but were generally overlooked or soon forgotten.

What was different about this three-decades-old model was that it predicted with uncanny precision what the consequences of sticking with the then-prevalent patterns of energy consumption would be: a raise in Earth's global mean temperature by 0.8 degrees by the year 2020. In other words, thanks in part to legitimate research that the company itself was conducting, Exxon had as clear a picture of anyone in the world about the dangers of global warming.

Sadly, the story dates back almost a decade *earlier* than the 1980s. In 1977, the company's senior scientist, James Black, told Exxon's management committee that there was "general scientific agreement that the most likely manner in which mankind is influencing the global climate is through carbon dioxide release from the burning of fossil fuels." And years later, he told management that humankind had to deal with energy strategies *quickly*—within five to ten years—or global warming could become a dire threat.[21]

What did ExxonMobil do with those warnings? It either ignored them, obfuscated around them, or denied them outright. For example, its website in 2007 attacked climate projections—including projections very much like its own—as fundamentally theoretical and therefore unreliable. Seven years later, CEO Rex Tillerson asserted that there was still a great deal of uncertainty about climate change. At the annual shareholders' meeting the following year, Tillerson said that the company should wait for better science before taking action on climate change: "What if everything we do, it turns out that our models are lousy, and we don't get the effects we predict?"[22]

What were the risks, and how did ExxonMobil manage them? Initially, it seems, the company saw only public-relations downsides and the potential for reduced profits and therefore embraced a strategy of denying and delaying. But over time, new risks began to emerge, in part because those superaccurate Exxon-generated predictions were still out there, waiting to be rediscovered and analyzed—and used as evidence in class-action lawsuits that legal experts are now beginning to liken to the successful suits filed against the tobacco companies decades ago.[23]

The parallels are compelling. When a company knows its products to be harmful and conceals that fact, it may well be held legally responsible for damage caused by those products. As *Science* summarized it:

Today, dozens of cities, counties, and states are suing oil and gas companies for their "longstanding internal scientific knowledge of the causes and consequences of climate change and public deception campaigns." The European Parliament and the US Congress have held hearings, US President Joe Biden has committed to holding fossil fuel companies accountable, and a grassroots social movement has arisen under the moniker #ExxonKnew. Our findings demonstrate that ExxonMobil didn't just know "something" about global warming decades ago—they knew as much as academic and government scientists knew. But whereas those scientists worked to communicate what they knew, ExxonMobil worked to deny it—including overemphasizing uncertainties, denigrating climate models, mythologizing global cooling, feigning ignorance about the discernibility of human-caused warming, and staying silent about the possibility of stranded fossil fuel assets in a carbon-constrained world.

"They knew as much as independent scientists did," said one of the authors of the *Science* article, "and arguably, they knew all they needed to know to start to take action and warn the public." In other words, they knew all they needed to know and still didn't manage the risks that were looming larger in front of them.

The end of this story has yet to be written. In 2019, in the first relevant case to come to trial, New York's Supreme Court ruled that the state's attorney general had failed to prove that Exxon had misled its shareholders about the true cost of climate change. For Exxon, the costs of losing would have been high: $1.6 billion in damages, untold reputational harm—and an open door for future litigation.[24]

Bad apples?

"Misconduct" in business—such as has occurred in some of the events cited previously—is often more completely and accurately framed as a *judgment* issue. Yes, there are legitimate bad apples out there—but as we've said in previous chapters, "bad apples" very often turn out to be manifestations of bad barrels, or even bad barrel makers.

Shifting the analysis of misconduct away from morals and ethics and toward judgment is not merely a definitional tweak; it's a prescriptive advantage. In our experience working with corporations and other organizations, this shift allows the issue of misconduct to be addressed in a more positive, aligned, and *actionable* manner. In other words, people pay less attention when someone tells them, "Let's work on improving your morals." They pay more attention when someone says, "Let's work on improving your judgment, decision-making skills, outcomes, performance, leader potential, and well-being." It's true: by and large, people want to get better at what they do, and they certainly want to succeed without blundering into misconduct. And it's worth noting that what gets labeled as "misconduct" is often perpetrated by a high performer who lacks Humility, comes up short on Collaboration, gets into trouble, and tries to fix it—only to get into deeper trouble. The person who's doing the "fixing" doesn't think of his or her actions as a cover-up but rather as a *remedy*. Think of Nick Leeson, for example, who had no intention of bringing down Barings Bank but merely sought (at first) to cover up for a team member's dumb mistake. But by so doing, he or she demonstrates poor judgment based on character deficiencies.

For all of these reasons, Enterprise Risk Management (ERM) programs shouldn't be seen as stand-alone algorithms—aimed at generating tools like risk dashboards and risk heat maps—but rather as processes that require experienced, nuanced, balanced judgment. The chairs of effective risk committees would not find this statement particularly surprising or controversial. What they *would* find surprising, however, is that the quality of judgment that goes into these ERM Dashboards and Maps is profoundly influenced by the strength of character of the individuals who produce and consume them.

What's the prescription here? As described in previous chapters, *think as broadly as possible about risk*, including both operational and cultural aspects—and the character that underpins them. Once an ERM process has been set up, the greatest contribution that can be made to effective risk management lies *not* in tweaking the ERM, but rather, in investing in the strength of character across their entire organization. Simply put, investment in leader character at the individual and organizational levels will foster and sustain the desired ERM culture.

Ultimately, and ideally, this character-infused judgment is invoked at each micro-moment of decision—and risks are thereby minimized and mitigated.

Notes

1 As with the Boeing section in the previous chapter, much of the 737 MAX account included here is distilled from Peter Robison's excellent account, *Flying Blind: The 737 MAX tragedy and the fall of Boeing,* published by Doubleday in 2021.
2 *Flying Blind,* p. 39.
3 *Flying Blind,* p. 83.
4 See, for example, "How the FAA ceded aviation safety oversight to Boeing," online at www.pogo.org/analysis/2019/03/how-the-faa-ceded-aviation-safety-oversight-to-boeing, accessed March 15, 2023.
5 *Flying Blind,* p. 136.
6 All of this tinkering was made necessary by the weight and forward placement of the 737's massive new engines, which tended to pull the plane's nose down.
7 *Flying Blind,* p. 140.
8 *Flying Blind,* p. 141–142. See also the June 21, 2020, article in the *Spokesman-Review,* describing Ewbank's subsequent whistle-blowing activities regarding the 737 MAX, online at www.spokesman.com/stories/2020/jun/21/boeing-whistleblower-alleges-systematic-problems-with/, accessed March 15, 2023.
9 See www.cnn.com/2019/10/02/politics/boeing-whistleblower-complaint-737-max/index.html, accessed March 15, 2023.
10 From an email exchange between Mark Forkner and Patrik Gustavsson, as reported in the *New York Times,* online at www.nytimes.com/2019/10/18/boeing-pilot-messages.html, accessed March 15, 2023.
11 See "Boeing engineer who led development of 737 MAX to retire" online at www.reuters.com/business/aerospace-defense/boeing-engineer-key-airplane-programs-michael-teal-retire-company-memo-2022-01-14/, accessed March 15, 2023.

12 See "Boeing's 777X chief project engineer Teal to retire, succeeded by Loffing" on-line at www.flightglobal.com/airframersboings-777x-cheif-project-engineer-teal-to-retire-succeeded-by-loffing/147135.article, accessed March 15, 2023.

13 See the Boeing 737 Technical Site, 09.13.20, online at www.facebook.com/b737tech/posts/keith-leverkuhn-who-was-vice-president-and-general-manager-of-the-737-max-progra/159479310, accessed March 15, 2023.

14 Dennis Muilenburg was ousted in December 2019. Boeing pointed out in a press re-lease that the departing CEO would *not* get additional severance or a 2019 bonus and that he was forfeiting $14.6 million in stock awards. See www.manufacturing.net/aerospace/news/21109798/boeing-ceos-golden-parachute-was-62-million, accessed March 15, 2023.

15 See IBM's white paper online at www.ibm.com/topics/risk-management, accessed March 15, 2023.

16 See "Summary of the FAA's Review of the Boeing 737 MAX" online at www.faa.gov/foia/electronic_reading_room/boeing_reading_room/media/737_RTS_Summary.pdf, accessed March 15, 2023.

17 See "Lessons in risk from the Boeing 737 MAX disasters" online at www.globalrein-surance.com/lessons-in-risk-from-the-boeing-737-max-disasters/1437327.article, accessed March 15, 2023.

18 This section draws heavily on a January 25, 2022 article published in *Manage-ment Learning* article entitled "Organizational learning through character-based judgment," by Mary Crossan, Brenda Nguyen, Dusya Vera, Ana Ruiz Pardo, and Cara C. Maurer. The article can be accessed here; https://journals.sagepub.com/doi/abs/10.1177/13505076221100918.

19 See the interesting NBC News story on this subject, online at www.nbcnews.com/news/world/everest-deaths-some-climbers-are-unprepared-underestimate-mountain-n1011821, accessed March 15, 2023.

20 See the article "Assessing ExxonMobil's global warming projections," written by Geoffrey Supran, Stefan Rahmstorf, and Naomi Oreskes, in *Science* online at www.science.org/doi/10.1126/science.abk0063, accessed March 15, 2023. For a journal-ist's perspective, see the January 12, 2023, article in the *Toronto Star*, online at www.thestar.com/news/canada/2023/01/12/oil-and-gas-giant-exxon-predicted-extent-of-global-warming-with-striking-precision-decades-ago-study-finds.html, accessed March 15, 2023.

21 See the article "Exxon knew about climate change almost 40 years ago," written by Shannon Hall, in the October 26, 2015 edition of *Scientific American,* online at www.scientificamerican.com/article/exxon-knew-about-climate-change-almost-40-years-ago/, accessed March 15, 2023.

22 See, for example, https://insideclimatenews.org/news/22122016/rex-tillerson-exxon-climate-change-secretary-state-donald-trump/, accessed March 15, 2023. Rex Till-erson later served (briefly) as one of U.S. President Donald Trump's Secretaries of State.

23 The sugar industry may be next. As of this writing, no such suits had been field—but they appear to be on the horizon. See, for example, www.hugheshubbard.com/news/targeted-by-historians-sugar-industry-may-face-litigation-risk, accessed March 15, 2023.

24 The judge in the case focused on the fact that the attorney general had promised to produce witnesses who would testify that as investors, they had been actively misled by Exxon—and then failed to do so. See www.cnbc.com/2019/12/10/exxon-did-not-mislead-investors-a-new-york-judge-ruled-on-tuesday.html, accessed March 15, 2023.

Chapter 9

Character, directors, boards, and governance

Charles W. Scharf first appeared before the US House of Representatives' Committee on Financial Services on March 10, 2020.[1] The former CEO of BNY Mellon and Visa, Scharf was then barely four months into his role as CEO and president of Wells Fargo & Company.

The hearing's name revealed the predisposition of at least a majority of its members: "Holding Wells Fargo Accountable: CEO perspectives on next steps for the bank that broke America's trust." As he took his seat at the witness table, Scharf had a dubious distinction: the third Wells Fargo CEO to testify before the committee in less than three and a half years.

Committee chair Maxine Waters opened the hearing on a somber note, calling the US's largest bank "a lawless organization that has caused widespread harm to millions of consumers throughout the nation."[2] By this point, Wells Fargo had already paid more than $17 billion in penalties assessed by multiple federal regulators. Two years earlier, in 2018, the Federal Reserve had issued a consent order requiring board governance and oversight changes, and regulators had imposed an unwelcome asset cap on the bank—effectively tying the bank's hands in terms of future growth. Scharf's immediate predecessor as CEO, Tim Sloan, had recently told this same committee that the bank had met those requirements, which if true might lead to a lifting of government-imposed sanctions. But it turned out not to be true. Sloan soon resigned under pressure, and Scharf was hired to succeed him.

Waters then itemized some of the bank's documented offenses:

Wells Fargo has opened 3.5 million fraudulent accounts in their customers' names, which cost consumers over $6 million; charged consumers for automobile insurance policies they did not need, resulting in some consumers losing their automobiles; engaged in illegal student loan servicing practices; charged consumers inappropriate overdraft fees; overcharged veterans for refinance loans; and fraudulently sold complex financial products to retail investors.

DOI: 10.4324/9781003341215-10

Last week, the committee released a Majority staff report on Wells Fargo's compliance with five consent orders issued by various regulatory agencies, in response to the company's widespread consumer abuses and compliance breakdowns. Among the disturbing findings uncovered in the report is that the Office of the Comptroller of the Currency (OCC) is aware of dozens of cases at Wells Fargo where the number of consumers or customer accounts requiring remediation for consumer abuse exceeds 50,000, or the amount of harm exceeds $10 million.

Over the course of preceding months and years, Waters and other committee members had already suggested that Wells Fargo—with some 265,000 employees, of whom 100,000 were considered customer-facing—had become too big to manage and might need to be broken up. Not so, said Congressman Patrick McHenry, in his introductory remarks: "Wells Fargo isn't too big to manage." Instead, he said, "the findings of these documents show that it was grossly mismanaged."

In his introductory remarks, Scharf said that he agreed with McHenry's harsh assessment of gross mismanagement, referring to

deeply disturbing conduct that is utterly unacceptable and has no place in our company. . . . We had a flawed business model in how the company was managed. Our structure and culture were problematic, and the company's leadership failed its stakeholders.

He then went on to list eight changes that he and his team were implementing at the bank. Most of these had to do with aspects of the bank's governance structure—that is, the collection of rules and practices that determined how Wells Fargo did business, including its corporate strategy, risk management, compensation, ethical behavior, environmental impacts, and so on. The changes Scharf described focused, in part, on the bank's cumbersome "federated" structures and processes—which led to, among other shortcomings, a decentralized risk-management function and a lack of representation of the bank's various businesses at the senior management table. Other changes had to do with an ongoing transition in leadership, which at that point included a 75 percent turnover of the bank's operating committee and the replacement of 14 of the board of director's 16 members. Toward the end of his eight-point recitation, Scharf touched on what he called "culture," although again, his focus was mainly on structure and process:

We are redefining our culture, especially regarding how we work together. We will have a strong centralized control infrastructure. We will ensure we have the right people in the right roles. We will move with a sense of urgency, we will hold each other accountable for our commitments, and we will judge ourselves based upon our outcomes, not our words.

At one point, a committee member pressed Scharf on how he proposed to change the culture at Wells Fargo. Scharf's reply:

> We have to be clear on how a series of things come together to form a culture, and then we as a senior leadership team need to make sure that we are behaving that way.
> That includes changing compensation, the way we evaluate people, the things that we look at to include risk and customer experience as part of that evaluation. Any time that we see any harm, we have to be the ones to deal with it as quickly as we can.
> If there is wrongdoing inside the company, don't just look at an individual and say that they did something wrong. Ask the question, do we have something in our structure that is wrong? And I think all of those things come together, with accountability probably being the most important thing. . . .

That response begins to get at a core question: *do we have something in our governance structure that is wrong?* Or phrased in more fundamental terms: *is there something missing in our culture?* But Scharf's approach—as he explained to the committee—centered on managing operational risks, which he said could be accomplished through an unspecified sort of "education":

> I think the biggest issue for us is just making sure that everyone across the company, including those on the front lines, understands that risk management, especially operational risk management, is everyone's job, and we need to educate them on what that means.

It's possible that Scharf was playing to his audience: The committee appeared to be pushing for a governance structure that would emphasize operational risk management over profits. In other words, going forward, "character" at Wells Fargo would be demonstrated and reinforced only indirectly, by minimizing risk and (as necessary) sacrificing profitability.

Scharf seemed comfortable with that. "We did not have the appropriate controls in place," he testified. "We didn't have the appropriate culture. We didn't have the right people in these jobs." To the extent that he defined the term, the "culture" he referred to was one of *accountability* rather than character.

But even Scharf's limited vision poses problems. How does that cultural quality of accountability arise? Who are the "right people," and where do they come from? Can they be developed internally? The answer to this last question appeared to be "no." Scharf leaned toward *replacing* people rather than developing them:

> I think one of the problems that we had across the company is we didn't always put the right people in the right jobs. I said that in my opening remarks. The culture of the company was more family-like, and family can be good but family can be bad. Making the tough decisions about who really is capable and who is not capable, who is performing and who is not performing, is extremely important, at all levels in an organization, and I don't think we have done that as well as we could.
>
> So if people don't have the right skills or don't have the right experience for things that we need, we need to get people who do, as long as we treat people with the utmost respect. So when we look at the people that we have brought in from the outside, or people that we promoted up from within, I think people, both inside and outside the company say that they fit the bill. They have the experience, they have the know-how, they have the proven ability to get the work done.

Scharf believed that internal communications—often a determinant and reinforcer of culture—had suffered in the bank's balkanized federated system and was therefore taking at least modest steps to improve those communication channels:

> We do employee surveys, and even more important than actually doing the survey is making sure employees know that you read them, you listen to it, and you are going to do something about it. So I have spoken about the results that I have seen in the employee survey, and many of the actions that we have taken are a result of what we have seen.
>
> We have town hall meetings. I host a town hall meeting every quarter with every employee inside the company, and I encourage people to give me feedback, and I get feedback. I get hundreds and hundreds and hundreds of emails any time I send something out—not just after those quarterly meetings, and even between them.

The following morning, two former members of the Wells Fargo board—Elizabeth A. Duke and James H. Quigley—took their turns at the witness table.[3] In one sense, this was a logical next step for the committee, given that a company's board of directors is the most important force determining corporate governance and that Duke had served until recently as board chair and Quigley was a former director and independent chair of Wells Fargo Bank.[4] But both Duke and Quigley had resigned from the board earlier in the week to "avoid distraction," in their words, and it was highly unusual for a house committee to question former corporate directors.[5] The committee decided, however, that because Duke and Quigley had been personally involved in some of the bank's recent compliance failures—and had not been particularly responsive to requests from the Consumer Financial Protection Bureau and the Office of the Comptroller of the Currency—they should be asked to testify.

In her opening statement, Duke painted a reassuring picture of an institution on the mend: a bank that was once again focused on customers rather than sales. She pointed to a "fully transformed board" that had adopted appropriate structural changes to improve its governance capabilities, an executive team that "balance[d] a new approach with institutional knowledge," a risk-management team and platform "under construction from the ground up," and a new CEO— Richard Scharf—who had the "ability to execute on the significant remaining work necessary to meet the company's regulatory commitments."

Duke did not attempt to minimize the damage done by and at Wells Fargo in the recent past. Indeed, citing her own humble professional origins as a bank teller and new-accounts representative, Duke testified that she was both "appalled by the harm [done] to customers [and] sickened to hear how our employees were treated by their managers."

In his own opening remarks, James Quigley also cited his relatively humble origins—pointing out that he was the son of a forest ranger and a schoolteacher—decried the bank's failings, and tried to make the case that in terms of governance, Wells Fargo was now on the right track. By way of evidence, Quigley said that since the end of 2017, the bank's compliance teams had added 3,300 new members, effectively doubling their size. Going back as far as 2006, he continued, Wells Fargo had hired a new chief operating officer, chief risk officer, general counsel, chief auditor, chief compliance officer, head of HR, and head of technology.

Quigley admitted that the remaining cultural and structural changes were formidable but expressed his confidence that they could and would be addressed:

> Because I believe deeply in the critical role of culture in an organization like Wells Fargo, I was especially supportive of the culture Mr. Scharf is working to establish, one with clear priorities, best-in-class standards of operational excellence and integrity, a unified bank with clear line of sight across the business, accountability of management, and most important of all, a renewed commitment to completing the work of doing right by our customers and satisfying our regulators.

In the questioning that followed, committee members at times engaged in some of the bickering, grandstanding, selective truth telling, and flattery and scolding of the witnesses that tends to characterize contentious congressional hearings. But a common concern expressed by Republican and Democratic representatives alike was that Wells Fargo—and its board—still had not done enough in terms of reforming its governance structures. According to this analysis, the bank's board was mainly focused on getting the burdensome federally imposed asset cap and consent decrees lifted rather than actually fixing its risk-management problems and holding senior management accountable for the excesses of the recent past.[6]

Duke responded by pointing out that of necessity, the bank's (and by extension, the board's) current focus was on interacting with regulators—and those interactions were significantly *time-consuming*. For example, said Duke, at the board's recent first formal meeting with newly installed CEO Scharf, there had been *no* items on the agenda dealing with the business itself; every single agenda item had to do with regulatory problems. This was compounded, she said, by a relentless turnover in the ranks:

> There are a number of places where the people who were working on those submissions [to the regulators] were changed. Someone else was working on them, in particular the ones that had to do with risk management. So, we got a new chief risk officer, we got a new chief compliance officer, we have been through four chief operational risk officers. We were changing out the people, looking for the people who could actually get the plans written in a complete fashion.

But both the way the question was posed and the way it was answered hint at the same nagging questions left over from the Scharf testimony on the preceding day: *Who are the "right people," and where do they come from?* Can they be developed internally? Like Scharf, the board's governance philosophy seemed to lean toward *replacing* people—"changing them out"—rather than developing them. At one point, committee member Blain Luetkemeyer recalled this same mentality prevailing at Wells Fargo during the tenure of CEO John G. Stumpf, Scharf's predecessor once removed:

> Mr. Stumpf was in here during that period of time, and I asked him point-blank, because he was firing about 1,000 people a year over a 5-year period and kept it up. I kept asking him, "Why have you not changed the culture in your bank? Because you keep firing people." He said, "Well, now we are fixing it." I replied, "No, you are not fixing it, if you keep firing 1,000 people every year. That is not fixing it. You should have fixed it so you do not have to fire everybody, so everybody is doing the right thing."

But how could *that* happen? Could it happen, for example, through investments in the work force? Perhaps. But between 2016 and 2019—as committee member Jesus "Chuy" Garcia pointed out—Wells Fargo had more than doubled the money it put into dividends and stock buybacks: from $12.5 billion to $30.2 billion. "Do you agree," Garcia asked Duke and Quigley, "that Wells Fargo could have used those billions to invest in its workforce, which may have, in turn, fixed its internal culture?"

How boards do and don't work

It was a good question, although certainly one not best answered by individual directors of the institution.[7] Why? Because, as suggested by our definitions of corporate governance laid out previously, directors don't micromanage their company's activities—including, for example, trying to satisfy consent-order requirements imposed by regulators (the *how*). Their mandate is far broader and less granular.[8] "The business of the company," according to the Wells Fargo corporate governance guidelines, "is managed under the direction and oversight of its board."[9]

In fact, board members play a number of critical leadership roles that can have substantial impact on corporate performance. They are, in a sense, in the eye of the strategic storm that also includes regulators, investors, executives, and other stakeholders. In the midst of that ongoing and always-evolving storm, they appoint CEOs and often other members of the senior management team and approve major management decisions. As noted, they set corporate policies, monitor management, maintain internal controls, and otherwise provide corporate governance.

As individuals, moreover, corporate directors are expected to provide independent thinking and thought leadership. Within clear bounds, as implied previously, they are expected to serve as *leaders*, with most having had considerable executive experience that has qualified them for their roles as directors. They are also expected to bring to the table valuable information and perspectives through their contacts with members of other boards and outside groups. And to the extent that the company operates within an ecosystem of regulation, media scrutiny, and other pressures, directors need to monitor, interpret, and report back to their fellow board members on those pressures in a broader context.

Boards are complex teams, with unusual characteristics that distinguish them from conventional work teams. For example, boards have many part-time members, meet only episodically, and tend to be larger than traditional work teams. Their members devote varying levels of time to the board's work between meetings. All of these characteristics make leadership efforts in the board context more challenging—and character considerations all the more critical.

Boards are highly disciplined and socialized mechanisms. Their rules, norms, and regulations help shape their behavior and decision-making, presumably in positive directions. And at the same time, many of the major corporate crises of recent years are partly the result of weak corporate governance, including the Volkswagen emissions scandal—as recounted in Chapter 1—the Theranos implosion (in our Chapter 5), BP's failure to deal with the biggest-ever environmental disaster in North America, the corruption and fraud scandal faced by the SNC-Lavalin Group, the collapse of Enron, and the faults and flaws in the banking sector that led to the financial crisis in 2008. Analyses of these and other meltdowns have tended to conclude that individual directors and corporate boards failed in their leadership and character obligations, often with severely detrimental effects for shareholders, customers, employees, and other stakeholders.

Wells Fargo certainly conformed to this poor-governance profile, according to a damning 2017 report issued by the Office of the Comptroller of the Currency. That report noted that the bank's board had received "regular" reports since 2005 about sales-tactics violations and had done nothing in response.[10] Perhaps even more troubling, by 2010, more than 700 whistleblower complaints had been logged regarding those tactics, and the board subsequently claimed to have heard nothing about them.

In all of these cases, and many others that achieved less notoriety, several layers of controls had to be circumvented—which begs the question why board members, individually and collectively, failed to provide adequate governance.

In part, the answer lies in the sheer complexity of the corporate world above a certain scale, including the speed at which that world changes. Wells Fargo can be faulted for failing to spot the approaching train of customer abuse—but regulators, too, can be faulted for "fighting the last war." The regulatory community focused on risk management as defined by the casino mentality of the 2008 banking crisis but failed to consider the exposures that a heavily retail-oriented (i.e., "low-risk") bank like Wells Fargo might be creating for itself.

But the answer also lies, in part, in the realm of *character*. A deeper exploration of how character affects individual behaviors and subsequent board processes is an important step in understanding how boards either add value and contribute to organizational performance and sustainability—or help send companies off the rails. In previous chapters, we've focused on the importance of Leader Character in the day-to-day functioning of the workplace, comprising leaders at all levels up to the C suite; here we extend that analysis to include boards and board members.

As we've already implied, the board setting is a particularly challenging context for group sense-making and decision-making. There's certainly enough anecdotal and empirical evidence to conclude that socialized mechanisms including group dynamics—such as norms and patterns of interaction—create pressures that can negatively affect group decision-making processes and therefore distort the decisions that boards ultimately make. Groupthink is only one example of a social-psychological process that creates negative contextual pressures.[11] Other such contextual pressures may include, for example, imposed time limits for discussion, limited information sharing on the part of management, a dominant board chair who discourages open debate, or a lack of trust among board members resulting from the group's inability to cultivate strong interpersonal relationships.

These and other contextual pressures to conform may contribute to board members developing a feeling of isolation. They may begin to question their own legitimacy, expertise, and ability to function on the board. For example, board members may ask themselves questions like, "Who am I to challenge the board chair? Do I really have the requisite knowledge and competencies needed to meaningfully contribute to this debate? Will I be perceived as a risk-averse person if I object to the decision, and if so, what will be the implications for my reputation?"

A case in point

In March 2021, Dominion Voting Systems—manufacturer of the voting machines used in many states in the 2020 US elections, which included the presidential contest between Donald Trump and Joe Biden—filed a defamation suit against the Fox Corporation, owner of the Fox News network, for the false claims that the network pushed after the election. Many of those claims included the assertion that Dominion's machines had been hacked in order to shift votes from Trump to Biden, thereby "stealing" the election from Trump.

By that point, Paul Ryan had been on the Fox Corporation Board of Directors for two years. Ryan previously served as the 54th Speaker of the US House of Representatives, joining the Fox board three months after leaving his House position. He soon began playing a prominent role on the board, serving as the chair of its Nominating & Corporate Governance Committee.[12]

In the weeks following the 2020 election, Ryan became increasingly concerned about Fox's post-election coverage, which questioned the outcome of the presidential election and presented conspiracy theories—including the subplots allegedly including Dominion and a competitor, Smartmatics—some 800 times.[13]

On December 6, 2020, Paul Ryan acted on what he thought were his director's responsibilities. He texted Fox head Rupert Murdoch and Murdoch's son Lachlan, telling them that he saw this postelection juncture as a "inflection point for Fox, where the right thing and the smart business thing to do line up nicely."[14] Ryan also reportedly told the Murdochs that it was time for Fox to "move on from Donald Trump" and "stop spouting election lies."[15]

It's worth noting that there's no evidence that Ryan took his concerns to the board table—a step which might have better embodied good governance and might even have forced the issue to some sort of resolution. The same is evidently true for Ryan's fellow board member Anne Dias, who was so shaken by the January 6, 2020, riot at the US Capitol that she told the Murdochs directly that Fox had to "take a stance" and change course.[16]

The Murdochs evidently agreed with Ryan and Dias that the stolen-election allegations were fake—but for competitive reasons declined to tell their on-air personalities to stop making those false claims. That turned out to be a grave mistake, and one that could certainly have been foreseen. According to Fox's 2022 annual report, for example, the company typically faces a number of risks in its operations, notably including an "unfavorable litigation" scenario:

> We are subject from time to time to a number of lawsuits, including claims relating to competition, intellectual property rights, employment and labor matters, personal injury and property damage, free speech, customer privacy, regulatory requirements, and advertising, marketing and selling practices. Greater constraints on the use of arbitration to resolve certain of these disputes could adversely affect our business. We also spend substantial resources complying with various regulatory and government standards, including any related investigations and litigation. We may incur significant expenses defending any such suit or government charge and may be required to pay amounts or otherwise change our operations in ways that could adversely impact our businesses, results of operations or financial condition.[17]

It's now abundantly clear that the Murdochs should have heeded Ryan's and Dias' individual pleadings. As of this writing, in parallel defamation cases, Fox is being sued by Dominion for $1.6 billion and by Smartmatics for $2.7 billion, with the potential for substantial punitive damages.[18] And perhaps ironically, the highly visible Ryan came under fire for not doing more—in our terminology, for not demonstrating more Leader Character in his role as a Fox director. "By silently going along with misconduct about which they are aware, all directors, including Paul Ryan, are guilty of complicity through their complacency," said Yale professor and head of the Executive Leadership Institute Jeffrey Sonnenfeld, in a CNN interview.[19]

In other words, for a board member, the *opportunity* to demonstrate Leader Character may well be an *obligation*.

The character of boards and governance

This means, in turn, that good corporate governance presupposes board members with strong character. Boards need people with the courage to speak up and bring a different perspective to the discussion, especially in the face of strong opposition. This is particularly true when the discussion involves a dominant CEO, who forcefully presents a strategy that may or may not deviate from the fundamental purpose of the company. At that point, directors may have to stand and be counted.

At the same time, it's critical for board members to show humility—that is, to take advantage of any opportunity to learn from someone else, to avoid tunnel vision, and to have the self-awareness and modesty needed to let them to listen to and learn from others. Board members need to demonstrate accountability, avoiding the temptation to skirt the difficult questions or trade-offs that the board faces. They also need good *judgment*—the ability to avoid making unfounded assumptions or jumping to conclusions but instead to add insight, direction, and clarity to problem-solving discussions.

Small wonder, then, that it's hard to find the talented individuals needed to build and maintain an effective board!

Breaches in corporate governance are the consequence of a collective failure of judgment, and yet, the subject of character has been largely neglected in research on board governance. Why is that? One answer lies in the difficulty in gaining access to what is often an elite and very private group of leaders. As a result, researchers have tended to emphasize the more visible and easily accessible dimensions of governance, including the separation of the CEO and chair roles, the composition of the board—specifically, the role of independent directors—and to a lesser extent, characteristics such as age, tenure, gender, race, managerial experience, industry experience, and heterogeneity and diversity of its members.

These dimensions are all important to understand and, in some cases, can help explain individual board member behavior. But it's imperative to take a deeper, more fine-grained look at leadership and decision-making on corporate boards and, more specifically, the role that character plays in decision-making. *Character is a critical missing link in explaining failures at the board level.* Poor decisions, misbehaviors, and even misconduct can be interpreted as a failure of judgment—and poor judgment can be framed, understood, and described as a weakness in a person's character.

To support good governance, therefore, *boards need to elevate the importance of character alongside competence.* Competencies alone are insufficient for an organization to achieve its goals because our ability to develop and employ our competencies is directly connected to our strength of character. It requires *courage*, for instance, to challenge a strategy that is already in place, *transcendence* to envisage a future different from today, *humility* to accept and apply constructive criticism, and *collaboration* to move ideas forward.[20]

Voices from the front lines

Looking at a particular scenario from the outside in and imputing character—or the *lack* of character—has clear limitations. That's one reason why the testimony of Wells Fargo leaders cited previously is compelling. Under oath, the company's CEO and two former directors reflected, at least tangentially, on the intersection of leadership and character.

But we need to hear more from board members themselves. Do they agree that character is a critical missing link in explaining failures at the board level and that boards need to elevate the importance of character alongside competence? Do they believe that Leader Character can be critically important to key board processes, including—for example—CEO or board selection, performance review, and renewal processes by those in governance roles? What dimensions of character do board members believe are over-weighted and underweighted on boards? What character dimensions would directors like to see more of in their fellow board members? Less of? Do directors believe character can be developed?

We can help answer some of these questions. We recently had a unique opportunity to collect data from the Canadian governance community and explore the role of Leader Character at the highest levels in organizations. Through this initiative, we sought to understand what individuals with deep expertise in corporate governance think about the role and importance of character in organizational success.

A total of nearly 800 directors attended the sessions. The session included an in-depth workshop on leader character, which familiarized attendees with the language, concepts, and application of leader character to themselves and their organizations. Each attendee was sent an internet-based survey within three days after the event, eliciting directors' perceptions about the relationship between the 11 dimensions of Leader Character and their importance for the effectiveness of directors. We also sought their views about how easy or difficult it is to assess and develop character in individuals and how well, as directors, they actually do this.

The survey contained three sets of questions about beliefs regarding the importance of Leader Character. The first set of questions asked the directors to indicate the extent to which they agreed or disagreed with ten statements regarding Leader Character and corporate governance. The second set asked the directors to rate the impact of each of our eleven character dimensions on individual director effectiveness. The character elements supporting each character dimension were listed on the survey to enhance clarity of the dimension and thereby create a common frame of reference for the respondents. The third set of questions asked the directors to reflect on their personal experience as a director and then to indicate, for each dimension of Leader Character, if they wish there had been more of or less of the character dimension in the directors on the boards on which they served.

The results

The data reveal that directors agreed or strongly agreed (91 percent) that the character of a CEO has a tremendous impact on the effectiveness of a board and that the board should assess and evaluate the character of the CEO and C-level executives (86 percent). We therefore found it interesting that the majority of respondents (55 percent) disagreed, or strongly disagreed, that boards spend sufficient time assessing a potential director's character before asking them to join a board.

Directors agreed or strongly agreed (78 percent) that it is difficult to assess character compared, for example, with assessing competencies. They also agreed or strongly agreed (59 percent) that character can be assessed through extensive and intensive reference checking and that effective interviewing reveals character strengths and defects in potential directors (59 percent).

Sixty percent of the directors disagreed or strongly disagreed that the educational system does a good job of developing character. Eighty-one percent agreed or strongly agreed that business schools need to address character issues more than they currently do.

Directors disagreed or strongly disagreed (55 percent) that character cannot be changed once someone has become an adult. Eighty-one percent of the directors agreed or strongly agreed that early workplace experiences have a substantial impact on the formation of Leader Character.

So, briefly stated, *directors agree on the importance of Leader Character in the C-suite, that character is difficult to assess, that our educational system does not do a good job of developing character, and that character is increasingly difficult to change as a person becomes an adult.*

The next set of results focused on the perceived impact of the 11 character dimensions on individual director effectiveness. To summarize the results, *all character dimensions were seen as beneficial to individual director effectiveness.* Judgment, Integrity, Accountability, and Collaboration received the highest scores for director effectiveness while Humanity received the lowest score.

We found it interesting that the spread between the lowest score (Humanity) and the highest score (judgment) for directors who attended the session was much narrower than for those who did not. This suggests that those who attended the session and thought about character in a structured way understood that *all* Leader Character dimensions have an important role to play in decision-making and that any dimension in deficiency or excess can be a negative. It suggests further that they understood the nuances associated with the different dimensions, and our caution that some dimensions that they had previously viewed as important in all situations—such as courage—might pose a problem when not supported by other dimensions like temperance.

Some of the respondents indicated on the survey that the questions about the importance of the dimensions for director effectiveness were "obvious," that it would be "almost impossible to rate these dimensions as anything but very beneficial," or that "all of these traits are important and beneficial. Differentiating among them is difficult." The results, however, showed considerable variance in responses. For example, there were respondents who reported that they felt that Drive (8 percent of the respondents), Humility (12 percent), and Humanity (16 percent) have either no impact or a detrimental impact on director effectiveness.

We asked directors to indicate which of the eleven character dimensions they wish there had been more or less of, based on their personal experience on the boards on which they have served. The scores for directors who attended the roundtable discussion were higher on all character dimensions than the scores for those who did not attend the session. This finding suggests that attending the roundtable discussion may have contributed to personal reflection and the building of self-awareness of Leader Character and hence the perceived need to further develop the character dimensions for effective functioning as a director. For those who attended a session, *transcendence* stood out from the other ten character dimensions as "want some or much more of," followed by judgment, accountability, and courage.

We found this particularly interesting, given that transcendence was also seen as among the most beneficial dimensions among those who attended the roundtable discussion. Conversely, transcendence received relatively lower scores from those who did not attend the session. A potential explanation of this finding is that "transcendence" remained a somewhat abstract, hard-to-pin-down construct for those who were not exposed to our presentation and a subsequent discussion.

Now let's explore the dominant themes that emerged during the roundtable discussions as well as from the comments submitted at the end of the survey. First, there was an overwhelming belief that *Leader Character matters to board governance and organizational effectiveness*. Directors expressed the opinion that the need to discuss, study, measure, and bring character to the forefront for leadership cannot be overstated. For example, one participant wrote, "I believe Leader Character is the bedrock of an organization. I believe over the long term, character becomes the destiny of the organization. Character helps to build and sustain a business over long periods of time." Directors also expressed the belief that the framing of character is critically important for it to get traction in the workplace. They are looking for real, hard evidence that character can make a tangible difference in individual, team, and—in particular—organizational performance. Many directors indicated they felt the need for a tool to help discuss Leader Character in a meaningful way during board meetings or evaluations.

Second, directors felt that *Leader Character tends to be brought up by boards only during or after a crisis*. In other words, boards tend to be complacent about character until a significant challenge flares up, at which time character gets noticed. For example, one participant asserted that "the importance of character is often magnified during a crisis. We shouldn't wait for a crisis for the opportunity to assess character. I think boards need to pay very close attention to indications of character—during good times as well as the bad."

Many directors also expressed the belief that the character dimensions and elements need to be encouraged and reinforced by the organization's culture. This observation leads to the third theme: *in selecting the CEO and/or board members, Leader Character tends to be either entirely neglected or considered only in the sense of, "Is this a good person?" "Do they have strong values?" "Will this person be a good fit?" or "What is his or her reputation?"* The consensus among directors was that greater efforts must be made to establish character as a central component of director recruitment and selection. For example, one participant commented, "I think people's criteria for selection is a competency one—not that character isn't considered, but if you are thinking of appointing someone to a board, you are looking to fill a competency gap; you are looking for a particular background or set of experiences. Character isn't considered as much." In the same vein, it appears that few companies actually discuss character elements with the search consultants they hire to develop a pool of candidates. Instead, they assume that character will be addressed somewhere in the hiring process and that an "absence of negatives" indicates positive character dimensions.[21]

Fourth, directors generally agreed that among board members, *there tends to be an overemphasis on certain character dimensions*. For example, many directors asserted that their colleagues emphasized dimensions such as integrity and accountability are essential for all directors but that they sometimes failed to recognize that some dimensions of character could be overweighted, leading to the risk that virtues could become vices. Other directors recognized the need to have access to the complete set of dimensions, consistent with the notion that all dimensions of character are essential to ensure that virtues do not act as vices (e.g., courage manifesting itself as recklessness). As one participant explained, "I think the one dimension that boards see in excess is collaboration. Boards are natural breeding grounds for groupthink—a belief that we need to come to consensus; boards are expected to come together. I think collaboration is an admirable goal, but in excess it can be detrimental to the board and the decisions it makes."

Fifth, *directors recognized the importance of the dimension of judgment as being pivotal to effective boards*. They appreciated that the character dimensions can be very beneficial depending on the specific circumstances the board is facing—for example, there are times when drive is very beneficial, but there are also times when temperance and humility are very beneficial. But without judgment, the directors tended to agree, decisions may be not only ineffective but even disastrous.

And last, directors believed that *the board is a place where character can be developed, and where clear norms for behavior should be set and enacted*. How the board responds to individual board members really speaks to its culture—whether it supports or negates the person who comes forward with courage or humanity. For example, one participant expressed the belief that if people have humility, they will learn from others or be corrected by others that help them to develop character. Similarly, individuals may be able to develop integrity if colleagues with a strong foundation of integrity conduct candid conversations with others and engage in coaching activities. We heard expressed the strong belief that individuals can bring certain character dimensions out in their colleagues. Participants stated that the board chair plays a particularly important role in facilitating the development of character and setting the expectation that others will engage in that process as well.

Stated more strongly, *the chair is expected to put Leader Character on the agenda*. As one director wrote, "A strong chair can pull the necessary impulses together to make the board functional."

Participants were keen to learn about the multiple ways in which board members help develop character in other board members, both in the board room and outside, and to better understand how strength of character—or the lack thereof—may affect their quality of judgment and decision-making. At the same time, there was ample testimony that board dynamics and culture do not always support the character dimensions.

This leads us to several higher-level concluding remarks. In our group discussions and survey results, *character emerged consistently as a key contributor to director effectiveness and board governance.* But despite this perceived importance of character—as reported by highly experienced corporate directors—character is *not* commonly invoked in workplace and board conversations. If it is obvious that character matters, and if leaders and corporate directors generally agree that organizations and their governing bodies do not do a very good job taking character into account in decision making, what prevents them from doing so?

We identified at least three reasons for the gap between simply understanding the importance of character and actually doing something to bring it to boards of directors. First, as articulated by many directors during the roundtable discussions, *character is seen as a subjective construct.* Many directors want additional evidence that character can be "pinned down" and related to hard measures of organizational performance. Second, *the business community feels that it lacks a contemporary, practice-focused vocabulary with which to address good and bad examples of Leader Character in governance.* As a direct result, individuals often have difficulty bringing character into conversations in an attempt to modify or strengthen behavior. Third, *individuals do not have access to valid and reliable instruments to assess Leader Character* and bring it into an organization's HR practices (e.g., recruitment, promotion, or talent development programs) or into the overarching governance process.

We disagree. Many of these purported obstacles to bringing Leader Character into the workplace—up to and including the board table—have been or are being addressed through empirical research, including our own. Character *can* be expressed as behavioral manifestations, in practitioner-oriented language, and it *can* be measured.

Leader character has proven its ability to improve individual, team, and organizational performance. The business community today has a clear opportunity to begin shifting from *thinking* and *talking* about character to *enacting* it.

Strategy, purpose, and culture

What are the primary responsibilities of a board? First, they approve and oversee the implementation of the organization's strategy. This task is considered as important as, and generally tightly linked with, another main role of the board: selecting the organization's CEO.

Less formally, but no less important, boards are responsible for their organization's culture—understanding it, assessing it, and trying to ensure that the actual culture aligns with the espoused culture. But as we've also seen in many of the real-world examples described in this and previous chapters, this can be a complicated journey, indeed.

Boards are also responsible for ensuring that their organization has articulated a purpose statement that concisely sums up why it exists—that is, *what issues the organization seeks to solve.* Such purpose statements rarely focus on basic transactional issues like enhancing shareholder value—even if that *is* a main focus of the company—but rather stress higher-level goals, such as the company's role in society.

And finally, boards are responsible for ensuring that all of these governance-related issues are internally consistent and mutually reinforce each other. If they don't, it's very likely that the organization's stakeholders—from shareholders to employees, suppliers, regulators, and host communities—will be confused about the organization's goals and success in *achieving* those goals will be more elusive.

How can boards achieve this kind of alignment? By pursuing the common thread that runs through all of them: the thread of leader character. Consider Figure 9.1.

Let's begin at the top of the chart, with *purpose.* Purpose is not an alternative to profit but rather an avenue toward it. When purpose is placed in the

Figure 9.1 The Purpose, Culture, and Strategy Triad

foreground, in other words, profits will follow as a natural consequence. One trio of researchers calculated measures of corporate purpose, drawing on input from 456,666 employees across 429 companies, six years, and a broad range of industries. They found that what they called "high *purpose-clarity* organizations" exhibited "superior accounting and stock market performance."[22]

By definition, a statement of purpose requires the capacity, intent, and ingrained habits to reach out to, listen to and learn from, and collaborate with others to define and achieve what are typically broader, more inclusive visions of success. If your leadership does not have the benefit of leader character, it will struggle to formulate and realize this purpose.

But it will require much more from the board of directors than simply telling their leadership ranks that they must now operate in a manner consistent with the organization's stated purpose. Refined and nuanced judgments require leaders to stay present, listen, be patient, courageous, accountable, humble, and humane. In short, they speak to the essence of who these leaders are as people—their *essential character*. At the same time, it seems disingenuous, and unfair, for the board to demand an evolution to the consistent demonstration of these characteristics without ensuring the organization provides guidance, training, and support.

Moving on to *strategy*: purpose without strategy is wishful thinking. Strategy needs to comprise at least four key subjects: how the organization will measure year-over-year success, what value it delivers to its stakeholders, what its portfolio of products and services is and in which markets it will serve, and finally, what core activities it relies on to deliver on the strategy components.[23]

Think of these four components as cascading down through lines of business, geographies, and even functional areas. On the one hand, this sounds logical and straightforward—almost inevitable!—but in fact, it rarely occurs so easily. There are many things that masquerade as "strategy," including budgets and strategic initiatives, that in fact mainly mask strategic deficiencies. Even when there *is* strategic clarity, the challenges associated with ongoing strategic renewal are significant. Underpinning all of this is *strategic competence*—and even more importantly, the strength of character that discussions of strategy rely on.

Think back to the Boeing scenario. The issues with the 737 Max were born out of a shift in strategy that squarely focused on financial metrics in its goals and thus eroded the company's longtime value proposition and compromised its core activities. Where were the directors and senior leadership—the ones who should have been exercising the strength of character needed to question the shift that was being made?

This is never easy. Directors and regulators may feel that they are not in a position to question the strategy because they are not in the trenches and don't know the business. But in fact, when it comes to strategy, what they need is to be people who are not afraid to probe areas where they aren't confident about their knowledge—and the board needs to be a place that fosters those kinds of discussions.

Again, as former and current board members, the authors understand how difficult this can be—difficult but far from impossible. There are many firms that have figured out how to thread this needle and foster this kind of culture—and yours can be one of them.

And finally, we look at *culture*. One of the key indicators of a robust strategy is a robust culture, with a strong foundation of character. We have already comprehensively examined the deep and enduring relationship between Character and culture in Chapter 7. To this discussion we add our conviction that only about 10 percent of culture is strategy specific. For example, a strategy that emphasizes sales (e.g., Wells Fargo) will have a different culture than one that emphasizes engineering (e.g., VW, or Boeing). But in our view, the remaining 90 percent of aspirational culture will be character-based.

The cultural behaviors described in the "Balanced or Strong Character" column in Figure 3.2 of Chapter 3 provide the common foundation for the realization of any legitimate, aspirational culture. We have worked with thousands of executives and have asked them to plot where they are on the chart. Most of the time they find themselves in a vice state on several dimensions. The good news is that they now know what to do to strengthen their culture by investing in the development of Leader Character. Without fail, when we ask whether they would be delighted if their culture reflected the behaviors in the middle column, there is a unanimous "yes."

Character is foundational

Let's conclude this chapter with five specific prescriptions for directors who wish to bring leader character to bear on their board's activities:

Start with yourself. Do you have the strength of character to underpin the quality of judgment you need on the board? The work of boards inevitably treads into territory outside the comfort zone of most individuals. Are you prepared to voice reservations and concerns and persist even when facing resistance? Or do you remain silent and let others whom you see as more competent dictate the agenda? Our research revealed that board members believe they tend to be overweighted on collaboration and underweighted on accountability—a lethal combination for character based judgment.

Extend it to the board. Do the practices of the board reflect a culture of character? Looking back to the diagnostics in Figures 2.2 and 3.2, where do your conversations lie? Can people still speak candidly when they are "at the edge of their thinking"? For example, perhaps you don't fully grasp what a properly functioning Asset Liability Matching program looks like. Perhaps you feel uneasy about what you're seeing presented, to the extent that you *do* understand it. If so, do you feel courageous enough to raise your concerns even if you can't confidently and clearly express them? Does the board chair provide that kind of psychological safety? If we attempted to grade the Theranos, Boeing, VW, Wells Fargo, FTX, and Silicon Valley Bank contexts, would we wind up questioning the degree to which they exercised their duty of care? Would we conclude that their collective lack of insight impaired their judgment?

Use it in selection. As we've seen, leader character is a diagnostic approach that can and should be used to help select the CEO, leadership team, and directors. As we discussed in Chapter 6, many organizations today are using leader character–based selection processes to elevate character alongside competence.

Measure. Seek evidence for if and how the organization is elevating character alongside competence. What are they doing? What is the evidence that they are paying attention to it?

Build culture. Seek evidence for character-based culture. Where does your organization locate itself on Figure 3.2 in Chapter 3? Are you weak, balanced, or unsupported? (How do you know?) What would it take to change things for the better?

In all of this, there is always the chance that some voice of authority will ask, skeptically, "Is this worth all the effort it's going to take?" In previous chapters—and in our concluding chapter, which follows—we offer compelling evidence that the answer is *yes*.

Notes

1 Charles Scharf testified before the committee again in September 2022. See www. banking.senate.gov/imo/media/doc/Scharf%20Testimony%209-22-22.pdf, accessed March 16, 2023.

2 A video of the hearing is online at www.youtube.com/watch?v=tyxEcDvneZI, accessed March 16, 2023. A transcript of that same hearing is online at www. govinfo.gov/content/pkg/CHRG-116hhrg42866/html/CHRG-116hhrg42866.htm, accessed March 16, 2023. Much of this section is drawn from that hearing.

3 This section is derived from the transcript of that hearing, online at www.govinfo. gov/content/pkg/CHRG-116hhrg42867/html/CHRG-116hhrg42867.htm, accessed March 16, 2023. The video of the hearing is online at www.congress.gov/event/116th-congress/house-event/110719, accessed March 16, 2023.

4 An "independent chair" is a corporate official who 1) focuses his or her attention on managing the board and 2) is free of conflicts of interest that would prevent him or her from serving the company's owners as a dispassionate fiduciary. Interestingly, *Board Intelligence* lists "character" as one of the three key attributes possessed by an independent chair: "Character is the key to it all: the single most important factor in the success or failure of any governance system. Without it, no processes and procedures are fool-proof. Unfortunately, it is also something that is impossible to codify in any meaningful way. 'You know it when you see it' may work as a rule of thumb, but it is not the sort of thing you could write a rule around." We agree that "character" deserves better treatment! See the 2018 post by Chris Hodge online at www.boardintelligence.com/blog/the-3-cs-that-define-an-independent-chair, accessed March 16, 2023.

5 The only precedent, at least in recent years, was when retired Enron directors were asked to testify.

6 See, for example, remarks to this effect by Representatives Nydia M. Velazquez and Roger Williams in the transcript cited in footnote 3.

7 This is especially true for two *former* directors, who by that point had no active relationship with the bank.

8 Much of this and subsequent sections are derived from the 2019 article "Leader character in board governance," published by Gerard Seijts, Alyson Byrne, Mary Crossan, and Jeffrey Gandz, in the *Journal of Management and Governance*, 23: 227–258, online at https://doi.org/10.1007/s10997-018-9426-8.

9 See those guidelines online at https://www08.wellsfargomedia.com/assets/pdf/about/corporate/governance-guidelines.pdf, accessed March 16, 2023.

10 See Matt Egan's article, "Wells Fargo scandal: Where was the board?", an April 24, 2017 article in *CNN Business* report, online at https://money.cnn.com/2017/04/24/investing/wells-fargo-scandal-board-annual-meeting/index.html, accessed March 16, 2023.

11 For example, researchers have related groupthink on the board level to the demise of Enron.

12 Paul Ryan's bio can be found here, www.foxcorporation.com/management/board-of-directors/paul-d-ryan/, accessed March 16, 2023.

13 See, for example, www.mediamatters.org/fox-news/rupert-murdoch-admits-new-dominion-filing-fox-knew-election-fraud-conspiracy-theories-were, accessed April 12, 2023.

14 This quote is taken from the article "Fox chair Murdoch says 2020 election was fair: Court filings," online at https://abcnews.go.com/Entertainment/wireStory/voting-tech-firm-spotlights-murdochs-defamation-suit-97693725, accessed March 16, 2023.

15 This quote is taken from the article "Watch Paul Ryan's Longtime Friend Hold His Feet To The Fire Over Fox News," online at www.huffpost.com/entry/paul-ryan-fox-news-challenged_n_640086c0e4b05f1e793dc17f, accessed March 16, 2023.

16 This is another revelation from the Dominion-related revelations, as reported in the February 28, 2023, edition of the *New York Times*, online at www.nytimes.com/2023/02/28/business/media/fox-news-trump-break.html, accessed March 16, 2023.

17 See Fox's 2022 annual report at https://investor.foxcorporation.com/static-files/1ed7c450-e52a-4259-8631-80db9e79be32, accessed March 16, 2023.

18 See www.smartmatic.com/us/media/article/faq-defamation-lawsuit-against-fox-corporation/, accessed March 16, 2023. Given that the company's net income on $13.9 billion in 2022 sales was just over $1 billion, these are truly significant sums of money.

19 The quote is taken from the article "Paul Ryan 'absolutely disagrees' with Tucker Carlson as he defends role on Fox News board," online at www.independent.co.uk/news/world/americas/us-politics/paul-ryan-tucker-carlson-election-lies-b2292301.html, accessed March 16, 2023.

20 See the 2019 article "Leader character in the boardroom," by Rahul Bhardwaj and Gerard Seijts, in *Organizational Dynamics*, 50, online at www.sciencedirect.com/science/article/abs/pii/S0090261620300024.

21 Again, see "Leader character in the boardroom."

22 See the 2019 article "Corporate purpose and financial performance" (by Claudine Gartenberg, Andrea Prat, and George Serafeim published). *Organization Science* 30(1): 1–18.

23 See, for example, Crossan, M., Maurer, C., Rowe, G., & Rouse, M. (2022). *Strategic Analysis and Action (tenth edition)*. London: Pearson Education.

Chapter 10

The compass of your life

In our introduction, many pages back, we retold a story from Herman Melville's classic novel *Moby Dick*. That passage focuses on a sequence of events aboard the *Pequod* the morning after a pounding typhoon's electrical discharges have destroyed the ship's compass. The helmsman, relying on the failed compass, declares the ship to be sailing east. But in fact, it's morning and the sun is rising behind them, so obviously, the *Pequod* is sailing west. This is a disaster—potentially life-threatening.

Under the anxious scrutiny of his crew, Captain Ahab cobbles together a makeshift replacement compass. It works—at least up to a point—and Ahab triumphantly declares himself to be the *lord of the level loadstone*.[1] The crew is reassured, but again, only up to a point. Yes, their captain has demonstrated a certain kind of nautical competence, almost magic. But he has also underscored in their minds his deep character flaws. "In his fiery eyes of scorn and triumph," narrator Ishmael concludes, "you saw then Ahab in all his fatal pride."

Spoiler alert: we move now to the dramatic climax of *Moby Dick*. At long last, the *Pequod* once again spots the great whale and, at Ahab's insistence, goes through near-disastrous engagements with Moby Dick on two successive days. Two whale boats and a crew member are lost, not to mention Ahab's wooden leg. The intelligent and generally stoic first mate, Starbuck—by all accounts, long on Courage, short on Drive, but possessed of pretty good judgment—lashes out at the captain:

> "Great God! but for one single instant show thyself," cried Starbuck; "never, never wilt thou capture him, old man—in Jesus' name no more of this, that's worse than devil's madness. Two days chased; twice stove to splinters; thy very leg once more snatched from under thee; thy evil shadow gone—all good angels mobbing thee with warnings:—
>
> "What more wouldst thou have?—Shall we keep chasing this murderous fish till he swamps the last man? Shall we be dragged by him to the bottom of the sea? Shall we be towed by him to the infernal world? Oh, oh—Impiety and blasphemy to hunt him more!"

DOI: 10.4324/9781003341215-11

Ahab responds with an icy resolve, telling Starbuck and the rest of the crew that he couldn't give up this chase even if he wanted to:

> "Ahab is forever Ahab, man. This whole act's immutably decreed. 'Twas rehearsed by thee and me a billion years before this ocean rolled. Fool! I am the Fates' lieutenant; I act under orders. Look thou, underling! that thou obeyest mine."

Meanwhile, back on Nantucket Island in faraway Massachusetts, the *Pequod*'s de facto board of directors knows nothing of Ahab's deepening madness. Two retired whaling captains and Quaker businessmen, Bildad and Peleg, are the principal owners of the ship, and they represent both their own majority shares in the enterprise and the minority holdings of other members of the Nantucket community. They have paid to outfit the *Pequod* for its voyage, hired Ahab—by all accounts, a highly competent captain—to serve as their de facto CEO, signed on other specialists as crew members, and determined everyone's "lay," or share of the profits of the voyage.

Perhaps if the venture had a risk committee, its members would have explored the fact that their captain had lost his leg to an "accursed whale" on his most recent voyage and might well be holding a certain grudge. Perhaps they would have dug deeper into Peleg's description of Ahab as a "grand, ungodly, god-like man." (Certainly, the business of commercial whaling was risky enough without vengeance and a grandiose personality—*the Fates' lieutenant!*—entering into the picture!) Perhaps they would have considered whether Ahab's indisputable Courage and Drive were sufficiently offset by other character dimensions, such as Temperance, Humility, Humanity, and—above all—judgment.

And perhaps they would have considered whether his character was on a level with his demonstrated competence and ferocious commitment.

Invoking the compass

In our book's title and introduction, we called upon the compass metaphor because it focuses our discussion on a tool that was, and is, useful for navigation. A compass is a tool for figuring out *orientation*, where you have been and where you are, and *navigation*, where you're going. It recalls the past, captures the present, and points toward the future.

We have developed a new kind of tool—Leader Character—that we believe can be useful for both individuals and organizations as they seek to navigate the realm of character—hence, the "character compass." Leader character is the compass that helps leaders steer their organizations through real, positive, and lasting change. It has the power to transform leadership for the 21st century.

In the preceding chapters, we've laid out where that tool came from, what it does (and doesn't) do, and how it can be put to use in real-world settings.

Conversely, we've shown through real-world examples what happens when it *isn't* embraced by companies and the people within them.

If you've read this far, you may already be on your way toward being a changed person. You may already be understanding yourself, others, and the world around you in more accurate, comprehensive, and actionable ways.

Going forward, if you put into practice what you've learned in this book—if you invoke the character compass—you will embody what we call leader character. You will become a better decision-maker. You will perform better. You will help generate better outcomes for yourself, your team, your organization, and the communities within which you live and work. Most likely, for all of these reasons, you will feel better about yourself and enjoy an enhanced sense of well-being.

The building blocks and basics of character

Let's briefly revisit some of the key aspects of character and, by extension, Leader Character.

Character is often confused with, or submerged within, topics like "ethics" and "morals." Those topics are indeed important, but we argue that character provides a far larger and more useful framework. It comprises the whole life of a whole person—in this case, *you*.

Our framework is based on eleven behaviorally based character dimensions, roughly parallel to the "virtues" identified by Aristotle many centuries ago. (We've represented this 11-dimension framework in several different ways throughout this book.) Each of our dimensions has a number of "elements" associated with it, which help make the dimensions understandable and accessible. Temperance, for example, comprises the elements of *patient, calm, composed, self-controlled,* and *prudent.* If you are temperate, you are (at least) those five things.

All of our dimensions interact with and influence each other. Ten of the dimensions contribute to what we consider the central dimension: *judgment.* Strength across all the dimensions is likely to produce the wisest and best judgments no matter what specific context you find yourself in. It's also likely to help generate a broader set of strategic alternatives—novel, creative, and effective—for you to choose from.

Keep in mind that dimensions that are in excess or deficiency are likely to become problematic. Stated more succinctly, when out of balance, *virtues can become vices.* This means that you need to figure out and stay mindful of your imbalances and take the necessary steps to correct them. Most often, this means "dialing up" a counterbalancing dimension rather than dialing something back a dimension that's in excess. There is no limit to the strength of a dimension once it's supported by the other dimensions.

This observation introduces a central underpinning of our framework: the idea that *your character is changeable.* It is not fixed at birth or immutable.

Character is not even all that hard to change if you understand what it is and how to change it. In fact, your character is probably changing every day, in one way or another, in response to the changing circumstances and pressures of the world around you.

Meanwhile, on a conscious level, you are *busy, busy, busy.* So if all of this is true, then you need to ask yourself a key question: *who are you becoming while you are so busy doing?*

Here's where our compass metaphor can be helpful again: no matter how busy you are, wrapped up as you are in the affairs of the moment, you need to be steering toward something. You owe it to yourself to take control over how your character is developing by taking a *mindful, intelligent,* and *intentional* approach to your life. You need to change your habits. (Again, this is advice from long ago, courtesy of Aristotle.) As those habits change for the better, *you* will change for the better—emotionally and even physically. Your brain will work better, you will feel better, and you will feel better about yourself. And it's not so much about finding more time in your day to develop your character but rather transforming your lived moments to both *activate* and *strengthen* your character.

The need for rigor

There are many, many prescriptions out there that purport to tell you how to change your life for the better. Most of them are well intentioned, and some may well include some useful advice—but by and large, they are not grounded in any kind of rigorous investigation.

Our framework is different. We've spent a decade and a half not only thinking through issues of character, drawing on great thinkers who have preceded us in this field, but also testing our emerging ideas in a variety of real-world contexts. In the preceding chapters, we've mostly submerged the scientific scaffolding that supports our framework, but if you're interested, we encourage you to *follow the science* that is detailed in the notes that accompany each chapter. We have included several examples of our ideas being tested in practice, and we've given examples—such as in Chapter 9—of how we go about involving practitioners in our evolving ideas and prescriptions.

In other words, we see the need for rigor in working through the fundamentals of Leader Character. At the same time, we are regularly reminded of the need for rigor in *applying* those fundamentals. If you elect to embrace Leader Character on the individual level, don't cut any corners. Yes, it's tempting to simplify the framework by ignoring or deemphasizing one or more dimensions. But that will lead to problems somewhere down the road, when you discover that what you expected to be a virtue is operating like a vice because you failed to account for a key dimension. *All the dimensions are equally important.* Great musicians don't decide to play only in selected keys. They know that as professionals, they *need to be able to play in all keys.* As they practice, they need to focus in particular on the ones that give them the most trouble.

Remember, too, that this is intentional work and that we never stop learning. Great musicians keep playing their scales across their entire careers. Great athletes keep practicing and learning.

And finally, be patient with yourself and others. Accept yourself where you are, and accept others where they are, on the leadership character path. Be generous, and help others at every opportunity. Don't just be positive; be *relentlessly* positive. This doesn't mean that you don't hold people accountable for unjust behavior—for example—but rather rely on Humility and Humanity to understand the source of the misconduct so that you can address the shortcomings.

All five principles—no shortcuts, hard work, patience, generosity, and positivity—also hold true for embracing leader character at the organization level. Promoting or practicing incomplete visions of leader character company-wide is very likely to backfire. If and when it does, you and your colleagues will find it that much harder to make the necessary progress in the future.

Character at the core

As stated in our introduction, we've structured *The Character Compass* in what we think is a logical and purposeful way, moving from a central focus on the individual to an increasing focus on the organizational. Accordingly, we looked in our early chapters at the anatomy of character: the *what*. Then we moved on to *character development*: the *how*, on the individual level. And in our closing chapters, we examined the *application of character*, putting an increased emphasis on implementation in the organizational setting. We focused on the human resource function, EDI, risk management, and board governance and development, but these are only several of the functions and corporate-wide activities that can benefit directly from the embrace of Leader Character.

This last focus—the *application of character*—brought us to the intersection of *strategy*, *culture*, and *character*, which we hope is useful to leaders at all levels of an organization. Making character part of your organization's DNA is a strategic asset. It informs, influences, and positively affects *all* of your activities, relationships, environments, and outcomes. It sets you up for stronger performance. It makes your organization more robust and better able to respond to challenges and pursue opportunities.

That may sound like a cliché, but it isn't. Our world today faces unprecedented technological, social, and environmental changes. Our leaders and our organizations can't respond to those changes with self-interest, injustice, and cynicism. They have to respond with *character*. This was demonstrated in the Great Financial Crisis and again during COVID-19; no doubt, it will be proven again in the future.

That said, all of these developments are the expected *outcomes* of your efforts—but they are not the reason to engage in this work. Leader character is at its core a *human* project. It is about helping every person flourish and reach his or her individual potential with dignity, agency, and respect.

Congratulations! You are now a member of the Leader Character community, which we hope and believe is taking shape on a global scale. We hope and believe that you now see the world differently, that you can't "unsee" what you've seen, you can't unlearn what you've learned, and you're determined to change yourself and the world around you.

Finally, we hope and believe that you will stay engaged, have faith, and *enjoy* the transformative journey that you have undertaken. Embrace, apply, and trust your character compass!

Note

1   A loadstone (or "lodestone") is a chunk of magnetite, a naturally magnetized mineral. It's useful for making magnets but less so for making compasses. Either Ahab doesn't know this distinction or he hopes his crew doesn't.

About the institute

Contacting the Ian O. Ihnatowycz Institute for Leadership

Since its inception in 2010, the Ian O. Ihnatowycz Institute for Leadership at the Ivey Business School, Western University (London, Canada) has been at the center of leadership thought, inquiry, and education into what makes a better leader through its focus on Leader Character. The institute's research is integrated into Ivey's degree and executive education programs. The institute conducts a wide range of outreach activities with the public, private, and not-for-profit sectors. Through its work, the institute elevates the importance of character alongside competence in the practice of leadership and supports the development of global citizens who have strength of character, strive to make a difference, and contribute to the flourishing of teams, organizations, communities, and societies.

For more information on the institute's research, teaching, and outreach, visit www.ivey.ca/leadership or email leadership@ivey.ca.

Index

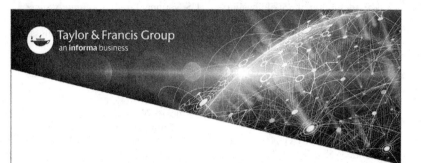

Printed in the United States
by Baker & Taylor Publisher Services